Trump's Populist America

Trump's Populist America

Steven Rosefielde
University of North Carolina at Chapel Hill, USA

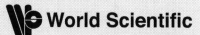 World Scientific

NEW JERSEY · LONDON · SINGAPORE · BEIJING · SHANGHAI · HONG KONG · TAIPEI · CHENNAI · TOKYO

Published by

World Scientific Publishing Co. Inc.

27 Warren Street, Suite 401-402, Hackensack, NJ 07601, USA

Head office: 5 Toh Tuck Link, Singapore 596224

UK office: 57 Shelton Street, Covent Garden, London WC2H 9HE

Library of Congress Cataloging-in-Publication Data
Names: Rosefielde, Steven, author.
Title: Trump's populist America / by Steven Rosefielde,
    University of North Carolina at Chapel Hill, USA.
Description: New Jersey : World Scientific, 2017. |
    Includes bibliographical references and index.
Identifiers: LCCN 2017020444| ISBN 9781944659486 | ISBN 9781944659493
Subjects: LCSH: Trump, Donald, 1946– | Populism--United States. |
    United States--Social conditions--21st century. | United States--Economic conditions--
    21st century. | United States--Foreign relations--21st century.
Classification: LCC E901.1.T78 .R67 2017 | DDC 973.933--dc23
LC record available at https://lccn.loc.gov/2017020444

British Library Cataloguing-in-Publication Data
A catalogue record for this book is available from the British Library.

Printed in Singapore

In Memory of David Rosefielde

Contents

Foreword

During the summer, before the American presidential election which took place in early November of 2016, Professor Rosefielde and I co-authored a book about the likely foreign policy of then presidential candidate Donald J. Trump. The book *The Trump Phenomenon and the Future of US Foreign Policy* was published two months before the election. It was surprisingly accurate and it played a role in the election campaign as a framework for Mr. Trump's foreign policy proposals. During the campaign, Mr. Trump and Mrs. Clinton each gave three major foreign policy speeches. The groundwork was laid by those speeches for a vigorous debate about the direction of American foreign policy. However, the mass media in the United States chose to virtually ignore all of the serious speeches of the two candidates in favor of a continual barrage of personal attacks, so that no serious discussion of American foreign policy ever took place during the campaign.

In November 2016, Mr. Trump was elected president of the United States. On January 20, 2017, he was sworn into office. There is now considerable curiosity about the likely direction of the Trump Administration. Professor Rosefielde has answered that curiosity with a new book *Trump's Populist America*, which is likely to be as accurate as the previous one and which considers both domestic and foreign policies. This is the most complete and objective material in any form now available about the new Administration's likely direction. As such, it is excellent for use in college courses, as background for journalists, and to inform general readers the world over as to the likely course of American policy in the upcoming years.

It is a great strength of Professor Rosefielde's work that he possesses an almost unequaled command of economic science and so is not misled by campaign rhetoric or promises about what can be undertaken. This book provides a realistic assessment of likely policies, not a set of promises. Nor is this book another of the myriad condemnations of Mr. Trump's proposals. The book is objective and hopeful, as is suitable to the initiation of a new democratically elected chief executive of a major country. Professor Rosefielde is knowledgeable about the topics of domestic and foreign policies which he addresses. There is no one in the United States better prepared and qualified to make the assessments he makes in this book. For anyone who wishes to understand the likely direction of the Trump Administration, this is the book to consult.

Daniel Quinn Mills
Harvard University

Preface

Trump's Populist America is a sequel to *The Trump Phenomenon and the Future of US Foreign Policy* co-authored by Quinn Mills and Steven Rosefielde; published by World Scientific in September 2016 prior to the November American presidential election. Trump's intentions could not be clearly decoded before the election, but his post-election appointments and statements have brought his purposes and programs into coherent focus. This volume documents the grievances of ordinary people that enabled Trump to win the 2016 presidential election and shows that he is moving boldly to redress the problem. It demonstrates that he is a populist and that US populism is an expression of the traditional America Dream. Trump's populist programs are desirable in many ways, but he has formidable opponents. The battle between populism (nationalism) and "globalism" is over the spoils, not a black and white matter of right and wrong. Trump's programs in many instances are well conceived. They can succeed, but will not be to everybody's liking and are sure to be contested vigorously. This volume has been written to facilitate a better understanding of the surging global populist tide and its historical implications.

Acknowledgments

Trump's Populist America was co-developed with Quinn Mills. Steven Rosefielde wrote the manuscript, but we jointly discussed and edited the entire work. The book is a joint labor, even though it was solo written.

Introduction

The American electorate has chosen Donald Trump to lead America in a new populist (nationalist) direction at home and abroad. The policies he espoused during and immediately after his successful presidential campaign depart radically from the "establishment" norm (joint Democratic–Republican party consensus). Trump contemplates rolling back America's social justice agenda to 1960 when equal opportunity and self-reliance still took precedence over affirmative action (privileged treatment for the "socially disadvantaged" in business contracts, jobs, pay, mortgage loans, university admission, financial aid and public services for selected minorities, women, gays and immigrants), and restorative justice (reparations for historical wrongs). He is thinking of rolling back America's worker protection policy to the 1930s when preserving jobs and shoring up wages took precedence over free immigration, and family was more important than cosmopolitanism. He is leaning toward rolling back federal government regulation and taxation to the 1920s, eradicating stifling executive orders, mandates, and controls, freeing private initiative and fostering prosperity. He inclines toward rolling back America's international commercial policy to 1913 when free trade and finance ruled the day without multilateral treaties. He desires to restore a conservative interpretation of the Constitution, reinstate small government, and resurrect the traditional American Dream.[1]

Trump denies being a racist, sexist and white male supremacist. He shuns anti-democratic rhetoric, storm trooper tactics and supports an open society. He says that he will employ conventional macroeconomic monetary and fiscal policies to spur economic growth, and endorses free international trade and finance so long as workers are adequately protected.

Trump's quarrel with the establishment is over the purpose and size of America's federal government. He wants to slenderize government regulation, reduce business taxes, curtail entitlements, affirmative action, restorative justice, and protect the middle class, especially blue-collar workers. Trump wants to limit immigration and expel millions of illegals because they harm employment opportunities for citizens, lower wages and drain public services. He is concerned about terrorist infiltration.

Trump's early post-election second thoughts suggest that he may not always stick to his guns.[2] He has decided to drop his promises to prosecute Hillary Clinton for national security violations; is reconsidering withdrawing from the Paris Climate Treaty and is no longer committed to waterboarding suspected terrorists.

A large number of Americans in the November 2016 presidential election shared Trump's view that the establishment had pressed its agenda too far.[3] They did not reject free trade, and did not advocate racism, sexism and social injustice, calling only for a moratorium on the expansion of establishment programs, elimination of abuses and the restoration of an open society.[4]

The establishment for its part responded with horror. It considers that it alone is qualified to rule and has mobilized against rolling back existing programs.

The battle between Trump and his adversaries is about the meaning of "national interest". Should America be ruled primarily for the benefit of the middle class (common man), or for the establishment's darlings (Wall Street, environmental and social activists, selected minorities, women, gays)? In the election campaign, Trump positioned himself as the people's champion, that is as a populist, while the establishment posed as the nation's moral conscience.[5] The establishment's battle cry was "no retreat, no surrender". Trump's motto was "never again".

Moreover, the establishment insists not only that its concept of the national interest is morally superior (the logical extension of the anti-slavery movement, feminism, gay rights, the French Revolution, Bolshevik Revolution, anti-colonialism and social democracy), but that Trump's populist objectives are self-contradictory.[6] Trump's critics claim that economic liberalization is inconsistent with high tariffs and restricted immigration. This is true, but not necessarily fatal. Government can and should sometimes limit the harm done to some, even though there is benefit for many. Trump seeks what he considers responsible liberalization consistent with prudent immigration quotas and fair commercial entry. He considers it unjust that China enjoys easy trade access to America's market, when it bars US exports.[7]

The establishment also faults Trump for opposing globalism; that is, the idea that America is obligated to impose the establishment's version of the American Dream on Russia, China and the Islamic world. It accuses Trump of failing to accept America's duty to lead. This is a half-truth. Trump intends to lead, but not in the way that the establishment desires. He favors a populist approach rather than the establishment's hegemonic one world strategy.

Trump's program under construction thus is neither immoral, nor infeasible. It merely gives priority to populist interests over those favored by the establishment. It is consistent with traditional values that the establishment claims as its own: democracy, liberty, competition, free enterprise, rule of law, equal opportunity and a social safety net. Trump has not called for the restoration of the Hawley Smoot tariff, authoritarian power, and/or minority oppression. He has only championed the protection of workers and the middle class against an establishment that seeks to impose a globalist agenda that privileges some against ordinary people at home and abroad.

Donald Trump won the American presidential election because the middle class was disgruntled with the joint Democratic and Republican party establishment.[8] The judgment is subject to qualification. Voters were influenced by a multitude of factors, and populist alienation does not exclude other influences. Middle class alienation does not include the entire middle class. It does not include professionals who consider it their ethical duty to grin and bear the strictures of "political correctness" (establishment priorities). It does not include retirees who no longer earn their livelihood and live contentedly on pensions, annuities, social security and/or wealth. The alienated middle class are wage and salary workers, business and professional people in competitive industries.

Their alienation is both objective and subjective, and opponents may consider it morally unjustified. However, the common people's grievances are not figments of their imaginations. The source of the problem is most evident from an economic perspective.

Real American wages have not increased for 40 years. Government salaries have been frozen, professional and small business incomes have been under pressure, while taxes have risen, benefits axed, and free public services have evaporated. Medical, dental, childcare, educational and food costs have skyrocketed. It is no longer possible for middle-class workers to support their children's many desires, and other state-imposed obligations and intrusions have diminished the quality of family life. A worker who started his/her career 40 years ago is substantially worse off today than when he/she began. There are no prospects for a brighter tomorrow. Ordinary people sense the threat of technological displacement and flooded labor markets. This is hardly the stuff of the American Dream. The future for the middle class seems grim enough to have put Donald Trump over the top. The situation in the United Kingdom is similar. [9]

The persistent erosion of the middle class's living standard was cushioned by pushing women out of the household into the factory. It now takes nearly two incomes to pay for the living standard of yesteryear. The situation for single and divorced workers is decidedly worse. These inferences are matters of simple arithmetic that belie sophisticated "you never had it so good" establishment counter-examples.

Moreover, the middle class senses that its declining fortunes in large measure stem from political abandonment. The gross domestic product has trebled since 1975, but workers and professionals gained nothing, and adding insult to injury they were compelled to shoulder a higher tax burden and lost public services. The political establishment could have prevented or mitigated the middle class's plight. It could have managed the labor pool including immigration. It could have supported unions, and managed the terms of employment. It could have outlawed unpaid internships. It could have mandated pensions and medical benefits. It could have mandated sharing some of the fruits of technological progress with workers. It could have kept the tax burden on workers and salaried personnel constant. It could have preserved free public services. It could have restrained the financial liberalization that culminated in the 2008 financial crisis. It could have lightened compliance burdens, discarded superfluous regulations and simplified taxes, but did none of these things, limiting itself instead to small election-time tax refunds.

The middle class also senses that politicians collude with Wall Street and social activities at their expense. The government it perceives is not "We"; it is "Them", an insiders' cabal spouting the rhetoric of inclusiveness, while in fact politicians are interested in ordinary people only enough to solicit their votes. Surveys repeatedly report that the middle class considers politicians of both parties to be liars, thieves and hypocrites. The establishment, including its "experts" is the people's enemy, and populists want it tossed aside.

Should Donald Trump actually subdue the establishment in the years ahead, he will be in a position to redress many populist grievances. He may not succeed.[10] He might acquiesce to establishment pressure. Nonetheless, the task itself is doable, despite adamant claims that any retreat will be catastrophic. It only requires undoing yesterday's mistakes. Labor markets can be tightened by restricting the supply of immigrants. The government can change workplace rules to increase labor incomes and benefits. Washington can cut a trillion dollars of federal spending that is little more than waste, fraud and abuse. It can reduce the tax burden on the productive middle class. It can deregulate, lighten compliance burdens, discard superfluous regulations, simplify taxes, restrain financial speculation and restore free public services. The task is more challenging than simply undoing the past because the middle class's attitudes on some important issues has changed.

The establishment opposes turning back the clock. It is committed to extending its reach. Moreover, even if politicians do accept government downsizing, President Trump would still be constrained by a poisoned legacy of bloated national debt, excessive monetary expansion and activist bureaucracy.

The only practical way forward in responding to populism's complaint is (1) a moratorium on expanding programs harming ordinary people, and (2) gradually reversing the politically correct tide in a compassionate and orderly fashion.

Neither will be easy. Wall Street and other special interests do not want immigration paused, or frozen and international trade and finance re-regulated. The establishment will not voluntarily cap its claims on middle-class incomes, nor shift the tax burden to either the rich or poor. It will not restore free public services. Social advocacy groups will resist moratoria and will not ally anew with the middle class.

Although, Trump is likely to make many pragmatic compromises with the establishment, there seems to be little room for conciliation on whose preferences will rule. Trump seems determined to impose selected moratoria and will haphazardly rollback the establishment tide.

This book surveys the emerging battleground shaping the middle class's economic and social futures both at home and abroad.[11] Part I focuses on domestic areas where Trump may press for moratoria or rollbacks. Part II addresses a few of Trump's foreign policy initiatives that may radically reverse the establishment's globalist paradigm.

None of these matters can be satisfactorily resolved by waving a magic wand. Each modification of the status quo is a potential morass. The dead hand of the past circumscribes Trump's room for maneuver. Sky-high national debt and cumulative excessive money expansion tie his hands on macroeconomic policy. Microeconomic reforms will take time to implement, and the media will demand immediate results.

Nonetheless, Trump's American counter-revolution has begun and deserves close attention.

Endnotes

1. Cf. Richard Haas, *A World in Disarray: American Foreign Policy and the Crisis of the Old Order*, New York: Penguin Press, 2017.
2. Karen Tumulty, "Trump Backs Away from Some of his Strident Campaign Promises", *Washington Post*, November 22, 2016. https://www.washingtonpost.com/national/trump-says-he-could-continue-to-run-his-company-in-theory-from-the-oval-office/2016/11/22/935745da-b0e3-11e6-be1c-8cec35b1ad25_story.html; Michael Wilner, "Trump Warms Israel: Stop Announcing New Settlements", February 2, 2017. http://www.jpost.com/Israel-News/Politics-And-Diplomacy/Trump-warns-Israel-Stop-announcing-new-settlements-480446.
3. Trump lost the popular election count. California voters tipped the scales for Hillary Clinton. Trump won the majority outside of California, and populism prevailed more broadly if Libertarians and Conservatives are added to Trump's tally.
4. The open society concept stresses civil competition, but liberals historically also have been willing to temper their attitude by restricting individual liberty for the greater good. See Richard Boyd, "John Stuart Mill on Economic Liberty and Human Flourishing", *AEI*, November 23, 2016. http://www.aei.org/spotlight/human-flourishing-js-mill/?utm_source=paramount&utm_medium=email&utm_content=AEITODAY&utm_campaign=112316.
5. Robert Daniels, *The Conscience of the Revolution: Communist Opposition in Soviet Russia*, Cambridge, Mass: Harvard University Press, 1960.
6. The open society is a concept originally suggested in 1932 by Henri Bergson, and developed during the Second World War by Austrian-born British philosopher Karl Popper. Henri Bergson, *Les Deux Sources de la morale et de la religion*, Félix Alcan, 1937, pp. 287–343. Karl Popper, *The Open Society and Its Enemies*, London: Routledge, 1945.
7. China's current account surplus with the United States exceeds $300 billion dollars. See Derek Scissors, "China Edges Toward a Big Mistake", *AEI*, November 22, 2016. https://www.aei.org/publication/

china-edges-toward-a-big-mistake/?utm_source=paramount&utm_medium=email&utm_content=AEITODAY&utm_campaign=112316.

8. Cf. Robert Reich, "Why We Need A New Democratic Party", *Huffington*, November 11, 2016. http://www.huffingtonpost.com/robert-reich/why-we-need-a-new-democratic-party_b_12920342.html; Robert Reich, *Saving Capitalism: For the Many, Not the Few*, New York: Alfred A. Knopf, 2015; Joseph Stiglitz, "What America's Economy Needs from Trump", *Project Syndicate*, November 13, 2016. https://www.project-syndicate.org/commentary/trump-agenda-america-economy-by-joseph-e--stiglitz-2016-11?utm_source=Project+Syndicate+Newsletter&utm_campaign=2068a5ccc1-stiglitz_trump_american_economy_14_11_2016&utm_medium=email&utm_term=0_73bad5b7d8-2068a5ccc1-93559677. "Donald Trump's astonishing victory in the United States presidential election has made one thing abundantly clear: too many Americans — particularly white male Americans — feel left behind. It is not just a feeling; many Americans really have been left behind. It can be seen in the data no less clearly than in their anger. And, as I have argued repeatedly, an economic system that doesn't 'deliver' for large parts of the population is a failed economic system. So what should President-elect Trump do about it?"

9. Will Martin, "Britain is Facing an 'Extraordinary and Dreadful' Income Crisis", *Business Insider UK*, November 24, 2016. http://www.businessinsider.com/institute-of-fiscal-studies-research-uk-wage-growth-2016-11. "British workers are set to suffer the 'dreadful' punishment of wages still not rising above 2008 levels by 2021 — the Institute for Fiscal Studies warned today. And this chart from the respected independent think tank shows how it is the young people who have suffered the most since the financial crisis (see Figure I.1).

The IFS analysis shows how while younger workers aged 22–30 have seen their real earnings plummet 7% since 2008 — at the same time older people have seen theirs increase by 11%.

Paul Johnson, the IFS director, said today it was the worst situation for people's pay since the end of the Second World War — or possibly longer. 'Overall real average earnings are forecast to rise by less than 5% between now and 2021. That means they will be 3.7% lower in 2021

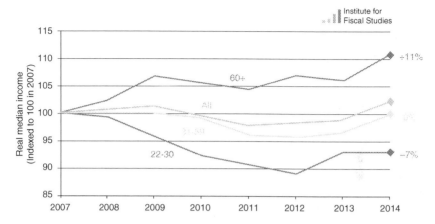

Figure I.1. What has been Happening to Living Standards? Real Median Income (2007–08 = 100).

Source: Figure 20.6 of *Living Standards, Poverty and Inequality, 2016*.

than was projected in March. To put it another way around, half of the wage growth projected for the next five years back in March is not now projected to happen,' he said.

'On these projections real wages will, remarkably, still be below their 2008 levels in 2021.'

The economist added: 'One cannot stress how dreadful that is — more than a decade without real earnings growth. We have certainly not seen a period remotely like it in the last 70 years.'"

10. Timothy Carney, "Trump's Attack Plan for Obama's Regulations", *AEI*, January 30, 2017. http://www.aei.org/publication/trumps-attack-plan-for-obamas-regulations/?utm_source=paramount&utm_medium=email&utm_content=AEITHISWEEK&utm_campaign=Weekly020416. "The courts slapped down some of his overreach, but much is still in place, and President Trump ran for office on a promise to declare war on Obama's regulations. When he started work on Friday, Trump began hitting some bullseyes in a target-rich environment.

Many conservatives expect a *blitzkrieg*, or a nuclear strike in which Trump wipes out Obama's executive actions with a few strokes of the pen. But while some of Obama's executive actions were simple orders that can be reversed, many are products of an extensive rulemaking process that will take time to take down."

11. Problems of international security are addressed in Quinn Mills and Steven Rosefielde, *The Trump Phenomenon and the Future of US Foreign Policy*, Singapore: World Scientific, 2016.

Part I
Trump's Domestic Agenda

Chapter 1

Establishment System

The target of Donald Trump's populist ire is the establishment system of American political, economic and social governance. America's founding principle in 1776 was democratic free enterprise (compassionate liberal democracy),[1] but the 20th century witnessed a silent revolution starting with the adoption of the federal income tax in 1913 (16th constitutional amendment) that bloated the government and gradually imposed the preferences of elected officials and big business on the electorate and private households.

The establishment positioned itself as the people's agent, beginning with a modest social security insurance program, sundry public works, and an anti-trust agenda, but over decades morphed into a regulatory empire covering health, education and welfare, promoting equal opportunity, entitlement,[2] affirmative action, restorative justice, open immigration, transnationalization, Wall Street and oligopoly in many industries. In recent decades, the boundaries between America and foreign nations have dissolved into the idea that the United States as the fountainhead of globalization should become the indispensable "global nation".[3] This oxymoron means that America should transform its culture into a progressive international blend, cede some of its national sovereignty to transnational institutions, and impose its universalized system on the world. Most establishment Democrats and Republicans are globalizers. They desire to rule the world from Washington in the name of all the planets' improved homogenized peoples, instead of the people they actually represent. The globalist posture gives them more degrees of freedom in pursuing their declaratory and hidden agendas at home and abroad. Both Democrats and Republicans find it convenient to tap Wall Street for financial support and promote globalization at home and abroad. Democrat and Republican politicians differ only in partisan emphasis and patronage networks. Democrats construct their collective identities around the theme of social justice, while Republicans focus on prosperity, promoting reduced taxation and economic growth. Democrats are the strongest proponents of globalism, but the Republicans also espouse the global nation dream.

Both encourage outsourcing as a device for turning government into a "public service" business. Government today often hires private companies to provide public services. Politicians own or control many of these firms allowing them to benefit directly and via under-the-table kickbacks and campaign contributions (super PACs).[4] Democrats and Republicans spend fortunes on their electoral campaigns because winning gives them control over patronage machines that not only provide public jobs, but also lucrative public contracts and protection for private interests via government industrial regulation. Some politicians may believe that big government is the best vehicle for serving their constituencies, but even those that do not, understand that expanded federal spending is the ticket to personal wealth and power.

The hallmarks of establishment rule are lucrative government programs, overregulation, open immigration and overtaxation borne by the middle class. Insiders enrich themselves directly and indirectly via tax loopholes. The poor, immigrants, "entitled", socially disadvantaged and rich at both ends of the income spectrum receive transfers from the common man's pocket. The lower and upper end beneficiaries never have enough, while the middle never has too little from the establishment's perspective.

Democrats drive the system toward social programs (affirmative action,[5] entitlements, and restorative justice[6]) when they hold the reins of power. Republicans drive the system toward business deregulation, with both factions oblivious to the secular decline induced by stultifying regulation and low labor force participation to join the entitled lower depths.[7] This establishment system tends to induce economic stagnation, and is self-perpetuating, if the middle class acquiesces and economic conditions are not too dire.

The establishment denies that big government, regulation, immigration, entitlements, affirmative action, restorative justice and taxation are excessive, but tacitly acknowledges the problem by relying on sky-high national debt, deficit spending, easy money and financial speculation to keep the economy afloat. First, it depresses the patient with barbiturates, and then tries to turbo-charge it with amphetamines, claiming that this serves the people best, even though the middle class knows better.

The discrepancy between the populist experience and the establishment's sunshine narrative is hidden by academia and the media.[8] Both are integral parts of the system. Academic economists divert attention from the middle class's plight by claiming that the establishment has the necessary tools at its disposal to assure that everyone prospers. Democrat and Republican establishment economists both insist more government is always better, ignoring the fact that ordinary people are paying the piper. They contend that sophisticated planning and management techniques mean that government programs are efficient; squabbling among themselves about best mix of monetary and fiscal stimulus. Instead of spotlighting the establishment's role in causing secular economic stagnation, most academics limit themselves to praising the system and choosing sides between Democrats and Republicans. The media drums home the message.

The failures of establishment system however are there for all to see. Despite trillions spent on eradicating poverty, the poverty rate has changed little in 50 years. Despite hundreds of billions spent on the war against drugs, the establishment can only report that it is legalizing pot. Despite a 20 trillion-dollar federal debt and a quadrupling of the money supply (m0) after 2010,[9] America's economy is barely able to grow at half its historical recovery rate. Despite countless promises, the middle class is becoming the new socially "disadvantaged". The establishment system is failing the middle class and spawning social discord, but politicians, the media and academics respond by denying this. It is an exercise in hypocrisy.[10]

The stealthy advance of the establishment system galls Donald Trump's populist supporters. Trump has sensed the anger and is tapping middle-class frustration. He could be co-opted, but his nationalist instincts and distaste for anti-nationalist excesses are prodding him toward advocating programs that re-empower the middle.

Endnotes

1. This means that consumer demand governs the supply of goods and services in the private sector and that the people's (demos) demand determines the supply of public programs.
2. "Entitlement" in the United States is used to identify federal programs that, like Social Security and Medicare, got the name because workers became "entitled" to their benefits by paying into the system. In recent years, the meaning has been used to refer also to benefits, like those of the food stamps program, which people become eligible to receive without paying into a system. Some federal programs are also considered entitlements even though the subscriber's "paying into the system" occurs via a means other than monetary, as in the case of those programs providing for veterans' benefits, and where the individual becomes eligible via service in the US military.
3. For a discussion of the concept see Strobe Talbott, "America Abroad: The Birth of the Global Nation", *Time*, July 20, 1992. http://channelingreality.com/Documents/1992_Strobe_Talbot_Global_Nation.pdf. "I'll bet that within the next hundred years (I'm giving the world time for setbacks and myself time to be out of the betting game, just in case I lose this one), nationhood as we know it will be obsolete; all states will recognize a single, global authority. A phrase briefly fashionable in the mid-20th century — 'citizen of the world' — will have assumed real meaning by the end of the 21st." "The best mechanism for democracy, whether at the level of the multinational state or that of the planet as a whole, is not an all-powerful Leviathan or centralized superstate, but a federation, a union of separate states that allocate certain powers to a central government while retaining many others for themselves.
   Federalism has already proved the most successful of all political experiments, and organizations like the World Federalist Association have for

decades advocated it as the basis for global government. Federalism is largely an American invention. For all its troubles, including its own serious bout of secessionism 130 years ago and the persistence of various forms of tribalism today, the US is still the best example of a multinational federal state. If that model does indeed work globally, it would be the logical extension of the Founding Fathers' wisdom, therefore a special source of pride for a world government's American constituents." Cf. https://www.pri.org/verticals/global-nation. This is a global nation advocacy group. Edward Goldberg, "America: Indispensable Nation, or Indispensable Partner?", *RealClearWorld*, October 12, 2016. http://www.realclearworld.com/articles/2016/10/12/america_indispensable_nation_or_indispensable_partner_112087.html. "America and its global role have been redefined during those 18 years; we are no longer the indispensable nation, we are the indispensable partner, and there is a big philosophical difference between those two ideas. The indispensable nation — like the individual entrepreneur, i.e., Donald Trump — takes independent risks to protect its own status. The indispensable partner leads and takes risks to protect the stability of its network — the new joint ventured world — and to grow that network."

4. Steven Rosefielde and Quinn Mills, *Democracy and Its Elected Enemies*, Cambridge: Cambridge University Press, 2013. Super PACs are a relatively new type of committee that arose following the July 2010 federal court decision in a case known as *SpeechNow.org v. Federal Election Commission*. Technically known as independent expenditure-only committees, super PACs may raise unlimited sums of money from corporations, unions, associations and individuals, then spend unlimited sums to overtly advocate for or against political candidates. Unlike traditional PACs, super PACs are prohibited from donating money directly to political candidates, and their spending must not be coordinated with that of the candidates they benefit. Super PACs are required to report their donors to the Federal Election Commission on a monthly or semiannual basis — the super PAC's choice — in off-years, and monthly in the year of an election. As of January 07, 2017, 2,408 groups organized as super PACs have reported total receipts of $1,797,657,369 and total independent expenditures of $1,119,480,236 in the 2016 cycle. https://www.opensecrets.org/pacs/superpacs.php.

5. Privileges given to socially disadvantaged individuals and groups including women and minorities are called "affirmative action".

6. Advocates of restorative justice like Black Lives Matter (BLM) demand compensation for the cumulative suffering inflicted on blacks by slavery and past racism rather than harm caused by perpetrators actually at fault. BLM is an international activist movement, originating in the African-American community that campaigns against violence and systemic racism toward black people.

7. Disability rates in America have soared because feigning disability pays better than working. Maxim Gorki, *The Lower Depths*, Wellesley, MA: Branden Publishing Company, 1906. Today's "rock bottom" social strata receive public housing, food and transportation subsidies, and upscale free healthcare.

8. Voltaire satirized this mentality nearly four hundred years ago by having Dr. Pangloss explain why syphilis is a national blessing. "It was a thing unavoidable, a necessary ingredient in the best of worlds; for if Columbus had not caught in an island in America this disease, which contaminates the source of generation, and frequently impedes propagation itself, and is evidently opposed to the great end of nature, we should have had neither chocolate nor cochineal" (Voltaire, *Candide, or the Optimist*, 1759).

9. http://www.tradingeconomics.com/united-states/money-supply-m0.

10. Sarah Chayes, "It Was a Corruption Election: It's Time We Realized It", *Carnegie Endowment for International Peace*, December 6, 2016. http://carnegieendowment.org/2016/12/06/it-was-corruption-election.-it-s-time-we-realized-it-pub-66381?mkt_tok=eyJpIjoiWXpnME5EWmpaR05tT kRObSIsInQiOiJac0FDDeUxjVllRSXYxcjVVeTIxWkhjOTRuT3VGRnR RT3pMekVWUXJSMnVKWVhxY0RWcWhVWEd5a3VZaTJJc3RzUX VoQ2xzWStRWWVrbU02Y3ZZTRYdjI5dDRWNk1GT2VJVFVFVJa3E 3eUx6QT0ifQ%3D%3D. American government has become thoroughly corrupt because of "Networks that weave together public officials and business magnates (think the food or energy industries, pharmaceuticals, or Wall Street) have rewritten our legislation to serve their own interests. Institutions that have retained some independence, such as oversight bodies and courts, have been deliberately disabled — starved of operating funds or left understaffed. Practices that, while perhaps not technically illegal, clearly cross the line to the unethical, the inappropriate, or the

objectively corrupt have been defended by those who cast themselves as bulwarks of reason and integrity". "Two candidates— Bernie Sanders and Donald Trump — made the word 'corruption' central to their campaigns. Together they drew easily more than half of votes cast. Yet to use this word to describe America remains almost taboo in polite circles. In the hundreds of pages of post-election commentary, how often has it been emphasized?" "In a country full of sophisticated lawyers and lobbyists and rationalizers, it is now urgent to ask whether we still understand what corruption is. To say it's what is proscribed by law is to fall into a logical sinkhole".

Chapter 2

Trump's Populism

Establishment critics call Donald Trump a populist and accuse him of heresy, of being a "retro" conservative enemy of equal opportunity, affirmative action, entitlement, restorative justice, competition and free trade.[1] His detractors view themselves as heirs of the French revolution (Declaration of the Rights of Man and state administrated progressive order) and treat Trump as a symbol of Thermidorian Reaction.[2] The bipartisan establishment perceives itself as the enlightened fusion of economic liberalization and compassionate social justice, dismissing Trump as the demagogic voice of nativist nostalgia. The establishment claims to harmonize social justice with prosperity, and accuses Trump of standing for the restoration of white male privilege, social conservatism, and callous individualism. The establishment portrays itself as the champion of anti-racism, anti-misogyny and anti-plutocracy, casting Trump as being insensitive to racial, religious, gender and economic inequality.

Is Trump intent on extinguishing social progress in favor of a conservative populist mix of isolationism, protectionism and white male domination? Does Donald Trump have a Dream? Or is he reacting as a contrarian against aspects of the establishment agenda without any intention of rolling back the clock to some romanticized future? The answers appear to be no, no and yes.

Trump is a force of nature. He is not an ideologue. He is a domineering entrepreneur, and a self-declared protector of the middle class who prefers military, business and veteran politicians to idealists,[3] but he has not espoused white male supremacy, nor opposed social justice. Trump is an unabashed individualist, not a collectivist. He is an ardent nationalist who seeks to make America a great force in Liberal Democratic global engagement. He is not a nostalgic isolationist.

Unlike Martin Luther King,[4] Trump has not explicitly articulated a dream. Like all politicians, he says that he wants to get America moving again, and resume its place as a great nation, but he has not embraced any specific social movement including libertarianism (Tea Party).[5]

Trump is a tycoon on the prowl for undervalued assets and hidden business opportunities wherever he finds them.[6] He treats experts as disposable hired guns and views the establishment as a cabal defending its economic, political and social privileges. He is a brash opportunist. Trump has wrested labor from the clutches of the Democratic Party. He has harnessed resentment against establishment programs and policies to his electoral advantage. He believes that establishment negotiators have been inept and has vowed to cut better deals.

Trump's temperament and background make him an advocate of a rough and tumble open society that frees initiative,[7] rewards the bold, and gives the bum's rush to motivated idealism.[8] He does not let other people's pieties and dreams foreclose his options. America's establishment maintains its authority by tabooing contrary opinion. It selectively chills legitimate dissent and free thought by treating dissenters as hate criminals (deplorable bigots),[9] and impairs efficient resource allocation in the name of entitlement. It tries to enrich itself by merchandizing public services. Trump opposes all of this and is right to do so. His contrarianism is not tantamount to an Enlightenment democratic vision, but his entrepreneurial spirit and efficiency mindedness incline him in the old fashioned "laissez-faire" direction.[10] Trump wants to salvage and rebuild a self-reliant, competitive America. He is a 21st century disciple of Ralph Waldo Emerson,[11] Frederick Winslow Taylor[12] and Fitzgerald's *The Great Gatsby*.[13] He is more an apostle of an open, can-do, cost-cutting Americanism than a social visionary, or counter-revolutionary defender of the ancient regime. The titles of his books capture his mentality: *Art of the Deal; Great Again; Think Big and Kick Ass in Business and Life*.[14]

High roller entrepreneurship is risky business. Trump's companies have filed for bankruptcy on numerous occasions.[15] He is likely to take the same approach as America's president, gambling with other people's money. His Thermidor may empower America, but buckle up. High stakes presidential contrarianism may mean that the nation is in for a wild ride.

Doing the Right Thing

Political legitimacy in America depends on persuading the public that governors are doing the right thing.[16] The establishment's authority rests on the claim that American rulers make right choices and their critics are "retro". Democrats and Republicans differ about priorities but hold a united front on the establishment's social mission, even though they square off against each other for electoral purposes. Both parties are supposed to support the consensus regardless of which party is in power.

Trump's legitimacy is rooted in a populist tradition that applauds self-reliance, productivity, admires tycoons and distrusts federal government. The outlook blends nativism with pragmatic self-reliance and audaciousness. The attitude suits the man, and underscores how far America has drifted from its founding values, but it is not failsafe.[17]

American Populist Policy

American populism is not an ideology.[18] It is a preference for nativist, democratic small government rather than an agenda for the socially and economically disadvantaged. Popular distrust of big government means that populists broadly favor a smaller federal presence in educational, health, social security and environmental affairs, but their attitudes toward defense, industrial policy and finance are fluid. Populists may advocate isolationism or robust national defense. They may support financial deregulation, or stringent control of banking and Wall Street, and they usually oppose oligopoly. Trump's reform agenda is congruent with the middle class's distrust of establishment government in the areas of education, health, social security and the environment, but his attitudes toward defense, big business, and Wall Street are more business friendly than ordinary people prefer. He seems to be a Teddy Roosevelt "trust-buster", but his pro-business orientation could well induce him to accommodate the mergers and acquisitions crowd.[19]

The chapters that follow scrutinize educational, environmental and social welfare aspects of Trump's populism, spotlighting his proclivities to clarify precisely where he stands *vis-à-vis* the establishment. The analysis identifies various technical problems with Trump's initiatives, but readers must decide the normative merits themselves.

Endnotes

1. The establishment has a composite American dream rooted in Franklin Delano Roosevelt's efforts to alleviate the plight of American workers through anti-competitive state intervention, state construction projects, economic relief and sky-high taxation in an isolationist era. His Democratic Congress tried to reverse foreign trade protectionism by passing the Reciprocal Trade Agreements Act of 1934, which allowed FDR to negotiate tariff reductions on a bilateral basis. Tariffs fell from 19 percent in 1930 to 13 percent in 1940, that is to the pre-Hawley–Smoot level. Roosevelt's attitudes toward race and religion are disputed. In June 1941, he issued Executive Order 8802, which created the Fair Employment Practice Committee (FEPC), but interned Japanese Americans during the war, and did little to impede Hitler's Holocaust.

2. The Thermidorian Reaction was a *coup d'état* within the French Revolution against the leaders of the Jacobin Club who had dominated the Committee of Public Safety. It was triggered by a vote of the National Convention to execute Maximilien Robespierre, Louis Antoine de Saint-Just and several other leading members of the revolutionary government. This ended the most radical phase of the French Revolution.

3. A populist is a member or adherent of a political party seeking to represent the interests of ordinary people.

4. Martin Luther King, Jr., "I Have a Dream", Speech by Martin Luther King at the "March on Washington", 1963. https://www.archives.gov/files/press/exhibits/dream-speech.pdf.

5. The Tea Party is an American political movement calling for a reduction of the US national debt and federal budget deficit by reducing government spending, and for lower taxes.

6. Foreigners applied the title "tycoon" [Taikun (大君)] to the *shogun* of Japan ["Nihon-koku Taikun" (日本国大)] in power between 1857 and 1868.

7. Karl Popper, *The Open Society and Its Enemies*, Princeton NJ: Princeton University Press, 2013.

8. Motivated idealism is a variant of the psychological term "motivated reason". It implies that idealism serves an ulterior purpose; that idealism is just an instrument for persuading others to accommodate you.

9. Hate speech is speech that attacks a person or group on the basis of gender, ethnic origin, religion, race, disability, or sexual orientation. The speech does not have to be hateful. Accusers claim the right to judge intent, and use the term indiscriminately. Alan Charles Kors, "Harassment Policies in the University", *Society*, Vol. 28, No. 4, (May/June 1991), pp. 22–30.

10. Abstention by governments from interfering in the workings of the free market.

11. Ralph Waldo Emerson, *Self-Reliance*, 1841. http://www.emersoncentral. com/selfreliance.htm. "So use all that is called Fortune. Most men gamble with her, and gain all, and lose all, as her wheel rolls. But do thou leave as unlawful these winnings, and deal with Cause and Effect, the chancellors of God. In the Will work and acquire, and thou hast chained the wheel of Chance, and shalt sit hereafter out of fear from her rotations. A political victory, a rise of rents, the recovery of your sick, or the return of your absent friend, or some other favorable event, raises your spirits, and you think good days are preparing for you. Do not believe it. Nothing can bring you peace but yourself. Nothing can bring you peace but the triumph of principles."

12. Taylor pioneered time and motion cost-cutting analysis, the forerunner of contemporary operations research.

13. F. Scott Fitzgerald, *The Great Gatsby*, New York: Charles Scribner's Sons, 1925.

14. Donald Trump, *Art of the Deal*, New York: Random House, 1987. Donald Trump, *Great Again*, New York: Simon and Schuster, 2015. Donald Trump, *Think Big and Kick Ass in Business and Life*, New York: First Collins, 2007.

15. Chris Isidore, "Everything You Want to Know about Donald Trump's Bankruptcies", *CNN Money*, August 31, 2016. http://money.cnn.com/ 2015/08/31/news/companies/donald-trump-bankruptcy/. "Trump has never filed for personal bankruptcy. But he has filed four business bankruptcies, which Bankruptcy.com says makes Trump the top filer in recent decades. All of them were centered around casinos he used to own in Atlantic City. They were all Chapter 11 restructurings, which lets a company stay in business while shedding debt it owes to banks, employees and suppliers".

16. Michael Sandel, *Justice: What's the Right Thing to Do?* New York: Farrar, Straus and Giroux, 2009.

17. Steve Mufson, "Trump Era Confronts Organized Labor with Gravest Crisis in Decades", *Washington Post*, December 9, 2016. https://www.washingtonpost.com/business/economy/trump-era-confronts-organized-labor-with-gravest-crisis-in-decades/2016/12/08/9f3fc584-bd5e-11e6-94ac-3d324840106c_story.html?utm_term=.62489b2f2f2a. "President-elect Donald Trump's Twitter attack this week on a union official, followed by his choice of a labor secretary who has criticized new worker protections, has rattled leaders of the American labor movement, who fear unions may be facing their gravest crisis in decades.

On Thursday, Trump announced that he would nominate as his labor secretary Andrew Puzder, a fast-food executive who has opposed additional overtime pay for workers and expressed skepticism about increasing the minimum wage. That followed a pair of Twitter messages Wednesday evening in which Trump attacked an Indiana union leader who had criticized him, saying the official had done a 'terrible job representing workers.'" "The list of potential setbacks for the labor movement is daunting. Some union leaders are worried that a Trump administration would attempt to introduce a national right-to-work law — allowing any employee anywhere to exempt themselves from participating in a union — and block unions from deducting dues from paychecks." "Some union leaders, who spoke on the condition of anonymity because they were not authorized to speak for the unions, said that labor leaders also fear that a Republican Congress and Trump White House would launch investigations of union finances while failing to enforce labor laws when employers underpay workers or violate occupational safety rules". "Trump's own views on worker issues have been mixed. He has argued for infrastructure spending to create jobs and to scale back trade deals that might imperil manufacturing workers. But he has also sparred with workers — the National Labor Relations Board ruled earlier this year that Trump's Las Vegas hotel violated the law when it refused to bargain with a union representing workers there. Trump is appealing."

18. Jan-Werner Müller, *What is Populism?*, Philadelphia: University of Pennsylvania Press, 2016.

19. "Election 2016: Trump on Antitrust", *National Law Review*, October 11, 2016. Kevin Carty, "An Unpredictable Upcoming Matchup: Donald Trump vs. Big Business", *Atlantic*, November 16, 2016. http://www.theatlantic.com/business/archive/2016/11/donald-trump-vs-big-business/507878/.

Chapter 3

Immigration

The establishment is incensed by Donald Trump's sound bites on immigration.[1] He is being assailed by Democrats as a "populist", "nationalist", racist and demagogue, and by free trade Republicans as an "anti-globalist".[2] He has fallen afoul of social justice advocates[3] and free traders both of whom disregard the interests of the middle class.[4] Are Trump's critics right? Is US immigration policy well-conceived? Is it balanced in the national interest?[5]

A sound immigration policy depends on net national benefit including compassion for immigrants and intangible foreign goodwill[6] with adjustments made for refugees fleeing life-imperiling political persecution. This requires a straightforward calculation of the expected economic and social contribution of each prospective immigrant to national well-being defined above (including foreign students and professionals temporarily working in the private sector), offset by counterpart economic and social costs. Immigration officers can compute applicants' expected lifetime earning streams and economic and social externalities based on educational attainments and skills. They can make parallel estimates of direct and indirect social service costs, including the burden of multilingual accommodation. They can calculate net benefits for individuals, families or groups, and estimate whether immigration spurs economic growth.[7]

Advocates, including Christian missionary groups,[8] and opponents claim that these calculations will support their views and provide copious statistical evidence. Both challenge each other's findings and selectively choose indicators. This suggests that the issue is not black and white and allows multiple interpretations,[9] but the big picture drawn from census data indicates that immigration is huge, rapidly rising[10] and concentrated in poor and unskilled Third World workers who intensively utilize social services and generate less income (value added) than native-born Americans[11] (see Figures 3.1, 3.2 and Table 3.1).[12] The data include illegals, but the statistical reliability of this immigration cohort is doubtful.

The basics are as follows: 42.4 million immigrants (foreign born) lived in the United States in 2014.[13] Approximately 11.5 million were illegals who entered the country without official authorization or overstayed their visas.

Nearly half (47 percent, that is 20 million) of all these foreign-born residents were naturalized as of 2014. Another 4.1 million were children of immigrants born in America. They are counted as citizens, not

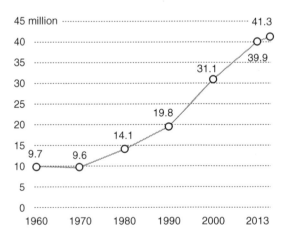

Figure 3.1. US Foreign-Born Population Reaches New High.

Source: U.S. Census Bureau, "Historical Census Statistics on the Foreign-Born Population of the United States: 1850–2000" and Pew Research Center tabulations of 2010 and 2013 American Community Survey (IPUMS). Estimates for 1960–2000 shown here may differ from other reported estimates since they are based on U.S. Census Bureau tabulations of the full sample data and not public-use subsamples from IPUMS.

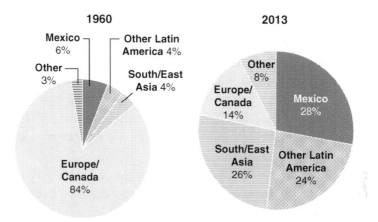

Figure 3.2. From Europe and Canada to Latin America and Asia: A Dramatic Shift in Immigration Origins.

Source: Pew Research Center tabulations of 1960 U.S. decennial census data and 2013 American Community Survey (IPUMS).

Table 3.1. Top Countries of Birth of Immigrants, 1960–2013.

	#1 Largest Country of Birth		#2 Largest Country of Birth		#3 Largest Country of Birth	
	Country of Birth	% of Immigrant Population	Country of Birth	% of Immigrant Population	Country of Birth	% of Immigrant Population
2013	Mexico	28	China	6	India	5
2010	Mexico	29	China	5	India	5
2000	Mexico	29	China	5	Philippines	4
1990	Mexico	22	China	5	Philippines	5
1980	Mexico	16	Germany	6	Canada	6
1970	Italy	10	Canada	9	Germany	9
1960	Italy	13	Germany	10	Canada	10

Note: China includes Taiwan, Hong Kong, Mongolia and Macau.
Source: Pew Research Center tabulations of 1960–2000 U.S. decennial census data and 2010 and 2013 American Community Survey (IPUMS).

immigrants, even though they are part and parcel of the larger immigration problematic.

More than a million illegal foreign-born children of immigrants are eligible for naturalization. Trump has promised to prevent this from happening. If he fails, then they will become permanent residents and citizens with full rights and duties. Immigrants granted citizenship of all types, legal and illegal would constitute nearly 8 percent of America's 318 million population (2014).

These trends are projected to continue through 2065, with a shift from Hispanic to Asian intensive immigration occurring in 2055[14] (see Figures 3.3, 3.4 and 3.5).

The fundamentals reveal that the problem is both big and little. On one hand, immigration, naturalization and citizenship automatically granted to the children of immigrants born in America is huge in comparison with global emigration to China, Japan or even the European Union.[15] On the other hand, the American immigration challenge is small compared with Israel. The Jewish state's population

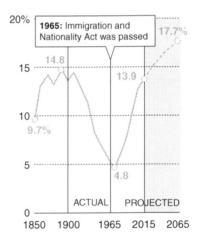

Figure 3.3. US Foreign-Born Share Projected to Hit Record Milestone by 2065.

Note: Data labels are for 1850, 1890, 1970, 2015 and 2065.

Source: Gibson and Jung (2006) for 1850 to 1890. Edmonston and Passel (1994) estimates for 1900–1955; Pew Research Center estimates for 1960–2015 based on adjusted census data; Pew Research Center projections for 2015–2065.

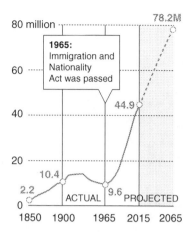

Figure 3.4. US Foreign-Born Population Reached 45 Million in 2015, Projected to Reach 78 Million by 2065.

Note: Data labels are for 1850, 1900, 1965, 2015 and 2065.

Source: Gibson and Jung (2006) for 1850 to 1890. Edmonston and Passel (1994) estimates for 1900–1955; Pew Research Center estimates for 1960–2015 based on adjusted census data; Pew Research Center projections for 2015–2065.

increased by nearly 20 percent in 1990–2000 due to the exodus of Jews (and some non-Jews) from Russia in the wake of the Soviet Union's demise with beneficial results.[16] Russian Jews quickly assimilated into Jewish Israel. The immigrants were better educated than the resident Israeli population and everyone prospered economically. Israeli economic performance was exceptional in 2000–2016, with the country flourishing during and after the global financial crisis of 2008.[17] Immigration was a boon, not a bane. America's experience, however, has been just the reverse. The global financial crisis traumatized the nation without any observable benefit from immigration.

These contrasting experiences suggest that the economic effects of immigration depend heavily on the human capital of newcomers and their attitudes toward assimilation. Where these factors are positive, as in the case of Israel, the middle class of all races, ethnicities and religions can prosper from immigration.[18] Where these factors are negative, as they have been in the United States, the middle class has suffered from immigration.

% of immigrant population

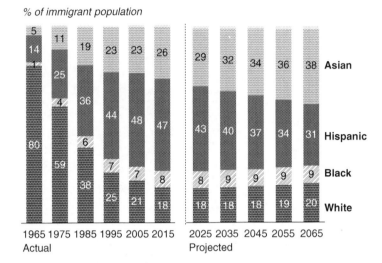

Figure 3.5.   Asians Projected to Become the Largest Immigrant Group, Surpassing Hispanics.

Note: Whites, blacks and Asians include only single-race non-Hispanics. Asians include Pacific Islanders. Hispanics are of any race. Other races shown but not labeled.

Source: Pew Research Center estimates for 1965–2015 based on adjusted census data; Pew Research Center projections for 2025–2065.

The composition of recent immigration to America is discomforting on both scores, and will remain so until 2055 when the increased inflow of highly educated, work oriented, upwardly mobile, entrepreneurial Asians from China, Taiwan, Hong Kong, Macau and India forecast by the Pew Research Center partly rectify the human capital imbalance. Until then, affluent Americans are and will continue benefiting from cheap labor (lower wages and servants), but the middle class will pay most of the bill for public services provided to immigrants. The American middle class will likely continue suffering income erosion and rising taxes to cover welfare costs. The intangible cost of social accommodation will also grow. Immigrants with engineering, medical and entrepreneurial skills will have little difficulty assimilating and embracing the traditional American way, even if they build strong ethnic communities in the US in the fashion of the Chinese and

Indians, but other groups, most conspicuously Islamic fundamentalists whose numbers are concealed in the aggregates will seek to impose their values on the nation.[19] Right or wrong, this may well cause intense sectarian strife of the sort visible in the Middle East in novel forms, and erode the cultural values (Protestant ethic) that supported America's superior economic performance in the past.

Trump's misgivings are valid from the middle class's perspective, even though ordinary Americans sympathize with newcomers, immigrant children and the globalist "American dream".[20] There is a legitimate case for slowing and reforming immigration within the racially, ethnically and religiously open framework established by Lyndon Johnson in 1965.[21]

The middle class is willing to accept gradual evolutionary changes in the scale and mix of immigration compatible with steady improvements in its well-being. The optimal rate and composition of immigration from the populist point of view depends on the net contribution immigrants make to the quality of middle class life in all respects, altruistically adjusted to accommodate refugees in life threatening circumstances. This determination takes compassionate account of net material benefits, environment factors (including congestion),[22] civic harmony,[23] the terrorist threat, international security and general global well-being.

Current immigration policy is at odds with the populist goal. It is skewed toward the poorly educated and low skilled with weak English language abilities, who require welfare assistance. It is also passive with regard to the terrorist threat. Reducing immigration quotas for the poorly educated and low skilled will ameliorate both problems.[24] Illegals of all types should be deported and terrorists and criminals should be expelled too, while permitting re-entry through established legal channels.

The numbers of well-educated and high-skilled immigrants can be adjusted up or down as circumstances dictate. The competitive forces of supply and demand should determine the scale of foreign students and long-stay professional immigration. Their impact is overwhelmingly positive in most respects.

Adjusting establishment immigration policy is not difficult. The reforms considered above accord with common sense and are neither unthinkable nor cruel as the establishment contends. Some people who might have brighter horizons immigrating to America will have to satisfice at home, but the well-being of ordinary Americans will improve. There are no free lunches.

The establishment energetically opposes the populist solution. Wall Street's endgame is to drive wage rates down to the global mean. Immigration for the financial and big business communities should only cease when foreigners are as well off at home as they are in America.[25] "Global nation" advocates have a different endgame. They want to replace America's founding culture with a "progressive" Third World-oriented internationalist blend consonant with the spirit of Karl Marx's Communist international. There is no authoritative global nation manifesto, but the loose text follows the line hewed by the Comintern.[26] If American globalists are consistent they should cap immigration when it no longer advances their notion of domestic social and economic justice.

Globalists and Wall Street, if they had their druthers would accelerate immigration including illegals and grant citizenship to anyone who wants it. They are not concerned about criminals or terrorists and some on the politically correct left may even support immigrant-led revolutionary violence. Both employ sophisticated quantitative analysis and compassionate rhetoric to plead their cases, but their ulterior motives are transparent. Wall Street wants profits and the Democrat party wants political power. Democrats are wagering heavily that the demographic revolution is the ticket to their perpetual electoral dominance; Republicans are gambling that they can have their cake and eat it too. Trump opposes both.

Endnotes

1. It is claimed that Trump's ideas on immigration are influenced by the polemics of Ann Coulter. See Ann Coulter, *Adios, America: The Left's Plan to Turn Our Country into a Third World Hellhole*, Washington, DC: Regnery Publishing, 2015. Ann Coulter, *In Trump We Trust: E Pluribus Awesome!*, New York City: Sentinel, 2016.

2. AEI and CATO which serve as think tanks for the Republican Party both staunchly support free immigration. Alex Nowrasteh, "Trump's Real Immigration Policy", *Cato Institute's Center for Global Liberty and Prosperity*, November 17, 2016. http://www.learnliberty.org/blog/ trumps-real-immigration-policy/?gclid=CI36iYXww9ACFUdYDQod w14OGQ. Steven Hayward, "The Great Liberal Freakout", November 9, 2016. http://www.powerlineblog.com/archives/2016/11/the-great-liberal-freakout.php.

   "The head of the Joint Center for Political Studies, which the Washington Post describes as a 'respected liberal think tank,' reacted to Republican candidate's election: 'When you consider that in the climate we're in — rising violence, the Ku Klux Klan — it is exceedingly frightening.' Castro, still with us, said right before the election: 'We sometimes have the feeling that we are living in the time preceding the election of Adolf Hitler as Chancellor of Germany.' Claremont College Professor John Roth wrote: 'I could not help remembering how economic turmoil had conspired with Nazi nationalism and militarism — all intensified by Germany's defeat in World War I — to send the world reeling into catastrophe... It is not entirely mistaken to contemplate our post-election state with fear and trembling.' Esquire writer Harry Stein says that the voters who supported the Republican candidate were like the 'good Germans' in 'Hitler's Germany.' Sociologist Alan Wolfe is up in the *New Left Review*: 'The worst nightmares of the American left appear to have come true.' And he doubles down in *The Nation*: '[T]he United States has embarked on a course so deeply reactionary, so negative and mean-spirited, so chauvinistic and self-deceptive that our times may soon rival the McCarthy era.' The *Bulletin of Atomic Scientists*, keeper of the "Doomsday Clock" that purported to judge the risk of nuclear annihilation, has moved the hands on the clock from seven to four minutes before midnight. Oh wait, did you think this was the reaction to Trump? Sorry — these are what the left was saying the day after Ronald Reagan's election in 1980. Some things never change."

3. Heidi Bierich, "The Nativist Lobby: Three Faces of Intolerance", January 31, 2009. https://www.splcenter.org/20090201/nativist-lobby-three-faces-intolerance.

4. The middle class for our purposes excludes both the rich and the poor. It is defined primarily by income and wealth criteria; rather than the role or

lack thereof members play in the productive process. Those not working for diverse reasons and low-wage earners including some clergy do not pay income taxes, and are mostly subsidized. The productive taxpayers in the new working class (middle class) are blue- and white-collar wage earners; salaried personnel, and the self-employed defined here as most individual service providers, small- and medium-size proprietors, and middle income professionals. In America, workers including the self-employed pay Social Security taxes and Medicare taxes. Self-employed individuals pay twice as much as individual workers, plus unemployment taxes. Everyone pays sales tax. The core of the nation's productive workers, are primarily those in the middle class with family incomes above $50,000 per year. The middle class also can be usefully conceptualized as families with taxable incomes in the 25 and 28 marginal tax brackets; that is between $10,000 and $190,000. Those with family taxable income north of $190,000 are classifiable as rich. See Steven Rosefielde and Quinn Mills, *Global Economic Turmoil and the Public Good*, Singapore: World Scientific, 2015.

5. Unlimited immigration is often presented as having a moral dimension — as being part of the moral high ground. It might be, if it were not accompanied by the impoverishment of millions and the enrichment of the establishment which advocates it.

   Immigration is appropriate when prosperity is advancing for the citizens of the recipient country, and when the establishment gains from immigration no more than other citizens of the host country.

   The massive legal and illegal immigration which has been sponsored in the United States by the left and acquiesced in by big business has not met these requirements. Immigration has been accompanied by increasing impoverishment of the American middle class and to some degree has contributed to the decline of the middle class — though it is not a prime cause. And recent immigration has benefited the Democratic establishment via voting for them and it has benefited the establishment generally by providing a source of cheap labor for their organizations.

   The right answer is limiting immigration until the two conditions are met and raising it slowly at that point.

6. The United States' openness to immigration is viewed by many foreigners as a positive aspect of the "American Dream". This is good for all concerned and facilitates US foreign policy goals including promotion of democracy, free enterprise, equal opportunity and the rule of law.

7. Michael Kremer, "Population Growth and Technological Change: One Million B.C. to 1990", *The Quarterly Journal of Economics*, Vol. 108, No. 3, 1993, p. 681. Dennis Ahlburg, "Julian Simon and the Population Growth Debate", *Population and Development Review*, Vol. 24, No. 2, 2002, pp. 317–327. Alberto Bucci, "Population Growth in a Model of Economic Growth with Human Capital Accumulation and Horizontal R&D", *Journal of Macroeconomics*, Vol. 30, 2008, pp. 1124–1147.

8. Christian missionary organizations of multiple denominations including evangelical have been actively promoting converts to emigrate to the United States. They have been especially active with refugees like the Karen, Hmong and middle American natives. Approximately 64,759 Karen came as refugees only from mid-2000s to July 1, 2015. Hmong communities in the United States have stabilized. The US government estimates indicate that between 170,000 and 186,000 Hmong were living in the United States by 2008. However, estimates from non-government sources have suggested that there may actually be between 250,000 and 300,000. About 60,000 Hmong reside in the state of Minnesota, with about 30,000 in the Minneapolis-St. Paul area alone.

9. George Borjas, *We Wanted Workers: Unraveling the Immigration Narrative*, New York: W.W. Norton, 2016.

10. "Foreign born" and "immigrant" are used interchangeably and refer to persons with no US citizenship at birth. This population includes naturalized citizens, lawful permanent residents, refugees and asylees, persons on certain temporary visas, and the unauthorized.

11. The Hispanic cohort has subpar education and skills. The Asian cohort has above par education and skills.

12. "Chapter 5: U.S. Foreign-Born Population Trends", *Pew Research Center*, September 28, 2015. http://www.pewhispanic.org/2015/09/28/modern-immigration-wave-brings-59-million-to-u-s-driving-population-growth-and-change-through-2065/.

13. Jie Zong and Jeanne Batalova, "Frequently Requested Statistics on Immigrants and Immigration in the United States", *Migration Policy Institute*, May 26, 2016. http://www.migrationpolicy.org/article/frequently-requested-statistics-immigrants-and-immigration-united-states?gclid=CP3ho5nextACFQlXDQodj-cMrA.

14. "Modern Immigration Wave Brings 59 Million to U.S., Driving Population Growth and Change Through 2065", *Pew Research Center*, September 28, 2015.

http://www.pewhispanic.org/2015/09/28/modern-immigration-wave-brings-59-million-to-u-s-driving-population-growth-and-change-through-2065/.

15. Immigration to the EU-28 from non-member countries was 1.9 million in 2014. Eurostat, "Migration and Migrant Population Statistics", *Eurostat: Statistics Explained*, May 2016. http://ec.europa.eu/eurostat/statistics-explained/index.php/Migration_and_migrant_population_statistics.

16. Assaf Razin and Steven Rosefielde, "Israel and Global Developments 1990–2015: Riding with the Global Flows", in Avi Ben-Bassat, Reuven Grunau and Asaf Zussman, eds., *Israel Economy in the 21st century*, MIT Press, 2017.

17. Assaf Razin and Steven Rosefielde, "Israel and Global Developments 1990–2015: Riding with the Global Flows", in Avi Ben-Bassat, Reuven Grunau and Asaf Zussman, eds., *Israel Economy in the 21st century*, MIT Press, 2017.

18. It should be noted that middle class blacks are prominent victims of wage compression. A close investigation of the micro immigration shows that the influence of blacks as a group is being diminished, and their presence in universities limited by Asian competition.

19. The Pew Canadian, European, African and Asia categories contain significant numbers of Muslims that are easily missed by casual readers.

20. The Statue of Liberty proclaims: "Give me your tired, your poor, your huddled masses yearning to breathe free, the wretched refuse of your teeming shore. Send these, the homeless, tempest-tossed to me, I lift my lamp beside the golden door!" The American middle class and foreigners remain responsive to this idealism.

21. The Immigration and Nationality Act of 1965 (H.R. 2580; Pub.L. 89–236, 79 Stat. 911, enacted June 30, 1968), also known as the Hart–Celler Act, changed the way quotas were allocated by ending the National Origins Formula that had been in place in the United States since the Emergency Quota Act of 1921. Representative Emanuel Celler of New York proposed the bill, Senator Philip Hart of Michigan co-sponsored it, and Senator Ted Kennedy of Massachusetts helped promote it.

22. Once upon a time, America was an open frontier. We are now overcrowded.

23. Immigrants before 1965 were expected to assimilate and did. Not so today. Islamic fundamentalists reject assimilation and many cosmopolitans support anti-assimilationist diversity.

24. American immigration policy has fluctuated historically with politics and economic conditions. See "History of U.S. Immigration Laws", *Federation for American Immigration Reform*, January 2008. http://www.fairus.org/facts/us_laws.

25. David Dollar and Aart Kraay, "Spreading the Wealth", *Foreign Affairs*, January/February, Vol. 81, No. 1, 2002, pp. 120–133. https://www.foreignaffairs.com/articles/2002-01-01/spreading-wealth.

26. The Communist International, abbreviated as Comintern and also known as the Third International (1919–1943). Today's progressives, unlike Comintern advocates, do not support the eradication of the state. They prefer a strong state that imposes their social agenda.

Chapter 4

Protectionism and National Sovereignty

The establishment is aghast at Donald Trump's advocacy of protectionism and national sovereignty.[1] Democratic and Republican advocates of America as the "global nation" and champions of the new world democratic free trade order have roundly condemned him.[2] The establishment contends that nationalist policies designed to protect industries and workers from foreign competition are a discredited relic of a bygone age. Democrats and Republicans warn that tampering with the World Trade Organization (WTO), International Monetary Fund (IMF), World Bank (WB), The North American Free Trade Agreement (NAFTA) and Trans-Pacific Partnership (TPP) including the 45 percent tariff Trump has threatened to impose on Chinese imports will trigger a worldwide trade war that will harm everyone including Trump's anti-establishment supporters.[3]

Democrats and many Republicans also oppose tampering with international institutions like the United Nations (UN), the International Court of Justice (ICJ) and other organizations that dilute American sovereignty and empower many anti-democratic elements. A significant segment of the establishment is sympathetic with transnational government like the European Union (EU) and Association of Southeast Asian Nations (ASEAN), and is continuously pressing the internationalist cause. Trump has expressed concern about this aspect of globalization.

The establishment contends further that multilateral free trade maximizes economic welfare everywhere, fosters economic development through direct foreign investment and technology transfer, and promotes the convergence of living standards worldwide to a common high frontier. Free trade is win–win.[4] Protectionism is lose–lose, they say.

Are Trump's critics right? Is US international trade policy sensible and balanced in the interest of the American middle class?

The consensus among professional economists is that the establishment is right and Trump is wrong on all three scores, but the details are opaque and the merit of outcomes depends on whose ox is being gored. The balance inclines toward Trump from the populist perspective, especially on the issue of national sovereignty.

Specialists in international macroeconomic theory believe that tariff wars and quotas are value destroying; that they lead to universal contractions in economic activity driven by negative Keynesian "multiplier" effects.[5] They argue that protectionist measures designed to save jobs in import-competing sectors reduce income and aggregate effective demand abroad, culminating in reduced foreign demand for American exports. Income destroying protectionism is derided as "beggar-thy-neighbor" job security that causes acute economic depression.[6] International macroeconomic theorists attribute the intensity and duration of the Great Depression of the 1930s in large part to Hawley–Smoot "beggar-thy-neighbor" job protectionist policies.[7] They recognize that tariff wars do not have to culminate in depressions,[8] but believe nonetheless that wage rigidities, liquidity traps[9] and other obstructions make this result probable.

The Soviet experience belies the claim. The USSR practiced autarky (economic self-sufficiency with abnormally low trade participation) from 1929 to 1989 without incurring any unemployment or depression.[10] The Kremlin banned inessential imports from non-Comecon countries,[11] and exported to satisfy critical needs without adverse cyclical macroeconomic consequences. This proves that protectionism does not have to have catastrophic cyclical outcomes and can provide job security if cleverly managed.[12]

However, the cyclical stability of Moscow's command economy was costly. Protectionism (autarky and command planning) allowed Soviet workers to "enjoy" over-full employment,[13] but only at the expense of inferior living standards because barriers to free competition impaired technology transfer and diminished consumer welfare.[14]

Sino-American Trade Deficit

The establishment consensus that protectionism on balance is apt to harm national well-being therefore is persuasive, but only if the alternative is free or workable competition.[15] This is the rub. The evaluation of protectionism becomes less clear when there are grounds for suspecting that state-managed market economies like China use beggar-thy-neighbor tactics to support domestic employment, subsidize exporters and protect import competitors to the detriment of America's middle class.[16]

The issue is slippery because the harm caused by China's state managed trade is less visible than it was immediately after the 2008 global financial crisis when American unemployment peaked at 10 percent.[17] The problems today are subtler. Millions of discouraged Americans have dropped out of the labor force, many claiming disability benefits because they cannot find jobs and are no longer counted as unemployed.[18] Inexpensive Chinese imports put downward pressure on wages unrelieved by increased American exports to China because of concealed protective barriers imposed by Beijing. The welfare loss sustained by American workers from China's beggar-thy-neighbor trade practices were partly offset by the gain realized by consumers from China's subsidized exports and purchases of US treasury bonds with excess dollar reserves.[19] Beggar-thy-neighbor foreign trade practices therefore are not necessarily detrimental because the consumer benefit of subsidized goods may offset the collateral damage,[20] even though they are unambiguously detrimental when they lead to depressions and/or negative side effects are shared unequally as they are today by American workers.[21]

Table 4.1 reveals the magnitude of the problem. It shows that China exported 483,245 million dollars of goods to America in 2015, but

Table 4.1. 2015: US Trade in Goods with China.

Month	Exports	Imports	Balance
January 2015	9,481.5	38,588.4	–29,106.9
February 2015	8,759.3	31,573.6	–22,814.2
March 2015	9,882.0	41,139.2	–31,257.1
April 2015	9,306.7	36,115.8	–26,809.2
May 2015	8,763.1	39,073.2	–30,310.2
June 2015	9,621.7	41,455.0	–31,833.3
July 2015	9,513.6	41,216.4	–31,702.8
August 2015	9,169.3	44,141.9	–34,972.6
September 2015	9,424.3	45,718.2	–36,293.9
October 2015	11,410.1	44,318.6	–32,908.4
November 2015	10,618.0	41,908.3	–31,290.3
December 2015	10,122.3	37,996.2	–27,873.9
TOTAL 2015	**116,071.8**	**483,244.7**	**–367,172.9**

Note: All figures are in millions of US dollars on a nominal basis, not season-ally adjusted unless otherwise specified. Details may not equal totals due to rounding. Table reflects only those months for which there was trade.

only purchased 116,072 million dollars' worth of imports in return. The current account imbalance was –367,173 million dollars. If Trump bans America from trading with China, domestic manufacturers will produce more than a third of a trillion dollars-worth of new import substitutes and exports, with a commensurate increase in jobs and a fillip for increased wages.[22] The numbers for 2016 through October are nearly identical.[23]

International trade theory teaches that the harm Trump perceives in the bilateral current account trade deficit between China and America (compounding losses from "offshoring") is misleading because Beijing and/or third parties ultimately should use dollar surpluses to buy American goods roundabout. The logic is sound, but global markets are not generally competitive. Aggregate effective demand often is deficient and unemployment can be endemic. The global market should effi-ciently adjust to current account and financial imbalances, but seldom does raising the question of whether it is better to limit the US–China current account imbalance by state to state agreement (after threaten-ing each other with economic war); eliminate diffuse barriers to perfect competition, use tax transfers to compensate displaced workers, or grin and bear it. The establishment on both sides of the aisle for the last decade has chosen to accept Beijing's claim that it does not indulge in beggar-thy-neighbor state trading. Democrats and Republicans have both urged patience, taking into account a host of factors including international security.

The establishment defends its passivity by arguing that time will heal the Sino-American current account deficit, but the situation warrants a comprehensive reassessment because there is no relief in sight. Although it can be plausibly argued that China does not intend to harm America's workers, its state trading system is structured to generate precisely this outcome across a wide spectrum of potential Chinese foreign exchange rates.[24] The import side of the Sino-American trade deficit is not mysterious. Beijing currently holds 3.1 trillion dollars-worth of foreign currency reserves.[25] It has the power as state trade manager to purchase American goods and services,[26] or give a large portion of its reserves to the Chinese people as a dollar denominated "tax" refund, allowing them to buy American goods themselves.[27] However, it has chosen to do neither, implicitly protecting China's import competing domestic sector. Beijing uses stealthy subsidies to encourage overexporting in the interest of Communist insiders.[28]

Trump's assertions that American workers are harmed by Beijing's state trading practices; that the market cannot resolve the Sino-American trade deficit alone[29] and that America's globalists do not care about American workers are all correct. There is a legitimate need for deft action to redress the imbalance,[30] including tit for tat trade renegotiations.[31]

Off-Shoring

Beijing's overexporting impairs America's export competitiveness and drives US manufactures to outsource part of their operations abroad. They may well do so anyway for other competitive reasons, but the Sino-American trade deficit is a contributing cause. The relocation of American manufacturing abroad is called "off-shoring". Donald Trump took action to curb off-shoring even before officially assuming the presidency. He announced on December 1, 2016 that he had called the CEO of Carrier Corporation who agreed to keep 1,000 jobs in Indiana instead of off-shoring them to Mexico,[32] and he suggested that the same technique would be applied broadly to fight job flight. Trump's method was to obtain a promise from Indiana's governor to provide a seven million dollar incentive package to Carrier.[33] The establishment immediately attacked him for using jobs as a pretext for giving Carrier "corporate welfare".[34] Supporters counter-argued that the subsidy merely offsets American off-shoring tax incentive credits.[35] Carrier workers were impressed.[36]

The issue is convoluted because although both sides of the establishment oppose off-shoring job losses,[37] Democrats and Republicans do not want to do anything about it. Democrats oppose solutions that benefit big business ("corporate welfare") and urge increased tax collection on unrepatriated multinational corporate profits held abroad to pay for worker relief.[38] Republicans reject solutions that impair free trade and oppose tax transfers to labor.

Trump himself does not condemn all aspects of off-shoring. He understands that there are valid economic arguments for outsourcing, and has concentrated his fire against the use of federal subsidies to facilitate the process. His deal with Carrier therefore is significant because it shows that Trump is willing to employ a wide range of protectionist tactics beyond punitive tariffs without repudiating free trade. The approach is pragmatic. It uses political power to achieve an acceptable balance between the merits of job protection and trade promotion, and differs from establishment practice by deprioritizing the globalist agenda in favor of American workers.

National Sovereignty

Trump is a staunch traditional nationalist who refuses to conflate the American interest as populists perceives it with globalism. The establishment wants America to lead and dominate globalization as the global nation; that is, a great power that transfers aspects of national sovereignty to international institutions (not the people of the world) as the *quid pro quo* for global hegemony.[39] For the Democrats this means America's transformation into a blended civilization reflecting Third World aspirations, affirmative action and restorative justice. Republicans take a somewhat different approach. They too are willing to transfer aspects of national sovereignty to international institutions, but seek foreign economic penetration in return. Trump rejects both strategies. He refuses to surrender US sovereignty to multinational institutions and multilateral trade agreements,[40] but is willing to pursue international agreements bilaterally, if sovereign America can negotiate acceptable terms. The distinction may appear trivial, but it is not in Trump's hands. Trump does not accept the establishment status quo. He will not request a waiver to bar America's embassy in Israel from relocating to Jerusalem as globalists urge to appease the EU establishment,[41] or kowtow to China's sensibilities about Taiwan.[42] He will veto the Transpacific Partnership (TPP),[43] Transatlantic Free Trade Area (TAFTA) and Transatlantic Trade and Investment Partnership (TTIP),[44] and disregard aspects of prior accords including NATO that infringe traditional American sovereignty as he sees it.[45]

Trump's position mirrors critics who fault the EU for its "democratic deficit".[46] French, Greek, Italian and Dutch nationalists, following the British lead, are demanding that their nations exit the EU partly because they contend that the unelected European Commission governs their economic, political and social lives in the establishment's interests against the people's will in each member state.[47]

Is Trump on the side of the democratic angels against the insider establishment? No summary judgment is possible at the present juncture. Democratic nationalism is compatible with the Enlightenment and has much to commend it on this score,[48] but democracy is not tantamount to doing the right thing, which needs to be assessed on a case by case basis. The notion of establishment infallibility, however, deserves Trump's scorn.

Endnotes

1. This includes Trump's opposition to the Offshoring Act (the Internal Revenue Code of 1985 that provides tax relief to companies relocating abroad

from the United States). He proposes establishing tariffs to discourage companies from laying off their workers in order to relocate in other countries and ship their products back to the United States. Some Congressmen have been pressing for this issue since 2010.

2. America was protectionist during the Great Depression, but reversed course after World War II when it began a sustained effort to negotiate a global reduction in tariffs and quotas under the auspices of GATT, the General Agreement on Trade and Tariffs. The process began in Geneva in April 1947 and continued in nine rounds through the Doha negotiations in 2001. The 75 existing GATT members and the European Communities became the founding members of the WTO on January 1, 1995. Tariff levels today are under 10 percent and negligible in transatlantic trade. See WTO, *Trade and Tariffs*, 2015. https://www.wto.org/english/thewto_e/20y_e/wto_20_brochure_e.pdf.

Post-war global trade was also positively affected by evolving exchange rate and financial systems that began when Western nations accepted the Bretton Woods fixed exchange rate system based on the dollar, but tied it to gold. The free trade tide gained momentum after the United States unilaterally terminated convertibility of the US dollar to gold on August 15, 1971. The Plaza Accord signed on September 22, 1985 at the Plaza Hotel in New York City between the governments of France, West Germany, Japan, the United States and the United Kingdom depreciated the US dollar in relation to the Japanese yen and German Deutsche Mark by intervening in currency markets, triggered a massive expansion in global international trade, and the creation of the IMF and WB contributed to the process.

3. Simon Denyer, "As Trump Prepares for Office, Concerns about China Trade Intensify", *Washington Post*, November 28, 2016. https://www.washingtonpost.com/world/asia_pacific/as-trump-prepares-for-office-concerns-about-china-trade-reach-a-crescendo/2016/11/27/472b5c26-b199-11e6-bc2d-19b3d759cfe7_story.html.

4. "Trump Confronting China on Trade Sets Up Corporate Backlash Risk", *Bloomberg News*, November 28, 2016. http://www.bloomberg.com/politics/articles/2016-11-28/trump-confronting-china-on-trade-sets-up-corporate-backlash-risk.

"If US President-elect Donald Trump delivers on campaign pledges to get tough with China on trade, lining up against him likely will be another powerful adversary: American multinational corporations. These companies have more than $228 billion in China investments at stake in the event of a trade conflict between the world's two biggest economies. Their track record of pushing back against Washington on trade indicates they'll back their own interests — and thus China — if enmity erupts".

5. John Maynard Keynes, *The General Theory of Employment, Interest and Money*, London: Macmillan Cambridge University Press, for Royal Economic Society, 1936.

6. Adam Smith, *An Inquiry into the Nature and Causes of the Wealth of Nations*, Book IV, Chapter III (part II), 1776: "… nations have been taught that their interest consisted in beggaring all their neighbours." Charles Kindleberger, *The World in Depression: 1929–1939*, Berkeley CA: University of California Press, 1973.

7. Joan Robinson, "Beggar-My-Neighbour Remedies for Unemployment", in *Essays in the Theory of Employment*, 2nd edn., Oxford, UK: Basil Blackwell, 1947, pp. 156–170.

8. Say's law contends that the invisible hand will quickly limit economic contractions. Jean-Baptiste Say, *A Treatise on Political Economy* (*Traité d'économie politique*), 1803. He wrote: "A product is no sooner created, than it, from that instant, affords a market for other products to the full extent of its own value". See Ben Bernanke, "Monetary Policy and the Global Economy", *Board of Governors of the Federal Reserve System*, March 25, 2013. https://www.federalreserve.gov/newsevents/speech/bernanke20130325a.htm.

9. Paul Krugman, "Thinking about the Liquidity Trap", December 1999. http://web.mit.edu/krugman/www/trioshrt.html.

10. Franklyn Holzman, *Foreign Trade under Central Planning*, Cambridge: Harvard University Press, 1974. Cf. Steven Rosefielde, *Russian Economy from Lenin to Putin*, New York: John Wiley, 2007.

11. The Council for Mutual Economic Assistance (Совет Экономической Взаимопомощи) was an economic organization from 1949 to 1991 under the leadership of the Soviet Union that comprised the countries of the Eastern Bloc along with a number of communist states elsewhere in the world.

12. Protectionism is frequently advocated to nurture "infant industries".

13. Soviet workers labored more hours per year than they would have if they received a competitive wage, and had the right to substitute leisure for labor. People working less than the state mandated were viewed as "parasites" and enemies of the people.

14. Paul Samuelson, *Foundations of Economic Analysis*, Cambridge: Harvard University Press, 1947.

15. John M. Clark, "Toward a Concept of Workable Competition", *The American Economic Review*, Vol. 30, No. 2, Part 1, June 1940, pp. 241–256.

16. Steven Rosefielde, "China's Perplexing Foreign Trade Policy: Causes, Consequences and a Tit for Tat Solution", *American Foreign Policy Interests*, Vol. 33, No. 1, January–February 2011, pp. 10–16. Steven Rosefielde, "Export-led Development and Dollar Reserve Hoarding", in Steven Rosefielde, Masaaki Kuboniwa and Satoshi Mizobata, eds., *Two Asias: The Emerging Postcrisis Divide*, Singapore: World Scientific, 2012, pp. 251–266. Steven Rosefielde and Huan Zhou, "Global Imbalances", in Steven Rosefielde, Masaaki Kuboniwa and Satoshi Mizobata, eds., *Prevention and Crisis Management: Lessons for Asia from the 2008 Crisis*, Singapore: World Scientific, 2012.

17. Bureau of Labor Statistics, Labor Force Statistics from the Current Population Survey, http://data.bls.gov/timeseries/LNS14000000. An Economic Policy Institute report, "Unfair China Trade Costs Local Jobs", March 2010 estimates that China's excess export practices have cost American workers 2.4 million jobs since 2001, when China joined the WTO. www.epi.org.

18. Steven Rosefielde and Quinn Mills, *Global Economic Turmoil and the Public Good*, Singapore: World Scientific, 2015.

19. Most of China's foreign-exchange reserves are held in US dollar-denominated financial assets such as US Treasury securities. Since 2008, when it overtook Japan in this respect, China is the largest foreign owner of US Treasury securities, accounting for about 22 percent of all US Treasuries held by non-Americans.

20. Subsidies can be viewed as gifts to the beneficiary. Ironically, if Beijing sent cash to American consumers instead of underpriced exports, few would complain.

21. Gottfried von Haberler, *The Theory of International Trade*, Geneva: League of Nations, 1936. Gottfried von Haberler, *Prosperity and Depression: A*

Theoretical Analysis of Cyclical Movements, 1937, New Jersey: Transaction Publishers, 2011.

22. Jobs would have been saved in low value-added industries subject to predatory competition, and jobs would have expanded in high value-added industries with correspondingly higher wages.

23. United States Census, "Trade in Goods with China". http://www.census. gov/foreign-trade/balance/c5700.html.

24. China's state managed foreign trade system can maintain huge trade surpluses across a wide spectrum of renminbi exchange rate through the application of hidden quantity controls and subsidies. For a discussion of China's managed exchange rate see Steven Rosefielde, "China's Perplexing Foreign Trade Policy: Causes, Consequences and a Tit for Tat Solution", *American Foreign Policy Interests*, Vol. 33, No. 1, January–February 20, 2011, pp. 10–16; Steven Rosefielde, "Export-led Development and Dollar Reserve Hoarding," in Steve Rosefielde, Masaaki Kuboniwa and Satoshi Mizobata, eds., *Two Asias: The Emerging Postcrisis Divide*, Singapore: World Scientific, 2012, pp. 251–266.

25. The composition of China's foreign currency reserves is a state secret. Foreign analysts agree that about two-thirds of Chinese foreign-exchange reserves are held in US Dollars, approximately one-fifth in Euros and almost all the rest in Japanese yen and British pounds. China's foreign currency reserves peaked in 2014 at four trillion dollars. http://www. tradingeconomics.com/china/foreign-exchange-reserves. The source is the People's Bank of China.

26. The official position is that Beijing cannot find enough Western goods worth importing, other than weapons technologies the Pentagon refuses to sell. The generals at the People's Liberation Army Academy of Science conference, "The Economic Crisis — Implications for Global Security", Beijing held in July 13–17, 2009 complained that America was responsible for China's huge dollar reserve holdings because it would not sell the PLA sensitive military technology.

27. Exporters are required by law to surrender their dollar earnings (at the border) to the state bank. Loraine West, "Reform of China's Foreign Trade System and Prospects for Freer Trade", Center for International Research, US Bureau of the Census, CIR Staff Paper No. 69, October, 1993.

28. Countries that competitively maximize consumer utility do not overexport because the state prioritizes the people's welfare over special interests.

29. Aparna Mathur, "Making Manufacturing Great Again Will Require a Two-Pronged Approach", *AEI*, December 21, 2016. http://www.aei.org/publication/making-manufacturing-great-again-will-require-a-two-pronged-approach/?utm_source=paramount&utm_medium=email&utm_content=AEITODAY&utm_campaign=122216. "Employment in manufacturing peaked in the late 1970s at over 19 million. Since then, despite occasional positive bumps, manufacturing employment has shown a long-term secular decline. Today, fewer than 13 million workers are employed in factory jobs." "Today, there are 322,000 vacancies that are unfilled. Clearly, manufacturing jobs exist, and employers are ready to hire, but for some reason workers and firms are not matching up to fill these jobs." "All of this suggests that to make manufacturing great again, we need a two-pronged approach. We must encourage workers to upgrade their skills with training in math, science and computing. For younger workers, paid apprenticeships with companies could produce big results. But aside from the skills gap, we also need to tackle the 'image-gap'— the unwillingness of some workers to take up these jobs because of their inherent bias against working in jobs that they perceive as similar to the factory jobs of the past."

30. Don Lee, "Fierce China Critic and UC Irvine Professor to Head Trump's New Trade Council", *Los Angeles Times*, December 21, 2016. http://www.latimes.com/nation/politics/trailguide/la-na-trailguide-updates-fierce-china-critic-to-head-trump-s-1482352818-htmlstory.html. "President-elect Donald Trump is establishing a new White House-based trade office that will be headed by a UC Irvine professor known for his fierce criticisms of Chinese trade and economic practices. In appointing Peter Navarro as director of trade and industrial policy and the head of the new National Trade Council inside the White House, Trump is signaling that he wants to follow through on his tough campaign rhetoric in which he blamed the Chinese for the large U.S. trade deficit and manufacturing woes." Peter Navarro, *Crouching Tiger: What China's Militarism Means for the World*, Amherst, NY: Prometheus, 2015. Peter Navarro and Greg Autry, *Death by China*, Upper Saddle River, NJ: Pearson Education, 2011.

31. Tit for tat solutions are flexible. The basic concept can be modified to include warnings, consultations and negotiations. If this fails, tit for tat

can be introduced gradually, beginning with small import ban quotas, gradually increased as required. Gradualism might be more powerful than some suppose because as third parties begin to capture part of China's export market, outsourcing and foreign direct investment will shift in tandem. Foreign direct investment and the free technology transfer it provides are important drivers of Chinese economic growth, and reducing these inflows is sure to catch party leaders' attention. For a discussion of tit for tat games and nuances in optimal decision making, associated with the "prisoner's dilemma" see Robert Axelrod, *The Evolution of Cooperation*, New York: Basic Books, 1984, and Anatol Rapoport, *Fights, Games and Debates*, Ann Arbor: University of Michigan Press, 1960.

32. Benjamin Zycher, "The Carrier Deal and the Law of Unintended Consequences", December 2, 2016. https://www.aei.org/publication/the-carrier-deal-and-the-law-of-unintended-consequences/?utm_source=paramount&utm_medium=email&utm_content=AEITODAY&utm_campaign=120216.

33. NPR staff, "Is Trump's Deal with Carrier a Form of Crony Capitalism?" *NPR*, December 2, 2016. http://www.npr.org/2016/12/02/504042185/is-trumps-deal-with-carrier-a-form-of-crony-capitalism?utm_medium=RSS&utm_campaign=storiesfromnpr.

34. *Ibid.*

35. Roya Wolverson, "Outsourcing Jobs and Taxes", *Council on Foreign Relations*, February 11, 2011. http://www.cfr.org/united-states/outsourcing-jobs-taxes/p21777. "The current U.S. corporate tax code incentivizes companies to move their business operations overseas, and by extension the offshoring of jobs that would have based in the United States".

36. Salena Zito, "This Town gives Trump a Second Look after the Carrier Deal", *New York Post*, December 3, 2016. http://nypost.com/2016/12/03/this-town-gives-trump-a-second-look-after-the-carrier-deal/. "Trump deserves great credit for pulling this off, and certainly he deserves a second look from those of us who dismissed him because of how crazy this election cycle was. And you know what? He also deserves credit for coming to places like here, the middle of nowhere that politicians only talk about, not talk to," he said. "Haynes said Carrier was perhaps the most potent symbol of what these voters believe: that the powerful in America manipulate the working class for their personal gain." "In striking a deal to keep these jobs in the US, Trump delivers on the fundamental underpinning of his campaign; that he, one of the powerful, sees you, hears you and will

deliver for you, putting your interests on the level or even above those of the powerful," he said.

37. Roya Wolverson, "Outsourcing Jobs and Taxes", *Council on Foreign Relations*, February 11, 2011. "Many policymakers and analysts, including President Barack Obama, have repeatedly criticized the outsourcing of jobs abroad by U.S.-based multinational corporations, arguing that it not only reduces job opportunities for U.S. workers at a time of high unemployment, but also hurts U.S. competitiveness in the global economy. The Obama administration has proposed policies to encourage companies to move back to the United States, while closing corporate tax loopholes that make it easier for multinationals to pay limited taxes on their overseas operations. Some Democratic lawmakers, along with union representatives, believe Obama's proposals will help address a weak job market and troubling budget deficits. But Republicans, some Democrats, and industry representatives fear higher taxes on U.S.-based multinationals will lead to an exodus of business, investment, and jobs."

38. The treatment of multinational corporate taxation necessarily effects offshoring, but the net effects are disputed.

39. Steven Rosefielde and Quinn Mills, *Democracy and Its Elected Enemies*, Cambridge: Cambridge University Press, 2013.

40. Michael Spense, "Donald Trump and the New Economic Order", *Project Syndicate*, November 29, 2016. https://www.project-syndicate.org/commentary/nationalist-approach-to-economic-policy-by-michael-spence-2016-11?utm_source=Project+Syndicate+Newsletter&utm_campaign=987cc36f93-varoufakis_trump_minotaur+_4_12_2016&utm_medium=email&utm_term=0_73bad5b7d8-987cc36f93-93559677.

"In keeping with Trump's main campaign slogan, 'Make America Great Again,' it was his 'America first' comments that were most revealing. While Trump might pursue mutually beneficial bilateral agreements, one can expect that they will be subordinated to domestic priorities, especially distributional aims, and supported only insofar as they are consistent with these priorities. Developed-country voters' frustration with the old market-driven global economic architecture is not unfounded. That order did allow powerful forces, at times beyond the control of elected officials and policymakers, to shape national economies".

"The new emphasis on national interests clearly has costs and risks. But it may also bring important benefits. A global economic order sitting atop a crumbling foundation — in terms of democratic support and national political and social cohesion — is not stable. As long as people's identities are mainly organized, as they are now, around citizenship in nation-states, a country-first approach may be the most effective. Like it or not, we are about to find out".

41. The Jerusalem Embassy Act of 1995 is a public law of the United States passed by the 104th Congress on October 23, 1995. It was passed for the purposes of initiating and funding the relocation of the Embassy of the United States in Israel from Tel Aviv to Jerusalem, no later than May 31, 1999, and attempted to withhold 50 percent of the funds appropriated to the State Department specifically for "Acquisition and Maintenance of Buildings Abroad" as allocated in fiscal year 1999 until the United States Embassy in Jerusalem had officially opened. A waiver has been signed annually thereafter by every American president to appease international sensibilities, but Trump probably would not do it. Leigh Munsil, "Obama Delays Relocation of U.S. Embassy to Jerusalem for Final Time", *The Blaze*, December 1, 2016 2:36 pm. http://www.theblaze.com/news/2016/12/01/obama-delays-relocation-of-u-s-embassy-to-jerusalem-for-final-time/.

42. Stephen Collinson, Nicole Gaouette, Elise Labott and Laura Smith-Spark, "China Lodges Complaint over Trump–Taiwan call", CNN, December 3, 2016. http://www.cnn.com/2016/12/02/politics/donald-trump-taiwan/.

"China's foreign ministry said Saturday it has lodged a complaint with the United States over a controversial phone call between President-elect Donald Trump and Taiwan's President that has overturned decades of diplomatic protocol. China views Taiwan as a renegade province and, since 1979, the US has acknowledged Beijing's claim that Taiwan is part of China, with US–China relations governed by a set of protocols known as the 'one China' policy.

This means there are no formal diplomatic relations between the United States and Taiwan — so Trump's decision to take Taiwanese President Tsai Ing-wen's call could risk a major upset.

'We have noticed relevant reports and lodged solemn representation with the relevant side in the United States,' said a statement Saturday from China's Foreign Ministry spokesman Geng Shuang.

'I must point out that there is only one China in the world and Taiwan is an inseparable part of the Chinese territory ... The 'one China' principle is the political foundation of China–US relations. Trump risks antagonizing China after call with Taiwan.'"

43. The TPP or Trans–Pacific Partnership Agreement (TPPA) is a trade agreement among 12 of the Pacific Rim countries — notably not including China. The finalized proposal was signed on February 4, 2016 in Auckland, New Zealand, concluding seven years of negotiations. It is currently awaiting ratification to enter into force. Simon Johnson, "The Politics of Job Polarization", *Project Syndicate*, November 27, 2016. https://www.project-syndicate.org/commentary/trump-politics-job-polarization-by-simon-johnson-2016-11?utm_source=Project+Syndicate+Newsletter&utm_campaign=987cc36f93-.

"In this environment, with so many people insecure about their economic prospects, the push by President Barack Obama's administration for the Trans-Pacific Partnership (TPP) was a tone-deaf approach, at best. The administration argued that TPP would create some good jobs — and that people who lost jobs as a result could be 'compensated'. But such compensation always proves to be minimal and is widely viewed as meaningless".

44. The "United States–European Union High Level Working Group on Jobs and Growth" recommended the start of negotiations on the TTIP in 2013. Robin Emmott and John O'Donnell, "Analysis: Canceled EU–U.S. Talks Complicate Trade Ambitions," *YahooFinance*, October 6, 2013. TAFTA talks in Brussels were canceled because of the US government's partial shutdown. The process has been marred by exemptions. France won a concession to leave European movies and entertainment out of the pact, to shield them from Hollywood and Silicon Valley, raising concerns Washington may pursue opt-outs for its shipping industry on security grounds. EU and the US officials say the deal, known as the TTIP, could boost economic output by some $100 billion a year on each side of the Atlantic, creating a market of 800 million people. Both sides sought to complete the deal by the end of 2014, but failed. Claude Barfield, "The Case for a

Rump TPP", *AEI*, November 30, 2016. http://www.aei.org/publication/the-case-for-a-rump-tpp/?utm_source=paramount&utm_medium=email&utm_content=AEITODAY&utm_campaign=120516.

"President-elect Donald Trump has announced that he will follow through on his vow to upend U.S. trade policy by withdrawing from the recently completed Trans-Pacific Partnership Agreement (TPP) on his first day in office. His trade team has also announced that the regional agreement will be replaced by a series of bilateral trade agreements. And they have openly avowed that U.S. market power will enable the Trump administration to force U.S. trading partners to bow to its demands or face crippling trade barriers."

45. The North Atlantic Treaty Organization is an intergovernmental military alliance based on the North Atlantic Treaty which was signed on April 4, 1949. The organization constitutes a system of collective defense whereby its member states agree to mutual defense in response to an attack by any external party.

46. Simona Piattoni, "Institutional Innovations and EU Legitimacy after the Crisis" in Bruno Dallago and John McGowan, eds., *Crises in Europe in the Transatlantic Context: Economic and Political Appraisals*, London: Routledge, 2016, pp. 119–136.

47. Steven Rosefielde, "Grexit and Brexit: Rational Choice, Compatibility, and Coercive Adaptation", *Acta Oeconomica*, Vol. 66, September 2016, pp. 77–91.

48. Steven Rosefielde and Quinn Mills, *Democracy and Its Elected Enemies*, Cambridge: Cambridge University Press, 2013.

Chapter 5

Inclusive Economic Growth

If Horses Had Wings

E very American president after the Second World War has promised to foster full employment, economic stability and social progress.[1] They added economic growth, harmonious trade and a balanced budget to the mix in 1978.[2] More recently, there has been agitation for a fairer distribution of income and wealth (inclusive economic growth),[3] which could help the middle class if the rich shouldered more of the tax burden.[4]

Donald Trump, like his former presidential electoral rival Hillary Clinton endorses all these goals, but the establishment claims that Trump's populist economic policies are internally contradictory; that he cannot fulfill his promises and that his hidden agenda is to reward the rich.

Assuming that Trump really does want to help the middle class, is this mission possible? If so, are his economic policies realistic? Is he the beard for the wealthy? The answers are yes, probably and maybe.

No post-war president has achieved economic utopia. There have been periods of growth and inflation, stagflation, secular stagnation, booms, busts, high and low interest rates, full employment, overfull employment and crushing unemployment. Income has been mal-distributed in myriad ways and has never been ideal. The American economy has been in a state of secular stagnation since 2008, and more abnormally slow growth was on the globalist horizon.[5]

Some establishment economic strategies have been more internally consistent than others but the United States has run large federal budgetary deficits after 1960 with only two minor exceptions and is projected to keep doing so *ad infinitum*.[6] The American national debt is 20 trillion dollars,[7] or 119 percent of GDP,[8] and the money supply (M2) has increased by 75 percent since 2008.[9] The Congressional Budget Office reports that income inequality has risen steadily after 1975 and grown fastest for the top one percent of income earners.[10] America spent tens of trillions of dollars in war on poverty, but there is little progress to report.[11] All these numbers require qualification; however, the broad impression conveyed is accurate. The American and global economies are failing to deliver the good life to large segments of the population. The American and global economies are in serious disequilibrium (secular stagnation and financial bubbles).[12] Public programs are inefficient and profound economic inequities, signal difficult times ahead for macroeconomic management, no matter whether Trump or the establishment is at the helm.[13] Trump's critics are right in asserting that he is unlikely to keep all his economic promises.

Trump's pledge to decrease taxes and cover the budgetary deficit from the proceeds of enhanced GDP growth is pie-in-the-sky to the extent that it ignores anti-competitive, distortionary and devitalizing forces besetting the economy. Monumental fiscal deficits and rapid money expansion during the last decade, together with an anti-productive tax code and suffocating federal regulation have generated very subpar economic growth and there is no reason to anticipate that doubling down on failed policies will be more effective.[14]

What Can Be Done?

Trump's economic advisors know this, but still claim that this time will be better because fiscal deficits will be pro-growth instead of pro-welfare. They have a point, but only a bold and comprehensive strategy addressing all sources of America's economic dysfunction has a chance of putting the nation on the path to sustainable shared prosperity.

The trick, given existing systemic constraints is to break out of the establishment's deficit spending/excess monetary expansion trap by radically restructuring public expenditures.[15] Under the existing unwritten rules of the game neither Democrats nor Republicans can substantially alter the level and composition of federal spending because two-thirds of government resources are dedicated to "entitlements" (Social Security, Medicare, other welfare programs and interest), and half of the residual discretionary spending is allocated to defense and international security assistance. This means that nearly three quarters of federal spending for all intents and purposes is "mandatory" (non-discretionary) (see Figure 5.1[16]). Democrats and Republicans can bicker over the division of the remainder, and add

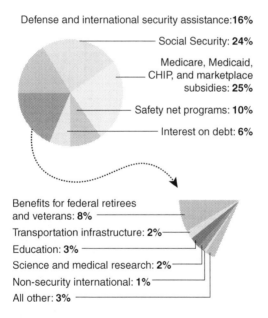

Defense and international security assistance: **16%**

Social Security: **24%**

Medicare, Medicaid, CHIP, and marketplace subsidies: **25%**

Safety net programs: **10%**

Interest on debt: **6%**

Benefits for federal retirees and veterans: **8%**

Transportation infrastructure: **2%**

Education: **3%**

Science and medical research: **2%**

Non-security international: **1%**

All other: **3%**

Figure 5.1. Most of Budget Goes Toward Defense, Social Security and Major Health Programs.

Center on Budget and Policy Priorities CBPP.ORC

Source: 2015 Figures from Office of Management and Budget, FY 2017 Historical Tables.

some fresh money, but the net effect on macroeconomic stability and GDP growth is apt to be small.[17]

If Trump stands any chance of accelerating sustainable economic growth and achieving collateral objectives, he must brush aside establishment taboos by looking inside the aggregates to undercover superfluous activities, waste, fraud and abuse that are misclassified as value added. The establishment insists that every dime spent by the federal government is essential, when countless scandals belie the assertion. Rosefielde and Mills have estimated that half of non-Social Security, non-Medicare and non-welfare expenditure can be eliminated with little loss to the nation.[18] Social Security, Medicare and other welfare expenditures also should not be sacrosanct, including block grants.[19] The establishment continuously tinkers with them, relaxing eligibility requirements and diluting returns to middle class contributors. Defense too is touchable. The establishment has larded the defense budget with social welfare mandates, funds for environmental protection and the "war against drugs trafficking" to shield these failed programs from public scrutiny. These featherbedded expenditures can be terminated, and the saving used to empower an investment driven "shared" growth economy.

A trillion dollars (a quarter of 2016 federal expenditures) can be cut,[20] and/or constructively reallocated to improve economic efficiency and accelerate economic growth. Some of these monies can and should be returned to taxpayers as a fillip to consumer demand and private investment. Trump proposed to dedicate some of these savings to public infrastructure rebuilding, which from Keynes's own perspective is a key to restoring full employment economic growth.[21] Other savings can be reallocated to growth promoting public expenditures,[22] and some savings can be used to pay down the national debt.

Trump could stimulate the economy further with corporate tax cuts (or permit corporations to expense investment instead of amortizing it).[23] In accordance with Ronald Reagan style supply side economics,[24] he is planning to reduce marginal tax rates across the board to stimulate profit-seeking and effort (see Figure 5.2).[25]

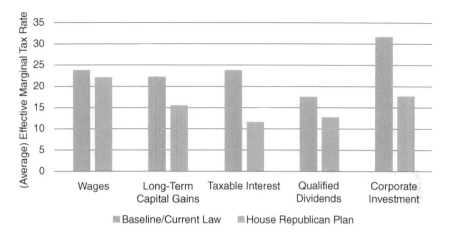

Figure 5.2. Effective Marginal Tax Rates Under Trump/House Plan.
Source: Alex Brill, "Tax Reform: Ryan-Brady Plan Is a Better Way." *Economic Perspectives*, American Enterprise Institue, October 2016.

He can also provide supplementary deficit financed public spending through a middle class "tax refund".[26] Trump can adopt a pro-competitive industrial policy, encourage investment based on present discounted value accounting rather than speculative financial returns. He can also nudge the nation toward a savings and investment culture, focusing policy on growth rather than Keynesian macroeconomic stabilization.

The establishment is trying its utmost to persuade Trump that he cannot operate outside the box,[27] but he does not have to straitjacket himself. He has many degrees of freedom. He can end excessive bureaucratic business regulation.[28] He can purge the tax code of its anti-growth provisions and rollback myriad executive orders and mandates that degrade America's economic competitiveness, and discourage foreign investment in the United States.[29] He can free resources placed off limits by federal bureaucracies.[30] He can appoint department and agency heads committed to reversing overzealous social policies that impede growth and efficiency.[31] The establishment strenuously resists tampering with anti-productive privileges concealed in the tax code, executive orders and mandates, but a populist outsider can sweep the street clean.

What Will Be Done?

Trump is likely to break out of the establishment box that prioritizes dependency, entitlements, transfers, affirmative action, anti-competitiveness (quotas, preferences, "fair wages"),[32] egalitarianism and government controls over effort, entrepreneurship and growth. He will try to restore growth through self-reliance, competition and innovation, while protecting workers from foreign predatory trade practices.

Trump should be able to increase defense and transport infrastructure spending. He will try to promote domestic production and protect workers by reversing some off-shoring and cool-headedly renegotiating trade pacts under the threat of imposing punitive tariffs and quotas.[33] He will cut taxes, reform the tax code, rescind most of Obama's executive orders,[34] amend or abolish the Dodd–Frank Wall Street Reform and Consumer Protection Act,[35] and try to rollback federal regulations, including those governing environmental protection, Occupational Safety and Health Administration, and obstructive affirmative action.[36]

Each of these actions should be positive from Trump's perspective, and most will help the middle class even though the battles will be fought tactically without a comprehensive and balanced vision of what ought to be done. The keys for the middle class are reduced taxation, restoration of public benefits, purging of price distortions in medical and educational services caused by federal misregulation, protection against foreign predatory trade practices and invigorated economic growth. Trump could deliver, but the proof will be in the pudding. Furthermore, it needs to be clearly understood that if he emphasizes deficit spending without cutting hundreds of billions of dollars of superfluous activities, waste, fraud and abuse from discretionary and "mandatory" federal spending as his designated budget director Mick Mulvaney is inclined to do,[37] his agenda will be jeopardized by an acute budgetary crisis. Macroeconomic magic and supply-side tax cutting are not enough to carry the day.

Trump has not provided any guidance about how he and his advisors plan to resolve the gargantuan revenue shortages that will necessarily arise if discretionary and mandatory programs are not slashed. should past deficit spending trends persist, national debt must continue its upward ascent at an accelerated pace and in the process debase bank balance sheets in the Federal Reserve system setting the scene for a mega global financial crisis,[38] and/or a bout of rampant inflation. Barack Obama and Hillary Clinton were both comfortable with rolling the dice in this way, and this likely will be the path of least resistance for Donald Trump.[39]

The best-case scenario for Trump's anti-establishment recovery package is milder secular stagnation. The 3–4 percent growth forecast by Steven Mnuchin is attainable, but not sustainable without comprehensive systemic reform.

Hard times are inevitable, if the national (and global) debt bubble bursts.[40] Hillary Clinton's economic plan would have been subject to the same danger, but this will be little solace to Trump if his program falters.

The only prudent way out of America's economic morass is to cut hundreds of billions of dollars of superfluous activities, waste, fraud and abuse from discretionary and "mandatory" federal spending. Trump could do it, but he does not yet fully grasp the unpalatable task awaiting him. At the end of the day, there is no such thing as a well-functioning, anti-competitive, inefficient, initiative suppressing, wasteful and corrupt economic system, whether it is governed by the establishment or Trump. There is no virtuous substitute for doing the right thing.[41]

Is Trump a Closet Plutocrat?

Is Donald Trump's populist economic program really well intended? Is he the middle class' best friend? He says that he wants to give the common man a fair shake, and is in the process of designing a program to improve the workers' lot by accelerating economic growth, adopting protectionist measures, reducing drug prices[42] and rewarding self-reliance. Some aspects of his agenda will benefit elements of the middle class; others will slice the other way. Cutting the nation's 35 percent top business tax rate to 15 percent obviously will increase corporate profits, but repatriating and collecting an estimated 1 trillion dollars of tax deferred profits held by foreign subsidiaries of large American corporations to increase federal tax revenues will reduce the stream of stockholders' future earnings.[43] Ditching the Dodd–Frank Wall Street Reform and Consumer Protection Act will help Wall Street grow richer,[44] but the protectionism Trump appears to envision will hurt the financial community's bottom line. Encouraging self-reliance will harm middle class beneficiaries of entitlement, affirmative action and restorative justice, but ordinary workers will gain.

The net impact of these and other conflicting forces cannot be accurately forecast. Trump might, or might not prove to be a closet plutocrat, even though the establishment's Democratic wing feels certain that his populist promises will be broken, but his policies will stimulate economic growth more than those advocated by Hillary Clinton. If she were in Trump's shoes, her policies of drastically raising taxes on the "1 percent" and raising the marginal federal income tax rate on millionaires to 70 percent would have stifled growth. She would have advanced the egalitarian cause, but sacrificed rapid GDP growth. Trump's strategy of stimulating business initiative is the better choice.

The incipient populist pro-growth counter-revolution that Trump appears to be engineering cannot produce economic utopia. An optimal economy is a textbook fantasy. Nonetheless, his stratagem could be superior to the status quo because it will enhance equal opportunity, self-reliance, consumer choice,[45] shared well-being, economic growth and might even increase distributive fairness.[46]

Endnotes

1. The Employment Act of 1946 Chapter 33, Section 2, 60 Stat. 23, codified as 15 U.S.C. § 1021, is an American federal law that makes the

government responsible for promoting full employment and business cycle stability, controlling inflation and spurring economic growth. Murray Weidenbaum, "The Employment Act of 1946: A Half Century of Presidential Policymaking, *Presidential Studies Quarterly*, Vol. 26, No. 3, Summer 1996, pp. 880–885.

2. The Full Employment and Balanced Growth Act (known informally as the Humphrey–Hawkins Full Employment Act), passed in 1978 provides the US federal government with a mandate to promote full employment, growth in production, price stability, and balance of trade and budget.

3. OECD, *All on Board: Making Inclusive Growth Happen*, Geneva: OECD, May 29, 2015.

4. Thomas Piketty, *Capital in the Twenty-First Century*, Cambridge, MA: Belknap Press, 2014.

5. Steven Rosefielde and Quinn Mills, *Global Economic Turmoil and the Public Good*, Singapore: World Scientific, 2015.

6. Office of Management and Budget, Table 1.1 — Summary of receipts, outlays, and surpluses or deficits (–): 1789–2021. https://www.whitehouse.gov/omb/budget/Historicals.

7. http://www.usdebtclock.org/.

8. The figure counts the money the government owns itself (borrowings from Social Security). If it is assumed that repayment of Social Security borrowing somehow does not matter, then the national debt falls to 74 percent of GDP. https://www.cia.gov/library/publications/the-world-factbook/geos/us.html.

9. M2 was 7451.4 billion dollars on January 7, 2008. It reached 13088.5 on September 19, 2016. US Money Supply (M2), http://www.data360.org/dataset.aspx?Data_Set_Id=10703. M0 has quadrupled over the same period.

10. "The Distribution of Household Income and Federal Taxes 2011". Congressional Budget Office, US Government. November 2014.

11. Robert Rector and Rachel Sheffield, "The War on Poverty After 50 Years", *Heritage Foundation*, September 15, 2016. http://www.heritage.org/research/reports/2014/09/the-war-on-poverty-after-50-years.

12. Yanis Varoufakis, "Trump, the Dragon, and the Minotaur", *Project Syndicate*, November 28, 2016. https://www.project-syndicate.org/commentary/

trump-chinese-debt-global-imbalances-by-yanis-varoufakis-2016-11?utm_
source=Project+Syndicate+Newsletter&utm_campaign=987cc36f93-
varoufakis_trump_minotaur+_4_12_2016&utm_medium=email&utm_
term=0_73bad5b7d8-987cc36f93-93559677.

13. Hans-Werner Sinn, *The Euro Trap: On Bursting Bubbles, Budgets, and Beliefs*, London: Oxford University Press, 2014.

14. *No Recovery: An Analysis of Long-Term U.S. Productivity Decline*, Gallup Report, December 7, 2016. http://www.gallup.com/reports/198776/no-recovery-analysis-long-term-productivity-decline.aspx?utm_source= ReportLandingPage. "We've been told that the economy is on its way back. In the seven years since the Great Recession, job growth in the United States has been steady and unemployment has fallen from 10% to just under 5%. Booming tech and professional services sectors should denote a healthy economy, but a new Gallup analysis identifies fundamental weaknesses in the U.S. economy that have emerged over decades. Economic growth has gradually fallen since the 1970s and 1980s, and three large sectors bear primary responsibility for the malaise: healthcare, housing and education. In 1980, healthcare, housing and education claimed 25% of national spending. By 2015, that share had ballooned to 36%. The costs to both national and per capita GDP are enormous." "In this study led by a Gallup senior economist in collaboration with the U.S. Council on Competitiveness, Gallup found that U.S. GDP per capita growth since 1980 has been nearly stagnant at 1.7% per year — and only 1% per year since 2007. Inflation and falling relative value in the healthcare, housing and education sectors are largely responsible."

15. The pure economic theory of optimal and satisficing economic system makes it clear that the plight of today's middle class can be remedied, and the well-being of the rest of the nation enhanced by radically overhauling the establishment economic mechanism. Economists are only able to prove the existence of a competitive general equilibrium, not its attainability. They can show how a competitive general equilibrium can be attained, and the existence of related bounded rational satisficing solutions, but cannot prove that such solutions are better for the middle class. Nonetheless, middle class welfare-improving solutions almost certainly exist because linking reward to productivity will

enhance labor and entrepreneurial per capita income. Also, it should be recognized that robotics and other labor saving technologies are putting pressure on American middle class jobs. Competition should overcome the problem in the long, but there may be a traumatic short run ahead that could thwart Trump's aspirations. See Steven Rosefielde and Ralph W. Pfouts, *Inclusive Economic Theory*, Singapore: World Scientific, 2014. The pertinent question however is whether better outcomes are possible with restricted reforms and the economic rejuvenation program envisioned by Trump's advisors.

16. "Policy Basics: Where Do Our Federal Tax Dollars Go?", *Center on Budget and Policy Priorities*, March 4, 2016. http://www.cbpp.org/research/federal-budget/policy-basics-where-do-our-federal-tax-dollars-go.

17. When one looks objectively at this budget, it is self-evident that increasing healthcare and retirement demands are going to make it difficult for the Federal government to use investment support programs to stimulate growth. Other approaches therefore will be essential to grow much faster to pay for these increasing costs, or there is going to be a big crash and then cuts will be made that none of us are now prepared to propose. What will have happened is merely that we will have chosen a path forward that goes through a crash rather than one that avoids it. Politicians in domestic policy, as in defense policy, cannot contemplate or accept a preemptive strike.

18. Steven Rosefielde and Quinn Mills, *Democracy and Its Elected Enemies*, Cambridge: Cambridge University Press, 2014.

19. The Federal government gave state $50 billion in block grants in 2014. See Robert Jay Dilger, "Block Grants: Perspectives and Controversies", *Congressional Research Service*, July 15, 2014. https://fas.org/sgp/crs/misc/R40486.pdf.

20. Paul LaMonica, "Trump Calls Fighter Jet Costs 'Out of Control'", *CNN Money*, December 12, 2016. http://money.cnn.com/2016/12/12/investing/donald-trump-lockheed-martin-f-35-tweet/index.html. "Trump tweeted Monday morning that the F-35 program and cost is out of control. Billions of dollars can and will be saved on military (and other) purchases after January 20th." Shares of Lockheed Martin (LMT), which makes the F-35 fighting jets, plunged 4% following

Trump's tweet. According to the fiscal 2017 Department of Defense budget released earlier this year, the Pentagon planned to spend $10.1 billion for F-35s — 43 F-35As for the Air Force, 16 F-35Bs for the Marine Corps and 4 F-35Cs for the Navy.

21. John Maynard Keynes, *The General Theory of Employment, Interest and Money*, London: Macmillan Cambridge University Press, for Royal Economic Society, 1936.

22. Real investment can be nudged up to 15% of GDP on a sustained, multi-year basis. This will create jobs and increase productivity and help restore the middle class. A corporate tax cut — yes. But only for real investment.

    A tax cut for the middle class — yes. Only for savings. This will help reduce the pressure on Social Security, which if more Americans save for retirement, will permit reductions of eligibility for Social Security. Increasing the Federal manipulated funds rate will bolster retiree's personal disposable income. Repatriation of profits held abroad by US firms — yes. Big incentives for real investment in the US. Massive reductions in federal regulations — yes. But major protections for the environment are continued. Massive reduction in size of federal bureaucracy — yes.

    Introduction of serious management into federal government activities — yes.

23. Experts disagree about whether reducing corporate tax rates would stimulate employment. Martin Feldstein argues that lower corporate taxes would be beneficial, but others disagree. See Martin Feldstein, "Would Reducing the US Corporate Tax Rate Increase Employment in the United States? in Michael Strain, ed., *The US Labor Market: Questions and Challenges for Public Policy*, Washington, DC: AEI, 2016, pp. 180–186.

24. James Gwartney, "Supply-Side Economics", in David R. Henderson, ed., *Concise Encyclopedia of Economics*, 2nd edn. Indianapolis: Library of Economics and Liberty, 2008.

25. Kevin A. Hassett, "Recovery through Tax Reform", *AEI*, December 9, 2016. http://www.aei.org/publication/recovery-through-tax-reform/?utm_source=paramount&utm_medium=email&utm_content=AEITHISWEEK&utm_campaign=Weekly121016.

26. Although middle class tax cuts benefit the middle class, their stimulatory effect on aggregate economic activity may be weak or non-existent.

Consumer can choose to save tax refunds instead of purchasing consumer goods and services.

27. There are many audacious possibilities for thinking outside the box. The US can discard the Federal Reserve System in favor of central banking. Social security could be terminated and replaced with an insurance program as originally intended. Cadillac medical care for the poor can be replaced with a Spartan alternative. Student loans need not be rescued. Environment restrictions can be radically pared.

28. Bret Stephens, "Doomed to Stagnate? Eight Years Ago It Took 40 Days to Get a Construction Permit. Now It's 81", *Wall Street Journal*, December 19, 2016. http://www.wsj.com/articles/doomed-to-stagnate-1482192461. "The World Bank, which does many things poorly, does one thing exceptionally well: It publishes an annual survey that scores and ranks countries according to the ease of doing business. Want to better understand the mess Greece is in? In 2006 it took an average of 151 days to enforce a contract in the Hellenic Republic. Today it takes 1,580. Want to measure Israel's progress? A decade ago, starting a business in the startup nation took about 34 days. Now it takes 12. What about the United States? When President Obama took office in 2009, the U.S. ranked third in the overall index, just behind Singapore and New Zealand. It has since fallen to eighth place. Eight years ago, 40 days were needed to get a construction permit. Now it's 81. When President Bush left office, it took 300 days to enforce a contract. Today: 420. As for registering property, the cost has nearly quintupled since 2009, to 2.4% of property value from 0.5%."

29. Ana Swanson, "Trump Announces Japanese Corporate Giant Is Investing $50 Billion in the U.S", *Washington Post*, December 6, 2016. https://www.washingtonpost.com/news/wonk/wp/2016/12/06/trump-announces-japanese-bank-investing-50-billion-in-the-united-states/?utm_term=.d9c043e2f504. The story suggests that expectations of reduced regulation affected Softbank's decision.

30. Valerie Volcovici, "Trump Advisors Aim to Privatize Oil-rich Indian Reservations", *Reuters*, December 5, 2016. https://www.fidelity.com/news/article/top-news/201612050622RTRSNEWSCOMBINED_KBN13U1B1_1.

"Now, a group of advisors to President-elect Donald Trump on Native American issues wants to free those resources from what they call a suffocating federal bureaucracy that holds title to 56 million acres of tribal lands, two chairmen of the coalition told Reuters in exclusive interviews."

31. Chris Mooney, Brady Dennis and Steven Mufson, "Trump Names Scott Pruitt, Oklahoma Attorney General Suing EPA on Climate Change, to Head the EPA", *Washington Post*, December 8, 2016. https://www. washingtonpost.com/news/energy-environment/wp/2016/12/07/ trump-names-scott-pruitt-oklahoma-attorney-general-suing-epa-on-climate-change-to-head-the-epa/?utm_term=.10c5a4207445.

"President-elect Donald Trump on Thursday nominated Scott Pruitt, the attorney general of the oil and gas-intensive state of Oklahoma, to head the Environmental Protection Agency, a move signaling an assault on President Obama's climate change and environmental legacy. Pruitt has spent much of his energy as attorney general fighting the very agency he is being nominated to lead. He is the third of Trump's nominees who have key philosophical differences with the missions of the agencies they have been tapped to run. Ben Carson, named to head the Department of Housing and Urban Development, has expressed a deep aversion to the social safety net programs and fair housing initiatives that have been central to that agency's activities. Betsy DeVos, named education secretary, has a passion for private school vouchers that critics say undercut the public school systems at the core of the government's mission".

32. James Damieson, "Donald Trump to Choose Fast-Food CEO to Be His Labor Secretary", *Huffington Post*, December 8, 2016. http://www. huffingtonpost.com/entry/donald-trump-andrew-puzder_us_584739b0e4b0b9feb0da1b7c. "In a rebuke to President Barack Obama's work on the labor front, President-elect Donald Trump is expected to choose a fast-food executive to be the nation's next labor secretary, tasked with enforcing workplace safety and wage laws on behalf of U.S. workers". "Like Trump, he argues that the federal government has made regulations too burdensome on businesses, stifling job growth. Two of the major regulations he has criticized — the minimum wage and overtime — are ones he would be tasked with enforcing". "In an op-ed he wrote for *The Hill*, Puzder argued that safety net programs like food stamps discourage poor people from working and need to be reined in". https://www.project-syndicate.org/commentary/no-mourning-dead-trade-

agreements-by-dani-rodrik-2016-12?utm_source=Project+Syndicate+
Newsletter&utm_campaign=702c748bf2-fischer_goodbye_to_the_
west_11_2_2016&utm_medium=email&utm_term=0_73bad5b7d8-
702c748bf2-93559677.

33. Dani Rodrik, "Don't Cry Over Dead Trade Agreements", *Project Syndicate*, December 8, 2016. "The seven decades since the end of World War II were an era of trade agreements. The world's major economies were in a perpetual state of trade negotiations, concluding two major global multilateral deals: the General Agreement on Tariffs and Trade (GATT) and the treaty establishing the World Trade Organization. In addition, more than 500 bilateral and regional trade agreements were signed — the vast majority of them since the WTO replaced the GATT in 1995." "The populist revolts of 2016 will almost certainly put an end to this hectic deal-making. While developing countries may pursue smaller trade agreements, the two major deals on the table, the Trans-Pacific Partnership (TPP) and the Transatlantic Trade and Investment Partnership (TTIP), are as good as dead after the election of Donald Trump as US president."

"What purpose do trade agreements really serve? The answer would seem obvious: countries negotiate trade agreements to achieve freer trade. But the reality is considerably more complex. It's not just that today's trade agreements extend to many other policy areas, such as health and safety regulations, patents and copyrights, capital-account regulations, and investor rights. It's also unclear whether they really have much to do with free trade."

Let us keep this in mind as we bemoan the passing of the era of trade agreements. If we manage our own economies well, new trade agreements will be largely redundant."

34. Kenneth Rogoff, "The Trump Boom?" *Project Syndicate*, December 7, 2016. https://www.project-syndicate.org/commentary/trump-business-confidence-growth-boom-by-kenneth-rogoff-2016-12?utm_source=Project+Syndicate+Newsletter&utm_campaign=702c748bf2-fischer_goodbye_to_the_west_11_2_2016&utm_medium=email&utm_term=0_73bad5b7d8-702c748bf2-93559677. "Consider regulation. Under President Barack Obama, labor regulation expanded significantly, not to mention the dramatic increase in environmental legislation. And

that is not even counting the huge shadow Obamacare casts on the health-care system, which alone accounts for 17% of the economy. I am certainly not saying that repealing Obama-era regulation will improve the average American's wellbeing. Far from it."

35. Justin Sink, Elizabeth Dexheimer, and Katherine Chiglinsky, "Trump to Order Review of Dodd-Frank, Halt Obama Fiduciary Rule", *Bloomberg*, February 3, 2017. https://www.bloomberg.com/politics/articles/2017-02-03/trump-to-halt-obama-fiduciary-rule-order-review-of-dodd-frank.

"President Donald Trump will order a sweeping review of the Dodd–Frank Act rules enacted in response to the 2008 financial crisis, a White House official said, signing an executive action Friday designed to significantly scale back the regulatory system put in place in 2010.

Trump also will halt another of former President Barack Obama's regulations, hated by the financial industry, that requires advisers on retirement accounts to work in the best interests of their clients. Trump's order will give the new administration time to review the change, known as the fiduciary rule."

36. Ylan Q. Mui and Max Ehrenfreund, "Trump Nominees Map Out Plans for Tax Cuts, Trade and Carrier-style Negotiations", *Washington Post*, November 30, 2016. https://www.washingtonpost.com/business/economy/trump-nominees-map-out-plans-for-tax-cuts-trade-and-carrier-style-negotiations/2016/11/30/54cfca98-b73d-11e6-a677-b608fbb3aaf6_story.html?utm_term=.27c5e9765c5c.

"Mnuchin Outlines 'Largest Tax Change since Reagan'", *USA Today*, December 1, 2016. http://www.usatoday.com/story/money/2016/11/30/mnuchin-outlines-largest-tax-change-since-reagan/94667050/. "There will be a tax cut for the middle class," banker, movie producer and former Goldman Sachs partner Steven Mnuchin told CNBC's Squawk Box in his first public comments on the incoming administration's economic priorities. "Any tax cuts that we have for the upper class will be offset by less deductions to pay for it." "Tax deductions for charitable contributions would still be allowed, he said. There would be a cap on mortgage interest payments, though 'some deductibility' would continue, said Mnuchin." "The proposed changes also include cutting the nation's 35% top business tax rate to 15%, along with an effort to encourage repatriation of the estimated $1 trillion that large U.S.

corporations hold in foreign subsidiaries to avoid the domestic tax bite. Trump has proposed a special 10% rate on overseas funds the companies shift back to the U.S." "We think by cutting corporate taxes we'll create huge economic growth and we'll have huge personal income, so the revenues will be offset on the other side," Mnuchin said in the interview. "I think we can absolutely get to sustained 3% to 4% GDP. And that is absolutely critical to the country," Mnuchin said. "To get there, our No. 1 priority is tax reform. This will be the largest tax change since Reagan."

37. Michael Shear, "Trump Picks Mick Mulvaney, South Carolina Congressman, as Budget Director", *New York Times*, December 16, 2016. http://www.nytimes.com/2016/12/16/us/politics/mick-mulvaney-office-management-budget-trump.html?_r=0. "Representative Mick Mulvaney of South Carolina, a conservative Republican member of the House and a fierce advocate of deep spending cuts, to be his budget director."

38. Lisa Lambert, "Stock, bond markets could see sharp declines- U.S. financial watchdog", Reuters, December 13, 2016. http://fidelity.com/news/article/top-news/201612131319RTRSNEWSCOMBINED_L1N1E80Z6_1. "The Office of Financial Research found stock valuations, measured by comparing prices to earnings, have reached the same high level that they hit before the three largest equity market declines in the last century."

39. Kenneth Rogoff, "The Trump Boom?" *Project Syndicate*, December 7, 2016. https://www.project-syndicate.org/commentary/trump-business-confidence-growth-boom-by-kenneth-rogoff-2016-12?utm_source=Project+Syndicate+Newsletter&utm_campaign=702c748bf2-fischer_goodbye_to_the_west_11_2_2016&utm_medium=email&utm_term=0_73bad5b7d8-702c748bf2-93559677. "It is hard to know just how much extra debt Trump's stimulus program will add, but estimates of $5 trillion over ten years — a 25% increase — seem sober. Many left-wing economics commentators, having insisted for eight years under Obama that there is never any risk to US borrowing, now warn that greater borrowing by the Trump administration will pave the road to financial Armageddon. Their hypocrisy is breathtaking, even if they are now closer to being right."

40. "A Pensions Time Bomb Spells Disaster for the US Economy", *Business Insider*, December 4, 2016. https://www.yahoo.com/news/pensions-time-

bomb-spells-disaster-213700584.htm. According to Danielle DiMartino Booth "underfunded government pensions to the tune of $1.3 trillion, with a gap that just can't be filled, is the ticking time bomb facing the US economy, which faces dramatic cuts in public services and potentially riots reminiscent of Athens six years ago." This deficit is in addition to the Social Security and Medicare shortfalls and other aspects of global leveraging.

41. "The Economy's Hidden Problem: We're Out of Big Ideas", *Wall Street Journal*, December 6, 2016. https://www.msn.com/en-us/money/markets/the-economys-hidden-problem-were-out-of-big-ideas/ar-AAldSxv.

    The big idea that is missing is the impossible idea of doing the wrong thing and making it right.

42. Yashaswini Swamynathan, "Dow, S&P Hit Highs; Trump Comment Hammers Drug Stocks", *Fidelity*, December 7, 2016. https://www.fidelity.com/news/article/top-news/201612070935RTRSNEWSCOMBINED_KBN13W1H7_1.

    "Trump, in an interview with the Time magazine, said he would bring down drug prices."

43. "Mnuchin Outlines Largest Tax Change since Reagan", *USA Today*, December 1, 2016. http://www.usatoday.com/story/money/2016/11/30/mnuchin-outlines-largest-tax-change-since-reagan/94667050/.

44. The Act provides major barriers to entry for the biggest banks, and so allows them an oligopoly position. Ben Protess and Julie Hirschfeld Davis, "Trump Moves to Roll Back Obama-Era Financial Regulations", *New York Times*, February 3, 2017. www.nytimes.com/2017/02/03/business/dealbook/trump-congress-financial-regulations.html?_r=0. "President Trump on Friday moved to chisel away at the Obama administration's legacy on financial regulation, announcing steps to revisit the rules enacted after the 2008 financial crisis and to back away from a measure intended to protect consumers from bad investment advice. After a White House meeting with executives from Wall Street, Mr. Trump signed a directive aimed at the Dodd–Frank Act, crafted by the Obama administration and passed by Congress in response to the 2008 meltdown. He also signed a memorandum that paves the way for reversing a policy, known as the fiduciary rule, that requires brokers to act in a client's best interest, rather than seek the highest profits for

themselves, when providing retirement advice. The executive order affecting Dodd–Frank is vague in its wording and expansive in its reach. It never mentions the law by name, instead laying out "core principles" for regulations that include empowering American investors and enhancing the competitiveness of American companies. Even so, it gives the Treasury the authority to restructure major provisions of Dodd–Frank, and it directs the Treasury secretary to make sure existing laws align with administration goals."

45. The establishment system emphasizes forced substitution (mandates) which degrades consumer choice. Curbing forced substitution is necessarily consumer utility enhancing.

46. Egalitarianism is not self-evidently fair. It forces some to transfer to others even when others are undeserving. Eliminating unmerited transfers will enhance economic justice.

Chapter 6

Education

Education provides individuals and nations with tools for advancing their well-being.[1] The concept includes the benefits of material consumption, but also takes account of moral, spiritual and intellectual excellence, as well as psychological factors like contentment and fulfillment. The contemporary understanding of well-being draws from Plato, Aristotle, Renaissance humanism, Freud's notion of mental health and spiritual concepts like Enlightenment. To attain a high state of well-being, individuals must be trained to cope with life's diverse challenges.

Individuals are multiple, not singular. They differ by potential, gender, temperament, talent, virtue, psychiatric, psychological and spiritual health, ethnicity, religion, identity, material resources, family, community, strata, caste, class and circumstance. If scarcity did not exist, and everything were known the ideal educational system would ascertain each individual's potential and teach him and her precisely what had to be learned to maximize well-being over the full course of their lives.

Scarcity however is ubiquitous. We do not know everything, and there are not enough resources to provide individuals with the education they need to fully actualize their human potential. Likewise, if the ideal is beyond the reach of individuals, it is also unattainable for the more demanding requirement that individuals modify their learning in the interest of the national good. Educators have to lower their sights.

They must fall back on the principle of "good enough". Although there is no attainable best ("bounded rationality"), there are a large number of "satisfactory" options.[2] Educational policymakers therefore should wisely promote individual well-being, taking account of the greater national good without insisting on utopia.

Satisfactory solutions are far removed from the ideal because students do not know their own minds, and their mentors are divided about what is satisfactory for students, themselves, the nation and the great global beyond. Educators, students, families, communities, interest groups and politicians are engaged in high-stakes battles for personal well-being, money and power. Students and families are most concerned about their well-being, but educators, interest groups and politicians have mixed priorities, which often are detached from individual and national well-being. They fight for their parochial interests under the guise of the public good.[3]

The public good as the establishment sees it boils down to promoting the Three Rs,[4] vocational preparation, civics, racial and ethnic equality,[5] special education,[6] and GDP growth. Economic productivity, efficiency and growth are mostly afterthoughts, based on the surmise that repairing the bottom (socially disadvantaged and poor) is the key to enhancing the performance of the whole (No Child Left Behind).[7]

America pays little attention to educating gifted primary and secondary school students.[8] Individual well-being is irrelevant beyond trying to keep immigrant, minority and special needs students from falling further behind the native, non-minority norm. The strategy addresses a legitimate sociological need, but this does not obviate its broad inadequacies: insufficient attention paid to middle-income working class and gifted students apparent in comparative international achievement statistics. The latest Program for International Student Assessment (PISA) report for 2015 published by the Organisation for Economic Co-operation and Development (OECD) reveals that American secondary students performed poorly in math

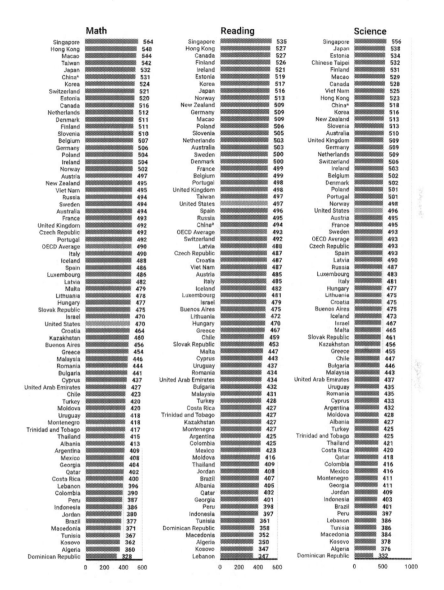

Math

Singapore	564
Hong Kong	548
Macao	544
Taiwan	542
Japan	532
China*	531
Korea	524
Switzerland	521
Estonia	520
Canada	516
Netherlands	512
Denmark	511
Finland	511
Slovenia	510
Belgium	507
Germany	506
Poland	504
Ireland	504
Norway	502
Austria	497
New Zealand	495
Viet Nam	495
Russia	494
Sweden	494
Australia	494
France	493
United Kingdom	492
Czech Republic	492
Portugal	492
OECD Average	490
Italy	490
Iceland	488
Spain	486
Luxembourg	486
Latvia	482
Malta	479
Lithuania	478
Hungary	477
Slovak Republic	475
Israel	470
United States	470
Croatia	464
Kazakhstan	460
Buenos Aires	456
Greece	454
Malaysia	446
Romania	444
Bulgaria	441
Cyprus	437
United Arab Emirates	427
Chile	423
Turkey	420
Moldova	420
Uruguay	418
Montenegro	418
Trinidad and Tobago	417
Thailand	415
Albania	413
Argentina	409
Mexico	408
Georgia	404
Qatar	402
Costa Rica	400
Lebanon	396
Colombia	390
Peru	387
Indonesia	386
Jordan	380
Brazil	377
Macedonia	371
Tunisia	367
Kosovo	362
Algeria	360
Dominican Republic	328

0   200   400   600

Reading

Singapore	535
Hong Kong	527
Canada	527
Finland	526
Ireland	521
Estonia	519
Korea	517
Japan	516
Norway	513
New Zealand	509
Germany	509
Macao	509
Poland	506
Slovenia	505
Netherlands	503
Australia	503
Sweden	500
Denmark	500
France	499
Belgium	499
Portugal	498
United Kingdom	498
Taiwan	497
United States	497
Spain	496
Russia	495
China*	494
OECD Average	493
Switzerland	492
Latvia	488
Czech Republic	487
Croatia	487
Viet Nam	487
Austria	485
Italy	485
Iceland	482
Luxembourg	481
Israel	479
Buenos Aires	475
Lithuania	472
Hungary	470
Greece	467
Chile	459
Slovak Republic	453
Malta	447
Cyprus	443
Uruguay	437
Romania	434
United Arab Emirates	434
Bulgaria	432
Malaysia	431
Turkey	428
Costa Rica	427
Trinidad and Tobago	427
Kazakhstan	427
Montenegro	427
Argentina	425
Colombia	425
Mexico	423
Moldova	416
Thailand	409
Jordan	408
Brazil	407
Albania	405
Qatar	402
Georgia	401
Peru	398
Indonesia	397
Tunisia	361
Dominican Republic	358
Macedonia	352
Algeria	350
Kosovo	347
Lebanon	347

0   200   400   600

Science

Singapore	556
Japan	538
Estonia	534
Chinese Taipei	532
Finland	531
Macao	529
Canada	528
Viet Nam	525
Hong Kong	523
China*	518
Korea	516
New Zealand	513
Slovenia	513
Australia	510
United Kingdom	509
Germany	509
Netherlands	509
Switzerland	506
Ireland	503
Belgium	502
Denmark	502
Poland	501
Portugal	501
Norway	498
United States	496
Austria	495
France	495
Sweden	493
OECD Average	493
Czech Republic	493
Spain	493
Latvia	490
Russia	487
Luxembourg	483
Italy	481
Hungary	477
Lithuania	475
Croatia	475
Buenos Aires	475
Iceland	473
Israel	467
Malta	465
Slovak Republic	461
Kazakhstan	456
Greece	455
Chile	447
Bulgaria	446
Malaysia	443
United Arab Emirates	437
Uruguay	435
Romania	435
Cyprus	433
Argentina	432
Moldova	428
Albania	427
Turkey	425
Trinidad and Tobago	425
Thailand	421
Costa Rica	420
Qatar	418
Colombia	416
Mexico	416
Montenegro	411
Georgia	411
Jordan	409
Indonesia	403
Brazil	401
Peru	397
Lebanon	386
Tunisia	386
Macedonia	384
Kosovo	378
Algeria	376
Dominican Republic	332

0   500   1000

Figure 6.1. 2015 PISA Average Scores.

Source: OECD. *China is represented by the provinces of Beijing, Shanghai, Jiangsu, and Guangdong   *Business Insider*

and only slightly above the OECD norm in reading and science despite spending substantially more per student (see Figure 6.1).[9]

The establishment spends large sums on education,[10] but still seeks to achieve its goals miserly by underpaying and overworking teachers.[11] It relies instead on setting universal standards, testing and administrative pressure (Common Core).[12] Ratcheting standards, testing and discipline have merit, but the tactic inevitably conflicts with the priorities of No Child Left Behind and is not a panacea. It is mostly a substitute rather than complement for addressing the problem of individual well-being.

The establishment is wedded to its No Child Left Behind/Common Core educational agenda that attempts to use education to solve both America's sociological and economic problems. It does not want to hear that it cannot have it all, without grasping that "having it all" short-changes the majority of students and is shallow.

Populist opposition to Common Core and the resource priorities of No Child Left Behind is strong. Donald Trump shares this middle-class concern, and he is contemplating taking radical action. He not only promised to scuttle Common Core, but he says that he is thinking about reducing the federal government role in the education business by drastically trimming the Department of Education.[13] The idea is not to defund education, but to transfer financial and administrative responsibility to the states and promote private participation in public education (public–private partnership) through "Charter Schools".[14]

Trump has appointed Betsy DeVos as Secretary of Education to carry out his mission. She is a seasoned advocate of delegating authority from the federal education department to states and localities, and a Charter School outsourcing entrepreneur.[15] DeVos intends to increase the role of publically financed for-profit business as a competitive vehicle for enhancing educational quality, with a subtext of rebalancing educational funding away from No Child Left Behind and toward the middle class, free from the constraints imposed by Common Core. The claim is that local public schools, including Charter Schools will adhere to surviving Common Core requirements, but otherwise will adopt better educational standards appropriate for the common man.

Critics, vociferously disagree contending that Trump's education strategy will harm No Child Left behind and its Charter School component is mostly about making money.[16] They may or may not have a point, but their complaint is subsidiary in the larger perspective.

Education reform for Donald Trump is mostly a wager on decentralization and the market without any serious assessment of content. He will welcome almost any result generated from downsizing the federal Education Department, with or without upgraded standards, testing and compliance. This is insufficient. The merits of both the establishment's and Trump's educational strategies depend more on their content than their institutional design, and both are seriously wanting. The establishment's neglect of middle class and gifted children is wrongheaded, and Trump's premise that business will get the job done right is naïve. There is popular support for local control and some business participation, but no basis for assessing whether these factors are really keys to improving America's poor educational performance.

Public Higher Education

Silence can be as revealing expert opinion. Donald Trump has said nothing about higher education. He may be unaware that American public universities are bedeviled by the same issues afflicting primary and secondary schooling, or holding his fire. The Department of Education has placed enormous pressure on public institutions of higher learning to promote the globalist affirmative action agenda through mandates and targeted research funding, while gradually reducing funding. State legislatures have followed suit, substituting part time instructors for professors, reducing teaching salaries, and causing public universities to rely increasingly on sundry forms of public–private partnerships without sober consideration of student well-being. The issue merits attention. America is not properly educating this generation of college and graduate school students for tomorrow's challenges. It is training them to be cheerleaders for globalism and big government. Trump does not seem to know that the problem exists. It will only be inadvertently addressed by DeVose, who may take some constructive action by reducing the Department of Education's footprint on public and private universities, but no concerted effort targeted at higher education is on the horizon. As with primary and secondary education, the tide is turning, but the core problems are not being forthrightly addressed.[17]

Endnotes

1. Steven Rosefielde and Ralph William Pfouts, *Inclusive Economic Theory*, Singapore: World Scientific, 2014.

2. Herbert Simon, *Models of Man: Social and Rational — Mathematical Essays on Rational Human Behavior in a Social Setting*, New York: John Wiley, 1957. Herbert Simon, "A Mechanism for Social Selection and Successful Altruism", *Science,* Vol. 250, No. 4988, 1990, pp. 1665–1668.

   Herbert Simon, "Bounded Rationality and Organizational Learning", *Organization Science*, Vol. 2, No. 1, 1991, pp. 125–134.

3. Total expenditures for public elementary and secondary schools in the United States amounted to $620 billion in 2012–2013, or $12,296 per public school student enrolled in the fall (in constant 2014 — $15, based on the Consumer Price Index). These expenditures include $11,011 per student in current expenditures for the operation of schools; $931 for capital outlay (i.e., expenditures for property and for buildings and alterations completed by school district staff or contractors); and $355 for interest on school debt. https://nces.ed.gov/fastfacts/display.asp?id=66.

4. Three Rs means reading, writing and arithmetic. This is the focus of "No Child Left Behind". The No Child Left Behind Act of 2001 (NCLB) was a US Act of Congress passed in 2001 which reauthorized the Elementary and Secondary Education Act (ESEA); it included Title I provisions applying to disadvantaged students. It supported standards-based education reform based on the premise that setting high standards and establishing measurable goals could improve individual outcomes in education.

5. American public school education seeks to narrow the class and racial achievement gap in the United States by creating common expectations for all. NCLB has shown mixed success in eliminating the racial achievement gap. Although test scores are improving, they are not improving equally for all races, which means that minority students are still behind.

6. Special education services students with learning disabilities, communication disorders, emotional and behavioral disorders, physical disabilities and developmental disabilities. Remedial services and programs for the gifted are separate categories. According to the Department of Education, approximately 6 million children (roughly 10 percent of all school-aged children) currently receive some type of special education services. As with most countries in the world, students who are poor, ethnic minorities, or do not speak the dominant language fluently are disproportionately identified as needing special education services.

7. The No Child Left Behind Act of 2001 (NCLB) was a US Act of Congress which reauthorized the ESEA. It included Title I provisions applying to disadvantaged students; supported standards-based education reform on the premise that setting high standards and establishing measurable goals could improve individual outcomes in education. The Act required states to develop assessments in basic skills. To receive federal school funding, states had to give these assessments to all students at select grade levels.

8. NCLB pressures schools to guarantee that nearly all students meet the minimum skill levels (set by each state) in reading, writing, and arithmetic — but requires nothing beyond these minima. It provides no incentives to improve student achievement beyond the bare minimum. Federal funding of gifted education decreased by a third over the first five years of NCLB. The Jacob Javits Gifted and Talented Students Education Act was passed in 1988 as part of the ESEA. Instead of funding district-level gifted education programs, the Javits Act has three primary components: the research of effective methods of testing, identification and programming, which is performed at the National Research Center on the Gifted and Talented; the awarding of grants to colleges, states, and districts that focus on underrepresented populations of gifted students; and grants awarded to state and districts for program implementation. Annual funding for grants must be passed by US Congress, and totaled $9.6 million in 2007.

9. Abby Jackson and Andy Kiersz, "The latest ranking of top countries in math, reading, and science is out — and the US didn't crack the top 10", *Business Insider*, December 6, 2016. http://www.businessinsider.com/pisa-worldwide-ranking-of-math-science-reading-skills-2016-12.

10. Anthony Smarick, "The $7 Billion School Improvement Grant Program: Greatest Failure in the History of the US Department of Education?" *AEI*,

January 17, 2017. http://www.aei.org/publication/greatest-failure-in-history-us-department-of-education/?utm_source=paramount&utm_medium=email&utm_content=AEITODAY&utm_campaign=012417. "The final IES report on the School Improvement Grant program is devastating to Arne Duncan's and the Obama administration's education legacy. A major evaluation commissioned by the U.S. Department of Education and conducted by two highly respected research institutions delivered a crushing verdict: The program failed and failed badly. (The Washington Post's article by Emma Brown does an exceptional job recounting the administration's $7 billion folly.) Despite its gargantuan price tag, SIG generated no academic gains for the students it was meant to help. Failing schools that received multi-year grants from the program to 'turn around' ended up with results no better than similar schools that received zero dollars from the program. To be clear: Billions spent had no effect."

11. Rebecca Klein, "An analysis released Tuesday by the Organisation for Economic Co-operation and Development looks at the state of education around the world, examining everything from intergenerational mobility in education to graduation rates to teacher pay", *Huffington Post*, November 11, 2015. http://www.huffingtonpost.com/entry/us-teacher-pay_us_56536f5be4b0258edb327d8f.

    "American public school teachers are underpaid compared to workers in the U.S. with similar education levels, the OECD found. Elementary school teachers in the U.S. make 67 percent of what college-educated workers in other professions earn. High school teachers earn 71 percent of what other college-educated workers make."

12. The Common Core State Standards Initiative is an educational initiative in the United States that details what K-12 students should know in English language arts and mathematics at the end of each grade. The initiative is sponsored by the National Governors Association (NGA) and the Council of Chief State School Officers (CCSSO) and seeks to establish consistent educational standards across the states as well as ensure that students graduating from high school are prepared to enter credit-bearing courses at two- or four-year college programs or to enter the workforce.

13. "Donald Trump on Education 2016 Republican Nominee for President; 2000 Reform Primary Challenger for President". http://www.ontheissues.

org/2016/Donald_Trump_Education.htm. Here are some of Trump's views on education:

- Department of Education: "You could cut that way, way, way down", South Carolina Tea Party Convention, Myrtle Beach, January 2015.
- Common Core curriculum standards: "I am totally against Common Core", South Carolina Tea Party Convention, Myrtle Beach, January 2015. "That's a disaster. That's bad. It should be local and all of that", Iowa Freedom Summit, Des Moines, Iowa, January 2015.

14. A public–private partnership (PPP, 3P or P3) is a cooperative arrangement between one or more public and private sectors, typically of a long-term nature. Jeffrey Delmon, *Public Private Partnership Programs: Creating a Framework for Private Sector Investment in Infrastructure*, Amsterdam: Kluwer, 2014.

15. Charter schools are publicly (tax payer) funded, privately managed institutions of K-12 education. As of December 2011, approximately 5,600 public charter schools enrolled an estimated total of more than 2 million students nationwide. Karl Zinsmeister, "From Promising to Proven: The Charter School Boom Ahead", *Philanthropy Magazine*, Spring 2014.

16. Sara Ganim and Linh Tran, "Trump's Choice for Education Secretary Raises Questions", *CNN*, December 6, 2016. http://www.cnn.com/2016/12/02/politics/betsy-devos-michigan-education-legacy/.

17. Trump has taken a strong position on student loans, but the subject is more about personal responsibility than educational strategy. Based on what Trump has said so far, here are his concrete plans:

(1). Consolidate ALL current repayment plans into a single Income-Based Repayment program (IBR) where students pay 12.5% of their income toward their loans each month and receive total loan forgiveness after 15 years.

(2). Plans to cover increased forgiveness amounts (and the higher cost to taxpayers) due to shorter repayment terms by lowering federal spending accordingly.

See http://www.studentdebtrelief.us/forgiveness/trump-student-loan-forgiveness/.

Cf. Goldie Blumenstyk, "What's In and What's Out for Colleges as Trump Takes Office",

Chronicle of Higher Education, December 21, 2016. http://www. chronicle.com/article/What-s-InWhat-s-Out/238727. "If you're a college leader who feels micromanaged by federal regulations, a university trustee who thinks that the U.S. Department of Education has been overly intrusive in overseeing colleges' handling of sexual-assault and discrimination cases, or a would-be education provider that is not a traditionally accredited college, you may well like some of the approaches of the coming administration of President-elect Donald J. Trump and the Republican-controlled Congress.

On the other hand, if you're a student stuck with debt for a program from a college that deceived you, a dean whose graduate students rely heavily on federal PLUS loans, or a professor whose courses and research touch on climate science or a host of other topics that have been demonized as "politically correct," then the next few years could be troubling". "Title IX enforcement on sexual assault. It won't go away completely, of course. But it's hard to imagine the next administration adopting the same aggressive posture taken by the current Office for Civil Rights, considering the way many Republicans, would-be Trump insiders, and even some colleges feel about the office's approach over the past several years. (Mr. Falwell, for one, says that the department has tried to turn colleges into 'police departments, judges, juries, and executioner — a lot of things colleges are not equipped to do.') Ditto for protecting the rights of gay and transgender people."

Chapter 7

Environment

America's environmental policy provides a tool for dealing with the effects of external diseconomies.[1] Private and public production sometimes pollutes other people's property and the wider environment. Some types of consumption like nude bathing may distress fellow beach goers. Private and public production occasionally generates external economies. A road for private use may reduce congestion on public highways. Economists agree that it is difficult and in some instances impossible to eliminate all external diseconomies, and capture the potential benefits of external economies with market methods.[2] There normally will be a place for markets in most environmental policy regimes, but a state presence also is indispensable. Governments use a variety of schemes to deter external diseconomies and capture external economies. They can create competitive market leasing rights for some public assets, regulate and enter into joint ventures with the private sector called public–private partnerships (PPP).[3]

Everyone is a stakeholder in the environment. All Americans breath air, use water, and cope with climate change. The costs of environmental protection affect business and developers. They reduce labor demand, increase consumer good prices and impair national security. American environment policies also affect other countries across the globe.

A virtuous environmental policy requires calibrating best solutions for all stakeholders using the right mix of regulatory techniques to eradicate environmental external diseconomies and maximize external economies. If successful, this will maximize individual stakeholder's well-being given limits imposed by bounded rationality.

This is the counsel of perfection. Just as in the case of education policy, scarcity and bounded rationality make it impossible to maximize each stakeholder's well-being, and to adjust individual outcomes in the national interest. Satisfactory solutions are feasible, but they are not ideal because stakeholders often sharply disagree with one another and American policymakers do not comprehensively compute environmental cost and benefits. Businesses and developers, workers, consumers, foreigners and environmental activists often have conflicting interests. They battle for their personal well-being, money and power. Businesses and developers seek profit; workers worry about jobs, consumers fret about being priced out of the market (housing), foreigners insist on having their say, and environmental activists fight for their causes.[4]

The American government is responsible for sorting out and comprehensively reconciling conflicting stakeholder claims, but there is no central authority tasked to do it. The Environmental Protection Agency (EPA) is well known.[5] However, there are 18 additional Federal Agencies with environment responsibilities.[6] Other government branches also participate. Environment policies carried out in this hodgepodge fashion, needless to say, must fall very short of the ideal well-being standard. Regulators make myriad ad hoc decisions with results that cannot be very good, even though those responsible invariably claim that they have done their best.

Some outcomes such as improvements in air quality are measureable, however the costs incurred achieving these benefits and specific effects on elusive stakeholders are difficult to compute. Bureaucrats are not required to maximize profit and often are oblivious to social costs. These ambiguities make environmental policy contentious.[7] Victims loudly complain, while winners overstate the public benefit.

The insensitivity of environment regulators to broad social costs of their actions explains Donald Trump's opposition to establishment environmental policy. He is keenly aware of the obstacles imposed by hodgepodge overregulation, bureaucratic passivity and hyper-activism that are invisible on the public radar screen,[8] and as an entrepreneur, he understands the corrupt games employed by motivated environmental bureaucracies.[9] His inclination is to rescind and relax overzealous environmental regulations, and abolish many overreaching government departments and subsections.[10] Trump's instinct is reasonable, but because it is so difficult to compute and weigh externalities, he can only push matters imprecisely in a pro-populist (anti-bureaucratic) and pro-business direction. Stakeholders, including the environmental bureaucracies themselves, who were yesterday's establishment winners, will almost certainly be tomorrow's losers in Trump's populist regime. His environmental policies will stimulate economic activity by reining bureaucratic overreach, and restoring states' constitutional jurisdictional rights, but these gains must take some environmental toll.

The same principle applies to the most contested, headline grabbing environmental issues: climate change and energy independence (including fracking).[11] The fear factor makes these concerns prominent. Many "chicken little" scientists contend that planet-wide greenhouse emissions are creating a hole in the earth's ozone shield,[12] and causing global warning with catastrophic implications.[13] The European Union has responded by establishing a complex carbon "trading" regime that flexibly limits emissions.[14] The Paris Agreement, which came into force on November 4, 2016, is the latest UN-based effort at extending the greenhouse emissions control process started by the Kyoto Protocol in 1992.[15] Its aims are:

(a) Holding the increase in the global average temperature to well below 2°C above pre-industrial levels and to pursue efforts to limit the temperature increase to 1.5°C above pre-industrial levels, recognizing that this would significantly reduce the risks and impacts of climate change;

(b) Increasing the ability to adapt to the adverse impacts of climate change and foster climate resilience and low greenhouse gas emissions development in a manner that does not threaten food production;

(c) Making financial flows consistent with a pathway toward low greenhouse gas emissions and climate-resilient development.[16]

President Obama, sidestepping Congress signed the Paris Climate Accord on September 3, 2016,[17] claiming that this was the only chance we have to save the planet.[18]

The deal as it currently stands does not legally require countries to curb emissions or take other steps to address climate change. It only obligates countries to release their targets and report emissions. The agreement's immediate impact is innocuous and is welcome by many in the global community.[19] Those opposing the Paris Agreement do not fret about its content. They worry about what they believe it portends. Their fear is that this innocuous beginning will inexorably grow into a bureaucratic nightmare. Scott Pruitt (designated EPA director), Cathy McMorris Rodgers (designated Secretary of Interior) and Donald Trump share this expectation, although their opposition could soften.[20] Their apprehensiveness reflects a legitimate aversion to post-war bureaucratic hyper-activism where projects begin modestly and then spiral out of rational control.

The heated debate over American energy policy turns on the same issue. Establishment activists are committed to replacing non-renewable fossil fuels (oil, gas, coal) and nuclear energy with eco-friendly renewable alternatives like gasohol,[21] wind, tidal and solar energy.[22] They oppose drilling and fracking and urge strict environment standards that raise extraction and refining costs. They also advocate national security energy reserves that keep fossil fuels in the ground. The combination of these policies, together with tolerance for cartels like Organization of the Petroleum Exporting Countries (OPEC) artificially inflate petroleum prices. The markup over the competitive equilibrium rate often is 10-fold, a disparity welcomed by the establishment because high fossil fuel prices make renewables attractive. Although the establishment appreciates that this harms American pocketbooks, it acts as if it feels that the environmental benefit from promoting renewables outweighs the public cost. The same logic drives the establishment to lavishly subsidize wind, tidal and solar energy projects, and mandate gasohol additives.

Scott Pruitt's, Cathy McMorris Rodgers's and Donald Trump's attitude toward the battle between advocates of non-renewable and renewable energy is broadly the same as for greenhouse emissions. They consider the establishment's hostility toward fossil fuels and nuclear energy unwarranted, and its promotion of wind, tidal and solar energy projects, and gasohol mandates overzealous. The issue for Trump populists is not science, or environmental insensitivity. It is the motivated bureaucratic overzealousness of the energy and environmental bureaucracies.[23]

The establishment's position is full speed ahead, no retreat, no surrender. The Trump-populist counter-position is that competitive renewables are fine, and small subsidies warranted, but the establishment's prevailing policies are unacceptable because they compel the middle class to pay an exorbitant tax burden in return for dubious benefits, with profits accruing to motivated renewables-friendly politicians, bureaucrats, entrepreneurs and militant activists. Trump's administration is sure to cut pro-renewable subsidies and mandates, relax restrictions on drilling, fracking and petroleum reserves with wide-ranging ramifications.[24] Fossil fuel supplies including natural gas will rise and prices fall. Fracking will cap OPEC's oligopoly power. Reduced regulatory costs will improve America's global competitiveness, and the public will receive a substantial windfall gain. Oil dependent states like Russia, Saudi Arabia, Iran and Iraq will suffer significant declines in national wealth and income. Non-renewable energy supplies will diminish. Greenhouse emissions will increase.

Trump considers all these changes positive on balance. He does not believe that the damage caused by curbing environmental overzealousness will be huge, or that it will not outweigh the gain, but as he himself acknowledges countermeasures will be required if at the end of the day it turns out that environmental activists were right.

Endnotes

1. The term external economies refers to the positive and negative effects that competitive individual profit and utility maximizing have on third parties.

2. Ronald Coase, "The Problem of Social Cost", *Journal of Law and Economics*, Vol. 3, 1960, pp. 1–44.
3. Yiyi Liu, "Public Private Partnerships and Joint Ventures: Smart Asian Governance", in Steven Rosefielde, Masaaki Kuboniwa, Satoshi Mizobata, and Kumiko Haba, eds., *Western Economic Stagnation, Social Strife and Decline: Asian Reverberations*, Singapore: World Scientific, 2017.
4. Benjamin Zycher, "Trump Nominee Scott Pruitt will Clean Up the EPA", *AEI*, December 14, 2016. http://www.aei.org/publication/trump-nominee-scott-pruitt-will-clean-up-the-epa/?utm_source=paramount&utm_medium=email&utm_content=AEITODAY&utm_campaign=121516.

"It is in the context of the benefit/cost analyses applied to draft and proposed regulations that climate science, economics and other disciplines outside legal analysis are relevant for the EPA administrator. Pruitt is absolutely correct that 'Scientists continue to disagree about the degree and extent of global warming and its connection to the actions of mankind.'

More to the point, Pruitt is very likely to put an end to the current EPA game of justifying its regulations on the basis of benefit/cost analyses that literally are bogus. An example: The EPA has published estimates of the effects of its greenhouse-gas efficiency rule for medium- and heavy trucks:

The results of the analysis, summarized in Table VII-37, demonstrate that relative to the reference case, by 2100 … global mean temperature is estimated to be reduced by 0.0026 to 0.0065°C, and sea-level rise is projected to be reduced by approximately 0.023 to 0.057 cm.

The EPA then states that 'the projected reductions in atmospheric CO_2, global mean temperature, sea level rise, and ocean pH are meaningful in the context of this action.' And so we arrive at the benefit/cost conclusion, given in all seriousness:

[We] estimate that the proposed standards would result in net economic benefits exceeding $100 billion, making this a highly beneficial rule.

Can anyone believe that a temperature effect by 2100 measured in ten-thousandths of a degree, or sea-level effects measured in thousandths of a centimeter, could yield over $100 billion in net economic benefits?"

5. Benjamin Zycher, "Trump Nominee Scott Pruitt will Clean Up the EPA",
   AEI, December 14, 2016. http://www.aei.org/publication/trump-nominee-
   scott-pruitt-will-clean-up-the-epa/?utm_source=paramount&utm_
   medium=email&utm_content=AEITODAY&utm_campaign=121516.

   The central job of the EPA administrator is to implement and administer the environmental laws enacted by Congress, and to limit agency
actions to those authorized in actual provisions of the laws promulgated
by the representatives of the people and of the states. (Remember the
quaint notion of the consent of the governed?) And the tools — the
regulations — used to implement and administer those laws also must
be consistent with those laws and the Constitution.

   It is emphatically not the job of the EPA administrator to pursue policies satisfying the political preferences of this or that interest group,
whether the fossil fuel industry or the environmental left or any others;
balancing of such competing demands is the job of Congress. It is not
the job of the EPA administrator to "save the planet," whatever that
means, or to satisfy the supposed imperatives underlying whatever slogan
happens to be the trendy one of the day.

6.

Federal Agency	Environmental Responsibilities
White House Office	Overall policy, Agency coordination
Office of Management and Budget	Budget, Agency coordination and management
Council on Environmental Quality	Environmental policy, Agency coordination, Environmental impact statements
Department of Health and Human Services	Health
EPA	Air and water pollution, Solid waste, Radiation, Pesticides, Noise, Toxic substances
Department of Justice	Environmental litigation
Department of the Interior	Public lands, Energy, Minerals, National parks
Department of Agriculture	Forestry, Soil, Conservation

(Continued)

(*Continued*)

Federal Agency	Environmental Responsibilities
Department of Defense	Civil works construction, Dredge and fill permits, Pollution control from defense facilities
Nuclear Regulatory Commission	License and regulate nuclear power
Department of State	International environment
Department of Commerce	Oceanic and atmospheric monitoring and research
Department of Labor	Occupational health
Department of Housing and Urban Development	Housing, Urban parks, Urban planning
Department of Transportation	Mass transit, Roads, Aircraft noise, Oil pollution
Department of Energy	Energy policy coordination, Petroleum allocation research and development
Tennessee Valley Authority	Electric power generation
Department of Homeland Security|United States Coast Guard	Maritime and environmental stewardship, National Pollution Funds Center (NPFC)

7. Benjamin Zycher, "Trump Nominee Scott Pruitt will Clean Up the EPA", *AEI*, December 14, 2016. http://www.aei.org/publication/trump-nominee-scott-pruitt-will-clean-up-the-epa/?utm_source=paramount& utm_medium=email&utm_content=AEITODAY&utm_campaign= 121516. During testimony last June before the Senate Finance Committee, Donald Trump's designated appointee as the administrator of the EPA argued "that the social cost of carbon analysis conducted by the Obama administration — led by the EPA — was the most dishonest exercise in political arithmetic I had ever seen produced by the federal bureaucracy." The modern EPA is a massive bureaucratic interest group out of control, effectively unconstrained by law or the constitution, a repository of environmental fanaticism utterly uninterested in the well-being of ordinary people or, for that matter, in the actual environmental effects of its edicts.

8. Bret Stephens, "Doomed to Stagnate? Eight Years Ago It Took 40 Days to Get a Construction Permit. Now It's 81", *Wall Street Journal*, December 19, 2016. http://www.wsj.com/articles/doomed-to-stagnate-1482192461.

9. Benjamin Zycher, "Trump Nominee Scott Pruitt will Clean Up the EPA", *AEI*, December 14, 2016. http://www.aei.org/publication/trump-nominee-scott-pruitt-will-clean-up-the-epa/?utm_source=paramount&utm_medium=email&utm_content=AEITODAY&utm_campaign=121516.

The EPA Mitigation Trust Fund, in which fines imposed by the EPA are deposited, then to be disbursed by EPA officials to its constituencies. Has anyone at EPA heard of the constitutional requirement that "No Money shall be drawn from the Treasury, but in Consequence of Appropriations made by Law …"

10. "EPA overreach means EPA regulatory efforts not authorized by the law — or, less politely, efforts by the EPA leadership to advance ideological preferences, and efforts by the EPA bureaucracy to increase its power to control the use of private property without regard to the costs of its actions or to their actual attendant environmental effects, both endeavors unconstrained by EPA's actual legal authority. EPA overreach also pertains to efforts eroding state prerogatives — the federalism underlying every one of our environmental laws — in favor of ever-more centralized control. That is the central thrust of the numerous states' application for a stay on implementation of the Clean Power Plan, granted by the Supreme Court last February." "Consider the proposed Clean Water Rule (the revised "Waters of the United States" definition), a blatant power grab under which the EPA claimed jurisdiction over most streams, dry beds, ponds and other such 'navigable waters' — the U.S. Court of Appeals for the Sixth Circuit issued a nationwide stay of that regulation in October 2015."

11. Hydraulic fracturing (fracking) is a well stimulation technique in which rock is fractured by a pressurized liquid. The process involves the high-pressure injection of "fracking fluid" (primarily water, containing sand suspended with the aid of thickening agents) into a wellbore to create cracks in the deep-rock formations through which natural gas, petroleum and brine will flow more freely. Hydraulic fracturing is highly controversial in many countries. Its proponents advocate the economic

benefits of more extensively accessible hydrocarbons. Opponents argue that these are outweighed by the potential environmental impacts, which include risks of ground and surface water contamination, air and noise pollution, and the triggering of earthquakes, along with the consequential hazards to public health and the environment. Hydraulic fracturing has been seen as one of the key methods of extracting unconventional oil and unconventional gas resources. According to the International Energy Agency, the remaining technically recoverable resources of shale gas are estimated to amount to 208 trillion cubic meters (7,300 trillion cubic feet), tight gas to 76 trillion cubic meters (2,700 trillion cubic feet), and coalbed methane to 47 trillion cubic meters (1,700 trillion cubic feet).

12. Edward Cowell, ed., *The Jataka; or, Stories of the Buddha's Former Births*, Cambridge: Cambridge University Press, 1897, Vol. 3, No. 322, pp. 49–52. Chicken Little bewails the end of the world by crying "the sky is falling".

    The metaphors used in the CFC discussion (ozone shield, ozone hole) are not "exact" in the scientific sense. The "ozone hole" is more of a depression, less "a hole in the windshield". The ozone does not disappear through the layer, nor is there a uniform "thinning" of the ozone layer. However, they resonated better with non-scientists and their concerns. The ozone hole was seen as a "hot issue" and imminent risk as lay people feared severe personal consequences such skin cancer, cataracts, damage to plants and reduction of plankton populations in the ocean's photic zone. Reiner Grundmann, "Climate Change and Knowledge Politics", *Environmental Politics*, Vol. 16, No. 3, 2007, pp. 414–432.

13. The Kyoto Protocol is an international treaty which extends the 1992 United Nations Framework Convention on Climate Change (UNFCCC) that commits state parties to reduce greenhouse gas emissions based on the premise that (a) global warming exists and (b) human-made CO_2 emissions have caused it. The Kyoto Protocol was adopted in Kyoto, Japan, on December 11, 1997 and entered into force on February 16, 2005. There are currently 192 parties (Canada withdrew effective December 2012) to the Protocol.

14. The European Union Emissions Trading System was the first large greenhouse gas emissions trading scheme in the world, and remains the biggest. It was launched in 2005 to fight Global warming and is a major

pillar of EU climate policy. As of 2013, the EU ETS covers more than 11,000 factories, power stations and other installations with a net heat excess of 20 MW in 31 countries — all 28 EU member states plus Iceland, Norway and Liechtenstein. The installations regulated by the EU ETS are collectively responsible in 2008 for close to half of the EU's anthropogenic emissions of CO2 and 40% of its total greenhouse gas emissions.

15. The Paris Agreement is an agreement within the UNFCCC dealing with greenhouse gases emissions mitigation, adaptation and finance starting in the year 2020.

16. "Paris Agreement, FCCC/CP/2015/L.9/Rev.1" (PDF). UNFCCC secretariat.

17. David Boyer, "Obama, Chinese President Ratify Climate-change Agreement", *Washington Times*, September 3, 2016. http://www.washingtontimes.com/news/2016/sep/3/obama-xi-ratify-climate-change-agreement/.

Deliberately sidestepping Congress, President Obama formally entered the U.S. into an international climate-change agreement Saturday with China and dozens of other nations to limit greenhouse gas emissions.

18. Byron Tau and Amy Harder, "Paris Climate Treaty to Take Effect in November", *Wall Street Journal*, October 6, 2016. http://www.wsj.com/articles/obama-lauds-historic-moment-as-paris-climate-agreement-takes-effect-1475701489. The agreement went into force on November 4, 2016 under the United Nations auspices. "The agreement aims to keep average global temperatures from rising more than 2 degrees Celsius above preindustrial levels through individualized national limits on greenhouse gas emissions, though the deal doesn't itself achieve that level of emissions cuts. World leaders hope to make more aggressive cuts within the deal in the years to come through the national plans to curb greenhouse-gas emissions. The deal doesn't legally require countries to curb emissions or take other steps on climate change — in the U.S. that would have likely required ratification by the Senate, which President Barack Obama was unlikely to get — but it does require countries to release their targets and report emissions." "The core of the Obama administration's commitment to the Paris deal, an EPA rule cutting power-plant carbon emissions, is facing legal pushback and also an

unusual temporary block from the Supreme Court until all litigation is over, which may not be until 2018."

19. Margareth Sembiring, "The Rise of Trump and Its Global Implications — Trump's Impending U-turn on Climate Change: Worry for Southeast Asia?", *S. Rajaratnam School of International Studies*, No. 307/2016, December 20, 2016.

20. "Trump Says He's Keeping an 'Open Mind' on Pulling Out of Paris Climate Accord", *Fortune*, November 22, 2016. http://fortune. com/2016/11/23/trump-open-mind-paris-climate-accord/. David Jackson and Eliza Collins, "McMorris Rodgers to be Trump's Interior Pick", *USA TODAY*, December 9, 2016. http://www.usatoday.com/story/news/politics/elections/2016/2016/12/09/mcmorris-rodgers-trumps-interior-pick/95197748/. Benjamin Zycher, "Trump Nominee Scott Pruitt will Clean Up the EPA", *AEI*, December 14, 2016.

    http://www.aei.org/publication/trump-nominee-scott-pruitt-will-clean-up-the-epa/?utm_source=paramount&utm_medium=email&utm_content=AEITODAY&utm_campaign=121516.

21. Renewable ethanol fuel mixtures used either as additives to automobile gas, or as substitutes.

22. Robert Alvarez, "An Energy Department Tale: Captain Perry and the Great White Whale", *Bulletin of Atomic Scientists*, December 1, 2016. http://thebulletin.org/energy-department-tale-captain-perry-and-great-white-whale10291?platform=hootsuite.

    "Energy Department's great white whale: responsibility for maintaining some 7,000 nuclear warheads and the rest of the nation's nuclear weapons complex. Military nuclear spending is the single largest piece of the Energy Department budget, making up nearly two-thirds of the total, and that budget area is experiencing out-of-control cost escalation." "Nuclear research and development consumed about $2 billion in the 2016 fiscal year — the single largest fraction (40 percent) of all Energy Department R&D funding".

23. Daniel Sutter, "Propagandistic Research and the U.S. Department of Energy: Energy Efficiency in Ordinary Life and Renewables in Electricity Production",

Econ Journal Watch, Vol. 14, No. 1, January 2017, pp. 103–120. https://econjwatch.org/articles/propagandistic-research-and-the-us-department-of-energy-energy-efficiency-in-ordinary-life-and-renewables-in-electricity-production.

"I treat two cases of what I believe can be characterized as research propaganda attributable to the U.S. Department of Energy (DOE). The first concerns the extent to which Americans are mindful of energy efficiency in their cars, appliances, homes, and machinery. The second concerns the mandating of the use of renewable fuels in electricity production. I contend that the DOE-based research is unsound and that the unsoundness rises to the level of propaganda."

24. Steven Mufson and Juliet Eilperin, "Trump Seeks to Revive Dakota Access, Keystone XL Oil Pipelines", *Washington Post*, January 24, 2017. https://www.washingtonpost.com/news/energy-environment/wp/2017/01/24/trump-gives-green-light-to-dakota-access-keystone-xl-oil-pipelines/?utm_term=.f0126752da69. "President Trump signed executive orders Tuesday to revive the controversial Dakota Access and Keystone XL oil pipelines, another step in Trump's effort to dismantle former President Obama's environmental legacy. He also signed an executive order to expedite environmental reviews of other infrastructure projects, lamenting the existing incredibly cumbersome, long, horrible permitting process."

"'The regulatory process in this country has become a tangled up mess,' he said."

Chapter 8

Social Welfare

Contemporary populism in the United States feeds on the dissonance between societal dreams and reality.[1] America's dream from the nation's founding until the Great Depression was based on the principles of democracy, freehold private property, civic rights, rule of law, equal opportunity, ambition and self-reliance. Its credo was that everyone could succeed, because American economic and social barriers were surmountable. Hard work, patience, prudence and frugality assured happy endings. People received what they earned, and reaped what they sowed. The virtuous prospered; the improvident had to bear the consequences because no one was entitled to anything beyond the value that they created, with the proviso that family and private charity would aid the needy.

This credo was always a declaration of faith. It did not capture America's complex reality. Society was stratified, and there were strong racial, religious and ethnic barriers to upward mobility. Nonetheless, the American dream was widely accepted, providing popular support for small government and self-reliance. Ordinary people believe that they could and would overcome.

People's faith in the American dream began to wane in the late 19th century with the closing of the Western frontier.[2] The decline gathered momentum until the Great Depression when Franklyn Delano Roosevelt introduced a variety of social programs to protect workers and the middle class, reduce barriers to upward mobility, restrain oligopoly, heavily tax the rich, and promote racial and religious justice. It seemed at first that these initiatives would empower the American dream by leveraging equal opportunity, but as the role of the federal government expanded, the emphasis shifted from hard work, patience, prudence and frugality to entitlement and affirmative action for those left behind. The American dream morphed from Turner's self-governing frontiersmen into the nanny state, where politicians and big business (the establishment) partnered for profit to provide middle-class living standards to everyone below the middle class at the middle class's expense.[3] This is root of America's populist discontent.

The middle class is not callous. It supports helping those left behind, welcoming the eradication of poverty, and empowerment of disadvantaged groups. It supports income transfers to the indigent (medical, educational and housing assistance) and limited affirmative action, but rejects establishment excesses. Federal government overreach bureaucratic overzealousness, big government's collusion with Wall Street, massive transfers of income and wealth to the rich repel populists upset by their own declining fortunes. The middle class wants the restoration of the American dream with inclusive equal opportunity, downsized affirmative action and modest compassionate transfers. It finds the establishment's politically correct globalist counter-vision irksome. Populists oppose privilege in the guise of unwarranted entitlements, affirmative action and dependency. They do not want the establishment to penalize them for working hard, or to surrender their freedom to faceless bureaucrats.

Their goals are reasonable and easily accomplished. The establishment can discipline itself. It can keep entitlements within bounds and spread the tax burden allowing everyone to share America's prosperity.

The establishment however is not prepared yet to do the right thing. It believes that it is wise to stay the course and shows no signs of accommodating the populist tide, forcing Trump to seize the day. He will certainly pare entitlements, affirmative action and return power to the states, but the rich rather than the middle class may well be the principal beneficiaries.[4]

The merit of Trump's populist endeavor at the end of the day will turn on whether a half-a-loaf is better than none. It is premature to judge, but two recent historical examples will illustrate why the details will matter more than lofty claims of virtuous intent.

The Establishment's Subprime Mortgage Affirmative Action Fiasco

The establishment hatched an affirmative action scheme in the mid-1990s to provide individual homeownership for millions of un-creditworthy people (mostly minority buyers). It gave unqualified minority home buyers a potential stake in the inclusive American dream by pressuring banks to issue subprime mortgages with no down payments at low initial interest rates,[5] gambling that the wealth created from real estate appreciation could be used to repay what would otherwise be unrepayable debts. Creditworthy home buyers (minority and non-minority alike) were benefiting from a real estate bubble, and credit-unworthy non-participants (predominantly minorities) wanted to join the party.

The establishment could have achieved the same purpose by directly paying part or all of the home purchase cost for the disadvantaged, but this would have been opposed for being overtly discriminatory, and the federal housing bureaucracy wanted the private sector to bear the risk and pay the subsidies.

It therefore chose to camouflage its purpose in broad non-discriminatory language, placate activists, increase the scope of the federal housing bureaucracy's domains, and use its mandating and regulatory powers to compel and entice various players into a destructive speculative game.[6] Housing was made affordable by subsidizing real estate developers and brokers. Wall Street underwriters were encouraged to create profitable mortgage-backed securities (MBS) and collateralized debt obligations (CDOs).[7] These financial instruments were used to securitize subprime loans, diminish mortgage lenders' risk and increase their profits.[8] These subsidies provided windfall profits to other financial and real estate speculators (including some of the credit-unworthy recipients of subprime loans), and lined the pockets of politicians selling these favors. Moreover, real estate developers, mortgage lenders, Wall Street underwriters, financial and real estate speculators, and politicians, all attempted to leverage the direct gains by capitalizing on the goodwill associated with assisting the disadvantaged.[9]

The scheme was shrewdly designed to conceal costs by funding them with insurance guarantees and indirect inflation taxes, and by shifting the remaining burden to those ultimately stuck with massive financial losses, including future generations obligated to pay the ever-mounting federal debt and forego retirement.[10] It also ignored catastrophic national risk, placing insider gain above the people's will and welfare. The results were predictable and were predicted,[11] but few participants were chastened because they bet correctly on winning themselves, and leaving the debt baby to others.[12]

Fannie Mae's promotion of subprime mortgages achieved this purpose initially by stoking the housing bubble, supplemented later by federal emergency deficit spending and diverse bailouts that were an integral part of the tax-transfer process from the middle class to establishment colluders. The process was not driven by good intentions gone wrong, but by bad intentions gone more or less as planned, obscured with finger pointing.[13]

The impact of Fannie Mae's drive to promote subprime loans is etched into the record. The subprime share of total originations was less than 5 percent in 1994. It jumped to 13 percent in 2000, and then catapulted to 20 percent in 2005 and 2006, just before the American real estate market collapsed. Six hundred and fifty three thousand subprime loans were originated in 2000 soaring to 4.13 million in 2004, before crashing to 472,000 in 2007.[14] Balloon loan originations skyrocketed from 50,000 at the start of the new millennium to 800,000 in 2006.[15] The share of subprime originations packaged as MBS more than doubled from 31.6 percent to 80.5 percent during the same period.[16] These trends were not entirely Fannie Mae's doing, but an appreciation of the fact that Fannie Mae and Freddie Mac stood ready to purchase all originators' bad mortgage loans was decisive.

The key point to grasp here is not the unsustainable claim that subprime loans alone caused the residential housing crisis of 2006–2007, but the demonstration that the establishment rigged the real estate market for its advantage to the middle class's detriment.[17]

Fannie Mae would have continued pressing subprime loans if the real estate boom had persisted, but the speculative fillip provided by its subprime campaign lost its potency in 2006 when experts, investors and other real estate participants became wary, fearing that the price appreciation, capital gains and ordinary profit growth trends in 2000–2006 could not be sustained. Home prices, which had risen nearly 9 percent per annum during these years (compared to 3 percent in the preceding decade) began dropping moderately,[18] raising the specter of capital losses on new real estate purchases. Interest rates began to rise, setting off alarm bells that homeowners could not pay the higher costs stipulated in their adjustable-rate balloon mortgages,[19] and the parlous state of over-indebted consumers made it plain that new market entrants were not going to pick up the slack. These factors depressed sales, profits, and price appreciation expectations soured. Suddenly, speculative demand for real estate properties plummeted, homebuilding stocks collapsed and the real estate market was flooded with subprime and prime property foreclosures. They jumped 42 percent in 2006 and 75 percent the following year to 2.2 million.[20]

The value of American subprime loans in 2007 was 1.3 trillion dollars, with over 7.5 million first-lien subprime mortgages outstanding.[21] Total home equity in the United States, which was valued at $13 trillion at its peak in 2006, dropped to $8.8 trillion by mid-2008. Total retirement assets, Americans' second-largest household asset, dropped by 22 percent, from $10.3 trillion in 2006 to $8 trillion in mid-2008. During the same period, savings and investment assets (apart from retirement savings) lost $1.2 trillion and pension assets lost $1.3 trillion. Taken together, these losses total $8.3 trillion.[22]

This however merely proved to be the tip of the iceberg because the real estate sector was indirectly hard hit by the delayed toxic effects of subprime mortgages in the global credit market during the 2008 financial crisis. As previously mentioned, mortgage lenders and Wall Street financial firms reaped enormous profits from Fannie Mae's affirmative action-driven decision to serve as a deep-pocketed buyer in the secondary mortgage market. Savings and loans, and other commercial mortgage originators used the Fannie Mae option to reduce their subprime risk exposure, while Wall Street turned the underwriting and trading of subprime MBS into what seemed to be a one-way street bonanza that did not survive the real estate crisis of 2006–2007. Demand for subprime MBS and related CDO began to weaken in 2007 and quickly evaporated in 2008 as investors began scrutinizing the risks of subprime mortgage default that might culminate in a run on shadow banks (nonbank financial institutions operating as credit creating *quasi* banks)[23] and a severe depression. Subprime mortgages were not the only cause of the global financial crisis, but they played a major role.

Their defaults contributed to the start of the global financial crisis when HSBC wrote down its holding of MBS by $10.5 billion on February 27, 2007,[24] and continued to play a key role thereafter.[25]

Total losses from the establishment's subprime prime mortgage gambit cannot be finely calibrated because they depend on the timeframe chosen, and cannot be cleanly separated from other contributing factors. Nonetheless, the figures in the real estate sector run well into the trillions and continued to mount in terms of foreclosures, cumulative unemployment, deficit spending and national indebtedness.

Four million and two hundred thousand properties were foreclosed in America in 2007–2008, at an average cost of $225,000 (the average home mortgage cost during the real estate boom), summing to nearly $1 trillion. The disadvantaged minorities that Fannie Mae claimed it was serving suffered most because of their large presence in the subprime mortgage market.

The subprime mortgage and MSB crises also contributed to collateral damage in the wider national economy. Unemployment ran about 5 million above normal for more than four years after 2008, the interest income earned by retirees dwindled to almost nothing, and the national debt more than doubled. No matter how the bottom line is tallied, the public was stuck with an astonishing bill brought about by establishment "reckless endangerment".[26]

The establishment's motto is to limit its damages and never retreat so that benefits and costs are always asymmetrically in its favor. The middle class always loses. Most of the principals in the subprime mortgage scheme were winners before the real estate and financial crashes;

took hits during the crashes, but had their winnings or losses cushioned immediately thereafter, and then resumed the tax-transfer subsidy game from the public to themselves in ways suitable to new conditions. They are doing well today. Others — workers, the middle class and passive rich — bore the losses.

Washington did not allow the market to punish those who created the bubble. It chose to selectively bail out key allies,[27] save its government-sponsored organizations (GSOs, Fannie Mae and Freddie Mac), and generate grand new opportunities for establishment enrichment with a quantum trillion dollar jump in annual deficit spending, and an easy money policy that provided windfall profits to financial institutions at savers' expense.

Congressional Budget Office (CBO) statistics as of November 2009 provide an illuminating overview of new federal commitments and expenditures intended to bail out real estate, financial concerns and others directly and indirectly connected to the subprime mortgage and MBS crises. These data reveal that Washington committed $11 trillion and spent $3 trillion specifically for these purposes,[28] with trillions more in emergency spending going to other purposes like extended unemployment relief and healthcare. Although big businesses like American International Group, Citibank and Bear Stearns are primary beneficiaries, there are also ample transfers granted to bureaucratic hyper-activists including $25 billion to help the Treasury Department launch its $75 billion, multipronged foreclosure prevention plan. That plan benefited the banks far more than homeowners.

Regulatory responses followed the same pattern. The federal government made a small gesture to restrict executive pay and diminish systemic risk. It expanded consumer protection, increased oversight over the shadow banking system and derivatives, and enhanced the Federal Reserve's authority to wind down some failing institutions. The Dobb–Frank Wall Street Reform and Consumer Protection Act signed into law in July 2010 addressed some of the causes of the crises, but also predictably made provisions to increase subprime mortgage lending to those claiming to be disadvantaged. There is no accountability.

Healthcare

The federal government is the dominant force in the American health-care system, even though the private sector provides the preponderance of medical services. The government paid 64.3 percent of the health spending bill in 2013, funded by Medicare, Medicaid, the Children's Health Insurance Program and the Veterans Health Administration. US healthcare spending grew 5.8 percent in 2015, reaching $3.2 trillion, or $9,990 per person. This amounted to 17.8 percent of GDP,[29] and 22 percent of personal disposable income,[30] costs disproportionately funded by the middle class, directly through Medicare payroll deductions (2.9 percent), income and sales taxes.[31] The middle class received a significant portion of healthcare benefits, but shouldered the bulk of the transfer burden.

The United States does not have a unitary healthcare system; however, it accepts the principle that everyone should have access to medical services without determining who must pay. The "commitment" is nebulous. It does not stipulate points of access, or patient choice. It does not specify the level, quality of care or patients' ability to select doctors and service providers. It does not address healthcare pricing, cost and patient responsibilities.

Just as in the subprime mortgage case, the establishment is certain of only three things. It is committed to overzealous bureaucratic affirmative action, coded as "equal access" and the "human right" of universal healthcare service. The establishment does not want to pay full freight through direct taxation, and is committed to inveigling the private sector into a destructive speculative game.

Just as in the subprime mortgage case, the establishment is clueless about administrative costs and efficiency. Administration of healthcare constitutes 30 percent of US healthcare costs.[32] The establishment's machinations are prime factors driving sectoral inflation and intermittent pain and suffering, despite penny wise, pound-foolish cost cuts. Doctors are being transformed into wageworkers with predictable results.

Pernicious incentives prevent people from getting the medical services they need. The government forces patients to substitute inappropriate for appropriate therapies, while simultaneously encouraging the over-use diagnostic and testing services. Patients are compelled to purchase boutique medial services when no-frill alternatives suffice, and fund pharmaceutical, medical device vendors' and insurers' excess profits. They are required to pay spiraling insurance premiums with reduced benefits, and must hire legal advocates when insurers invent excuses to deny legitimate claims.[33] They are overwhelmed with unfathomable paperwork that drives the infirm and elderly into bankruptcy. A 2013 study found that about 25 percent of all senior citizens declare bankruptcy due to medical expenses, and 43 percent are forced to mortgage or sell their primary residence.[34]

Just as in the subprime mortgage case, the government sweeps the inequities and failures of the healthcare system under the rug by falsely reducing a problem created by the establishment into an opaque choice between patient financial self-reliance and a utopian universal coverage. A saner populist approach must start with a sober assessment of the middle class's willingness to fund medical services that others cannot afford, followed by fixing a schedule of priorities within this budget. A central health authority can then pay legitimate claims on a priority basis, with windfall loses covered by philanthropy. The rest of the system can be left to the private sector and responsible bureaucratic regulation. The administrative cost saving of this efficient solution should come to hundreds of billions of dollars,[35] providing a glimpse of the total loss imposed on the middle class by the establishment's style of doing affirmative action business.

Representative Tom Price, Donald Trump's designated health secretary has a working knowledge of the establishment's healthcare paradigm.[36] He and Trump are determined to reform or rescind Obamacare (Patient Protection and Affordable Care Act); a scheme that vastly expands healthcare access to superior medical services for those who cannot or refuse to pay. Comprehensive insurance coverage is a legitimate issue, but also lends itself to Ponzi schemes that pose serious systemic risk.

Overzealous regulatory activism is a cancer. The social security system is another catastrophe under construction,[37] but does not require further elaboration here. The key points to grasp regarding the establishment approach to providing social services is that populist complaints are not frivolous. The establishment cannot control itself. Its strategies keep making things worse. Trump's solutions are not panacea either, but they are likely to nudge the system in the right direction.

Endnotes

1. Cf. Kishore Mahbubani and Danny Quah, "The Geopolitics of Populism", *Project Syndicate*, December 9, 2016. https://www.project-syndicate.org/commentary/populism-driven-by-geopolitical-change-by-danny-quah-and-kishore-mahbubani-2016-12. "Of course, all societies should look out for their poorest members and maximize social mobility, while also rewarding entrepreneurship and challenging people to improve their lot. But focusing on such policies would not address the public disaffection underlying the populist uprising, because inequality is not its root cause. Feelings of lost control are."

2. Frederick Jackson Turner, *The Frontier in American History*, 1920. http://xroads.virginia.edu/~hyper/turner/. John Faragher, ed., *Rereading Frederick Jackson Turner: The Significance of the Frontier in American History*, New York: H. Holt and Company, 1984.

3. John Kenneth Galbraith, *The New Industrial State*, Princeton, NJ: Princeton University Press, 1967.

4. Jonah Goldberg, "History's Lessons on Trump's Wealthy Cabinet", *AEI*, December 16, 2016. https://www.aei.org/publication/historys-lessons-on-trumps-wealthy-cabinet/?utm_source=paramount&utm_medium=email&utm_content=AEITODAY&utm_campaign=121916. "The net worth of Donald Trump's cabinet appointments so far reportedly exceeds $14.5 billion (if you include Trump's deputy commerce secretary pick, Todd Ricketts)." "President Woodrow Wilson enlisted the help of corporate titans to help with the war effort. These 'dollar-a-year men' descended on Washington to help Wilson win World War I to make the world 'safe for democracy.' The dollar-a-year men certainly helped with the war-mobilization effort, but they often did so by creating rules that helped their own industries, mostly by establishing cartels, which almost abolished competitive bidding. The War

Industries Board, for instance, staffed almost entirely by eminent industrialists, also fixed prices on commodities, froze wages, commandeered railroads, and the like. Grosvenor Clarkson, the head of the WIB, boasted how firms run by 'individualistic' people (code for free-market advocates) who didn't play along were steamrolled: 'The occasional obstructor fled from the mandates of the Board only to find himself ostracized by his fellows in industry.'"

5. The adjective subprime refers to mortgages issued to borrowers with poor credit credentials who normally would not qualify for loans at the competitive rate because their income prospects were poor or uncertain, or their credit histories unsatisfactory. Many prospective borrowers in this category are minorities, immigrants, young, indigent, low income, unemployed, imposters, speculators and deadbeats. Most either live with relatives and friends, or in traditional public housing, but desire to improve their living standard by owning their own homes, or to make quick profits from flipping properties in an appreciating real estate market. These individuals are not directly excluded from homeownership because of their age, gender, sexual orientation, race, ethnicity, religion, nationality or immigration status. They cannot buy homes under normal competitive, non-discriminatory conditions because statistically they cannot be expected to fully repay their obligations independently, or with the assistance of co-signers (family, friends and benefactors).

6. Fannie Mae began requiring commercial lending institutions to prove that they were not redlining (refusing loans to minorities in desirable neighborhoods), which as a practical matter forced them to accept minority mortgage lending quotas.

7. A mortgage-backed security (MBS) is a type of asset-backed security that is secured by a mortgage or collection of mortgages. The mortgages are sold to a group of individuals (a government agency or investment bank) that securitizes, or packages, the loans together into a security that investors can buy. A collateralized debt obligation (CDO) is so-called because the pooled assets — such as mortgages, bonds and loans — are essentially debt obligations that serve as collateral for the CDO.

8. Private banks were reluctant to issue these high risk loans, but were mollified in part by Fannie Mae's willingness to hedge their risk by purchasing their subprime paper. This put politicians squarely in the business of

giving the un-creditworthy title to assets many ultimately would be unable to afford, with the implicit promise of covering bad loans losses variously from future tax revenues, increased national indebtedness and inflations taxes. Big commercial banking quickly grasped the unwritten rules flooding the market with subprime loans including adjustable-rate "balloon" mortgages, often with no down payment even though they knew that these mortgages could not be repaid in hard times.

9. Goodwill in business and economics is defined as market asset value created when buyers and communities look favorably on sellers' commercial activities.

10. See Anne Kadet, "Working 9 to 5 — at 75: How the Fastest Growing Group in the American Work Force is Changing What It Means to be 'Retired'," *Wall Street Journal*, March 21, 2012.

11. The probability of default is at least six times higher for non-prime loans than prime loans. Robert Shiller, *Irrational Exuberance*, Princeton, NJ: Princeton University Press, 2005. James R. Barth, Tong Li, Triphon Phumiwasana and Glenn Yago, *A Short History of the Subprime Mortgage Market Meltdown*, Santa Monica: Milken Institute, 2008. Souphala Chomsisengphet and Anthony Pennington-Cross, "The Evolution of the Subprime Mortgage Market", *Federal Reserve Bank of St. Louis Review*, Vol. 88, No. 1, January/February 2006, pp. 31–56.

12. Robert Shiller and George Akerlof, *Animal Spirits: How Human Psychology Drives the Economy and Why It Matters for Global Capitalism*, Princeton, NJ: Princeton University Press, 2009.

13. The distinction here is analogous to the difference between manslaughter and murder in criminal law.

14. Souphala Chomsisengphet and Anthony Pennington-Cross, "A Look at Subprime Mortgage Originations: 2000–2007". http://www.ftc.gov/be/workshops/mortgage/presentations/Cross_Chomsisengphet_Subprime_2008.pdf.

15. Souphala Chomsisengphet and Anthony Pennington-Cross, "A Look at Subprime Mortgage Originations: 2000–2007". http://www.ftc.gov/be/workshops/mortgage/presentations/Cross_Chomsisengphet_Subprime_2008.pdf.

16. James R. Barth, Tong Li, Triphon Phumiwasana and Glenn Yago, *A Short History of the Subprime Mortgage Market Meltdown*, Santa Monica: Milken Institute, 2008.

17. Some observers argue that the role of subprime mortgages in the real estate and financial crises is exaggerated because subprime loans at the end of the day did not perform materially worse than prime loans. This may not be true because most federal mortgage relief assistance went to subprime loans creating the false impression of creditworthiness. Nonetheless, and be this as it may, the MBS shadow bank run that triggered the global financial crisis was based on the expectation that subprime mortgages at the end of the day would prove to be junk.

18. James R. Barth, Tong Li, Triphon Phumiwasana and Glenn Yago, *A Short History of the Subprime Mortgage Market Meltdown*, Santa Monica: Milken Institute, 2008.

19. Subprime borrowers' diminished ability to pay their monthly mortgage bills was exacerbated by the practice encouraged by Fannie Mae and other lenders of taking out second mortgages based on the appreciation of their homes, and using the money for current consumption. When the housing market crashed subprime mortgagees (and prime mortgagees) not only had to make first mortgage payments, but second mortgage payments as well.

20. RealtyTrac Staff, "More than 1.2 Million Foreclosure Filings Report in 2006", *RealtyTrac*, February 8, 2007; RealtyTrac Staff, "U.S. Foreclosure Activity Increase 75 Percent in 2007", *RealtyTrac*, January 29, 2008.

21. "How Severe is the Subprime Mess?," *Associated Press*, March 13, 2007. Ben Bernanke, "The Subprime Mortgage Market", *Speech*, Chicago, Illinois, May 17, 2007.

22. Roger Altman, "The Great Crash, 2008", *Foreign Affairs*, January/February 2009.

23. The term includes hedge funds. In a June 2008 speech, President of the NY Federal Reserve Bank Timothy Geithner, who later became Secretary of the Treasury, placed significant blame for the freezing of credit markets on a "run" on the entities in the "parallel" banking system, also called the shadow banking system. These entities became critical to the credit markets underpinning the financial system, but were not subject to the same regulatory controls as depository banks. Paul Krugman described the run on the shadow banking system as the "core of what happened" to cause the crisis. Paul Krugman, *The Return of Depression Economics and the Crisis of 2008*, New York: W.W. Norton Company, 2009.

24. "Timeline: Subprime Loses", *BBC News*, 2008.

25. HSBC was the world's largest bank in 2008.

26. Reckless endangerment in law is defined as the crime of knowingly and wantonly creating a substantial risk of serious bodily or material injury to another person. "Reckless" conduct involves the culpable disregard of foreseeable consequences to others from the act or omission involved. The accused need not intentionally cause the resulting harm. The ultimate question is whether under the circumstances, the accused's (here politocracy's) conduct was that of heedless nature that made it actually or imminently dangerous to the rights or safety of others.

27. "U.S. Regulator Feels Pressure Over Freddie, Fannie: Report", *Yahoo! Finance*, March 26, 2012. "Some officials in the Obama administration, the Federal Reserve and Congress have called on Fannie Mae and Freddie Mac to write down the value of mortgages they own or guarantee as part of an effort to help the U.S. housing market recover from a deep slump that saw one third of property values wiped out since 2006."

28. David Goldman, "CNNMoney.com Bailout Tracker". http://money. cnn.com/news/storysupplement/economy/bailouttracker/index.html. The subcomponents of these totals are: Troubled Asset Relief Program, Federal Reserve Rescue Efforts, Federal Stimulus Program, American International Group, FDIC Bank Takeovers, Other Financial Initiatives and Other Housing Initiatives.

29. https://www.cms.gov/research-statistics-data-and-systems/statistics-trends-and-reports/nationalhealthexpenddata/nationalhealthaccountsh-istorical.html.

30. Personal disposable income is the total amount of money available for an individual or population to spend or save after taxes have been paid. The income is from all sources including wages, salaries, retirement benefits, rental incomes, dividends and capital gains.

31. The individual contribution rate to Medicare is 1.45 percent. It is 2.9 percent for self-employed professionals.

32. Jeffrey Pfeffer, "The Reason Health Care is So Expensive: Insurance Companies", *Bloomberg*, April 10, 2013. https://www.bloomberg.com/news/articles/2013-04-10/the-reason-health-care-is-so-expensive-insurance-companies.

33. Heart attack victims (cardiac infarction) with no prior heart conditions are denied benefits for failing to pre-notify and receive treatment approval for life threatening events that cannot be reasonably foreseen.

34. A. Kelley, K. McGarry, S. Fahle, S. Marshall, Q. Du and S. Skinner, "Out-of-Pocket Spending in the Last Five Years of Life", *Journal of General Internal Medicine*, Vol. 28, No. 2, 2012, pp. 304–309.

35. Recall that 30 percent of America's 3.2 trillion-dollar health bill is attributed to administrative cost. If have this amount were saved, the benefit would be a half-trillion dollars.

36. Robert Pearnov, "Tom Price, Obamacare Critic, Is Trump's Choice for Health Secretary", *New York Times*, November 28, 2016. http://www.nytimes.com/2016/11/28/us/politics/tom-price-secretary-health-and-human-services.html?_r=0.

37. Laurence Kotlikoff, "Social Security Just Ran a $6 Trillion Deficit and No One Noticed!", *Forbes*, July 17, 2016. http://www.forbes.com/sites/kotlikoff/2016/07/17/social-security-just-ran-a-6-trillion-deficit-and-no-one-noticed/#3d91809258a4.

Part II

Trump's Foreign Agenda

Chapter 9

Populist Foreign Policy

Donald Trump believes that the harm the establishment inflicts on ordinary Americans extends to foreign affairs. He contends that American foreign relations are anti-populist; that they serve the establishment's globalist goal of building a new world order on principles that partly cede national sovereignty to foreign interests and transnational institutions. Trump wants to replace establishment globalism with a populist agenda that allows Washington to preserve America's sovereignty intact, and build foreign relationships in America's national interest on a case-by-case basis. For example, Trump has indicated that he may be prepared to support Taiwan's national independence, even though recognition would set back efforts to socio-politically transform and economically subordinate China in the manner the establishment desires. America's interest as Trump sees it is incompatible with establishment globalism. It might once have been wise to prod the Baltic States into joining the North Atlantic Treaty Organization (NATO), but drawing Ukraine into the organization now in accordance with establishment doctrine entails unreasonable risks of nuclear war with Russia.

Trump's approach to foreign policy mirrors his attitude toward the Environment Protection Agency, the US Department of Housing and Urban Development (HUD), the Department of Education and Obamacare. He wants to corral political correctness and address issues pragmatically instead of deferring to the establishment's globalist dogma.

Establishment Foreign Policy Framework

The premise framing the establishment's foreign policy agenda is that the United States can maintain its position of global leadership (soft hegemony) by championing its global nation version of the American dream. The establishment claims that its vision is the world's best dream; that the United States is the best, and that reason will compel rivals to join the bandwagon. Once competitors conclude that globalist democracy, "managed" free enterprise, "fettered" liberty, "approved" civic rights, "selective" equality, "establishment" rule of law, egalitarianism, affirmative action and restorative justice are the best, American leaders as custodians of the improved American Dream infer that they should be able to globally govern with a free hand. America as they see it is destiny's indispensable global hegemon. Their Wittgenstein tautology (a logically consistent theory disconnected from the facts) acknowledges the possibility of transitory clashes of civilization based on national, religious or ideological grounds, but sees them as bumps in the road.

Faith in the geopolitical power of American dreams is deeply felt because the traditional version has withstood the test of time. It weathered the storms of communism and fascism during the 1920s, 1930s and 1940s when Soviet Russia, Hitler's Germany, Mussolini's Italy and Hirohito's Japan expanded their domains, and confidence in America's superiority allowed the United States to overcome post-war East–West polarization by outlasting the USSR during the Cold War.

Staunch Marxist–Leninists did not expect this denouement. They were sure that American leaders were wrong; that the communist dream was better. They promised the politically disaffected One World Government, comprehensive social security, universal prosperity, full racial, gender and religious equality, justice and harmony with considerable initial success, but ultimately lost the dream war because communism failed to provide the good life most people desired. The traditional American Dream became the last universal dream standing, encouraging American leaders to believe that the future would always be theirs.

Russia, China and militant Islam however have refused to adhere to America's script. They have rejected political and economic globalization on America's "improved" terms (democracy, free enterprise, rule of Western law, affirmative action and restorative justice). They are defending their turf, expanding their regional and out-of-region spheres of influence, buttressed by new nationalist (or theocratic) dreams of their own. America's establishment is adhering to its belief that the United States must ultimately prevail, but the tide of history for the moment seems to be moving against it.[1]

Establishment Foreign Policy Agenda

The establishment's contemporary foreign policy agenda is easily decoded. American leaders want to control economic, political and social behavior everywhere to promote their goals and enrich themselves. Concretely, they seek to:

1. Foster a global American-led transnational order that prioritizes free immigration, Third World economic development, poverty alleviation, worldwide egalitarianism, gender, racial and Islamic affirmative action and restorative justice. The approach necessarily dilutes US sovereignty.
2. Eliminate rivals through "color revolutions", regime change or appeasement. Specifically, American leaders want to overthrow the governments of Russia, North Korea, most of the countries of the Middle East, and Myanmar, while accommodating China on Taiwan, and its expanding sphere of influence in the South China Sea. The establishment is supportive of Vietnam, Cuba and socialist-leaning nations everywhere. America's leaders want to eradicate militant Islam.
3. Badger Russia into rescinding its annexation of Crimea, reduce the Kremlin's sphere of influence, and persuade Moscow to accept a minor role in global affairs, including the Middle East. Coax China into democratizing (delegitimizing its communist party), and freezing

its sphere of influence. American leaders want to establish an independent Palestinian state (two state solution) on risky terms for Israel, and perhaps compel Israel to accept the right of Palestinian return. They also want to tame Islamic fundamentalism.

4. Reverse Brexit and deter Grexit, Frexit and Nexit preserving the German led European Union as the principal affirmative action partner in America's global control agenda.[2]

5. Maintain cooperative alliances with strings-attached assistance.

6. Compel North Korea to cease transforming itself into a full-fledged nuclear power. Slow Iran's entry into the nuclear club. Retard nuclear proliferation. Deter nuclear arms races. Press global nuclear disarmament. Press conventional arms reduction and insofar as possible adopt a policy of minimal deterrence.

7. Promote Western-oriented economic and political development in the Third World.

8. Achieve the objectives enumerated above without taking the steps needed to revive America's flagging economy. The establishment opposes diverting funds from domestic programs, and wants to gradually reduce defence spending. Nonetheless, it frequently goes to war relying on a strategy of minimal deterrence, and is unwilling to build creditable conventional military deterrents for deployment against Russia, China or hostile forces in the Middle East and Central Asia.[3]

These goals are riddled with inconsistencies. The establishment can neither bully nor persuade Russia into accepting American domination, if it refuses to mount credible military force along Russia's periphery or extricate America's economy from secular stagnation.

Likewise, the establishment consensus in many instances is a façade, camouflaging bitter disagreements within and between the Republican and Democratic parties. Republican support for the establishment's social transformation agenda is wafer thin, and Democrats are divided over compromising Israel's security to further the Islamist cause.

The establishment is trying to maintain a united public veneer, but the leftward drift of the Obama years is eroding the consensus.

Trump's Foreign Policy

Donald Trump's foreign policy in many important aspects is the antithesis of the establishment's eight-point agenda. He does not want to transform and control economic, political and social behavior everywhere to promote an American-led globalist order. Trump wants America to be a global Liberal Democratic leader, with a populist agenda and muscular management style. Just as with his domestic policy, he prefers a populist open competitive environment to centralized illiberal authority.

Concretely, Trump seeks to:

1. Foster American global leadership without entanglement in a web of multilateral international institutions. Trump intends to follow a populist course in foreign policy in accordance with the traditional American Dream.

   Contrary to the establishment approach, this means that he will turn Washington away from an American-led transnational world government with diluted US sovereignty, free immigration, worldwide egalitarianism, gender, racial and Islamic affirmative action and restorative justice. He will reduce the power of international institutions like the United Nations, and renegotiate terms of America's financial participation.

2. Trump is not committed to pressing his agenda through "color revolutions" and regime change, even though he is opposed to appeasement. Specifically, Trump does not want overthrow the governments of Russia, Israel, most of the countries of the Middle East and Myanmar. His attitude toward North Korea is unclear beyond opposing Pyongyang's emergence as a formidable nuclear power.[4] He will counter rather than accommodate China over Taiwan and the South China Sea, and refuse assistance to socialist-leaning nations everywhere.

3. Trump will try to achieve a Nikita Khrushchev style "peaceful coexistence" *modus vivendi* with Russia. If he had his druthers, he would prefer to see Moscow rescind its annexation of Crimea, and reduce the Kremlin's sphere of influence, but at least initially will settle for

pushing business deals. Trump will not try to coax China into democratizing, or freezing its sphere of influence, but will press instead for better terms of trade. He will parry China's actions in the China Sea with a counter naval build up. Trump will protect Israel against a disadvantageous two state solution, and may well discard the entire historical framework for Middle Eastern settlement. He will not support the Islamist cause and will attempt to contain militant Islamic fundamentalism more vigorously than Obama.

4. Brexit, Grexit, Frexit and Nexit are populist repudiations of the establishment. Trump will have kind words about these movements, and stand aside as Germany salvages what it can of the pre-Brexit European Union. He will cooperate bilaterally with the United Kingdom, the European Union and any new EU defectors. Affirmative action will become a peripheral aspect of the transAtlantic relationship. Trump will try to strengthen NATO and renegotiate terms of American participation.

5. Trump will maintain cooperative alliances with strings-attached assistance.

6. Trump will terminate the 2016 P5+1, plus Iran nuclear deal, fundamentally renegotiate its terms, and/or take vigorous action to slow Iran's entry into the nuclear club. He is also likely to press nuclear non-proliferation more energetically than the establishment, and is committed to upgrading America's aging nuclear arsenal. He will dismiss global nuclear disarmament out of hand, and disregard establishment calls for conventional arms reduction.

7. Trump will slacken the pace of assistance to Western-oriented economic and political development in the Third World.

8. He will strive to achieve the objectives enumerated above in tandem with reviving America's flagging economy. He will divert funds from domestic programs, and increase defence spending. He will attempt to build creditable conventional force deterrents for deployment against Russia and China, or hostile forces in the Middle East and Central Asia.[5]

Trumps goals are neither radical, nor impractical. He does not seek to conquer the world, and understands that his program may require diverting funds from domestic social programs to defence. He is solicitous of Taiwan and Israel and unsympathetic to Cuban communism, but this is not sinister. It is a matter of taste. The establishment's shrill indictment of Trump's foreign policy is also a matter of taste. The establishment cannot accept Trump's pragmatic populism because it is married to its global nation nirvana. It claims that if Trump prevails Armageddon will be at hand with Russia, China and the Middle East.

There are causes for concern, but they are not primarily of Trump's making. The establishment's color revolutionary policies in Russia, China and the Middle East have become increasingly destabilizing, leaving Trump with a combustible legacy. Trump appears to be offering some plausible solutions, but faces stiff opposition.[6]

Endnotes

1. Danny Quah and Kishore Mahbubani, "The Geopolitics of Populism", *Project Syndicate*, December 9, 2016. https://www.project-syndicate.org/commentary/populism-driven-by-geopolitical-change-by-danny-quah-and-kishore-mahbubani-2016-12. Cf. Yuri Friedman, "What the World Might Look Like in 5 Years, According to US Intelligence", *Atlantic*, January 11, 2017. http://www.defenseone.com/ideas/2017/01/what-world-might-look-5-years-according-us-intelligence/134511/?oref=d-river. "Even America's own government analysts see the American Era drawing to a close. Every four years, a group of U.S. intelligence analysts tries to predict the future. And this year, in a report released just weeks before Donald Trump assumes the presidency, those analysts forecast a massive shift in international affairs over the next five years or so: 'For better and worse, the emerging global landscape is drawing to a close an era of American dominance following the Cold War,'" the study argues. "So, too, perhaps is the rules-based international order that emerged after World War II." The National Intelligence Council (NIC), a unit within the Office of the Director of National Intelligence, is essentially marking the potential end not just of America's status as the world's sole superpower, but also of the current foundation for much of that power: an open international economy, U.S. military alliances in Asia and Europe, and liberal rules and institutions — rules like human-rights protections and institutions like the World Trade Organization — that shape how

countries behave and resolve their conflicts." "Today, however, major powers are struggling to cooperate on issues of global consequence and acting aggressively in their respective parts of the world, the NIC observes. In the coming years, the council envisions the current international system fragmenting 'toward contested regional spheres of influence.'"

2. Brexit is shorthand for British exit from the EU. Grexit, Frexit and Nexit reflect the desire of Greece, France and the Netherlands to follow the British example.

3. The Obama Administration cut hundreds of billions of dollars from defense and ignored the warnings of their own Defense Secretary about the minimum defense budget necessary for national security. *The Weekly Standard*, Feb. 3, 2015. The Obama–Clinton Administration tried repeatedly to dismantle the Navy's cruisers, the backbone of missile defense, even as the threat of ballistic missiles by Iran and North Korea grew rapidly. *Navy Times*, April 19, 2016. Under Obama–Clinton, the US Navy has been depleted to the point where key regions of the world have lacked any American aircraft carrier presence for months at a time. *Navy Times*, January 7, 2016.

4. James Action, "Can Trump Enforce His Red Line on North Korea?", *The Atlantic*, January 5, 2017. https://www.theatlantic.com/international/archive/2017/01/trump-twitter-north-korea/512450/. "In a New Year's address, North Korea's supreme leader, Kim Jong Un, had stated that his country had 'entered the final stage of preparation for the test launch of intercontinental ballistic missile.' In response, Trump tweeted that 'North Korea just stated that it is in the final stages of developing a nuclear weapon capable of reaching parts of the U.S. It won't happen!'"

5. Increase the size of the US Army to 540,000 active duty soldiers, which the Army Chief of Staff says he needs to execute current missions. Rebuild the US Navy toward a goal of 350 ships, as the bipartisan National Defense Panel has recommended. Provide the US Air Force with the 1,200 fighter aircraft they need. Grow the US Marine Corps to 36 battalions. Invest in a serious missile defense system to meet growing threats by modernizing our Navy's cruisers and procuring additional, modern destroyers to counter the ballistic missile threat from Iran and North Korea. Emphasize cyber warfare and require a comprehensive

review from the Joint Chiefs of Staff and all relevant federal agencies to identify our cyber vulnerabilities and to protect all vital infrastructure and to create a state-of-the-art cyber defense and offense. Pay for this necessary rebuilding of our national defense by conducting a full audit of the Pentagon, eliminating incorrect payments, reducing duplicative bureaucracy, collecting unpaid taxes, and ending unwanted and unauthorized federal programs. https://www.donaldjtrump.com/policies/national-defense.

6. "At Least Four Senior U.S. State Department Officials Leave Posts — Officials", *NewsOK*, January 26, 2017. http://www.cnbc.com/2017/01/26/several-senior-diplomats-resign-as-trump-administration-takes-shape.html. Josh Rogin, "The State Department's entire senior administrative team just resigned", *Washington Post*, January 26, 2017. https://www.washingtonpost.com/news/josh-rogin/wp/2017/01/26/the-state-departments-entire-senior-management-team-just-resigned/?utm_term=.84d0eec29d70. "Secretary of State Rex Tillerson's job running the State Department just got considerably more difficult. The entire senior level of management officials resigned Wednesday, part of an ongoing mass exodus of senior foreign service officers who don't want to stick around for the Trump era. Then suddenly on Wednesday afternoon, Kennedy and three of his top officials resigned unexpectedly, four State Department officials confirmed. Assistant Secretary of State for Administration Joyce Anne Barr, Assistant Secretary of State for Consular Affairs Michele Bond and Ambassador Gentry O. Smith, director of the Office of Foreign Missions, followed him out the door. All are career foreign service officers who have served under both Republican and Democratic administrations."

Chapter 10

Russia

The establishment's post-Soviet policy toward Russia degenerated into an on-again, off-again low intensity Cold War II despite auspicious beginnings because American leaders refused to temper their geopolitical ambitions, assemble credible conventional military deterrents in the Baltics and Ukraine, and avert secular economic stagnation. The disintegration and collapse of the Soviet Union offered the establishment an opportunity to spread its global hegemony across the Soviet space, including the Kremlin's East European, Central European and Balkan spheres of influence. The American Dream, both in its traditional and affirmative action guises had wide appeal, especially to liberal segments of communist Eurasia. Independence-minded elements of the Soviet Estonian, Latvian, Lithuanian, Ukrainian, Belarusian, Kazakhstan and Moldovan communist parties, and the communist parties of Poland, Hungary and the German Democratic Republic (GDR), as well as the broader electorate were attracted to the West's prosperity, competitive markets, democracy and the rule of law.

This attraction allowed America's establishment to expedite communism's demise throughout the region,[1] cripple Russia's armed forces,[2] open up the East's economies for financial, commercial and proprietary penetration, and foster the integration of Russia's former vassals into the European Union (EU) and North Atlantic Treaty Organization (NATO).[3] Within what historically is a blink of an eye, the post-Soviet space split into 15 independent nations, and the GDR merged with West Germany. Latvia, Lithuania, Estonia, Poland, Hungary, Czechia, Slovakia, Romania, Bulgaria and Slovenia joined the EU and NATO. Albania has not acceded to the EU, but has joined NATO. All former members of the Warsaw Pact except Russia, switched sides, and tacitly allied against Moscow.

Boris Yeltsin and his liberal entourage not only tolerated this reversal of Kremlin fortunes, they abetted it, with Russia itself participating in the G-7, NATO,[4] and flirting with EU membership. The high water market for the establishment's effort to integrate Russia into its global nation network came just before the 2008 worldwide financial crisis. The Baltic States, Visegrad Group (Poland, Czechia, Hungary and Slovakia), Romania and Bulgaria were absorbed into West, and the EU was flourishing. The establishment wanted to go further extending its net to Albania, Macedonia, Montenegro, Serbia, Bosnia, Herzegovina, Kosovo, Georgia, Moldova, Ukraine, Azerbaijan and Central Asia,[5] and has not given up,[6] but Russia is no longer cooperating. The Kremlin now views these efforts as acts of aggression in the cases of Georgia, Moldova, Azerbaijan and Central Asia,[7] and as a *casus belli* in Ukraine.

Russia's transformation from partner to adversary took the establishment by surprise because it was blinded by post-Soviet triumphalism. De-communization, demilitarization, the integration of the Baltic States, Visegrad Group, Bulgaria and Romania into the EU and NATO, and Russia's own partial westernization had seemed so inexorable that the establishment failed to see the *revanche* that was brewing from within.

The economic and political collapse of the USSR and the subsequent reconfiguration of spheres of influence were the fallout of a liberal palace coup within the Russian communist party and the fraternal communist parties of the Baltics, Ukraine, Belarus, and the Visegrad Group against the power services: armed forces and secret police.[8] The "siloviki" as they are called in Russia saw the handwriting on the wall as early as 1987, but temporized acquiescing first to Mikhail Gorbachev's policies of "new thinking" (*novoe myslenie*), "democratization" (*demokratizatsiia*), and radical economic reform (*perestroika*). They mounted a *coup d'etat* on August 19, but it failed, and then bit their tongues during the Yeltsin years waiting for revenge and vindication until they found their champion in Vladimir Putin, Russia's second elected president.[9] The *siloviki* are battle hardened and will not be deceived by liberal wiles again.

Putin was a loyal son of the *siloviki* who rose up the ranks of the Soviet secret police (KGB), and then successively became the head of the Russian Security Council, the Federal Security Service (FSB) successor to the KGB and Prime Minister shortly before his election to the presidency in 2000. He shared a desire for triple revenge with his fellow *siloviki* against what the power services saw as Gorbachev's liberal "stab in the back", Yeltsin's "stab in the chest", and America's betrayal. Gorbachev in their eyes had treasonously permitted the secession of the Baltic States, Russia, Ukraine and Belarus from the USSR,[10] and the scourge of "katastoika",[11] catastrophic economic "shock therapy". Yeltsin compounded the felony by paring Russia's armed forces to the bone,[12] defanging the secret police,[13] adopting a catastrophic economic transition program "katakod", and aiding the enemy, that is, America's quest to become the sole global hegemon.[14] The United States was a villain from the *siloviki*'s perspective not only because it had co-masterminded the Soviet Union's demise with Gorbachev, but also because it had made various unfulfilled pledges for a "Grand Bargain" to economically assist Russia,[15] and to refrain from expanding NATO.[16] These broken promises proved the West's treachery in *siloviki*'s eyes.

Various authorities including several establishment insiders contest the *siloviki*'s interpretation of these events.[17] They could be partly or wholly correct, but this does not negate the fact that the establishment should have foreseen the possibilities of *revanche*, including the restoration of Russian military superpower,[18] and defused the situation. This could have been easily accomplished by counseling Yeltsin against shock therapy in line with the World Bank Group's economic advice to Deng Xiaoping[19]; showing restraint at Pristina in 1999[20]; keeping the Baltic states, Visegrad Group, Bulgaria, Romania out of NATO, and accepting Russia's historical sphere of influence over Georgia, Moldova, Ukraine, Azerbaijan and Central Asia. Robert Gates, former CIA Director and Secretary of Defense, appears to concur.[21]

The establishment instead pressed forward, ignoring the *siloviki*'s grievances and Putin's pledge to restore Russia's military superpower and rollback the establishment's sphere of influence in Europe within a decade.[22] Nor was Washington fazed by Russia's counter-offensives.

Russia annexed Crimea (in violation of Article 2(4) of the UN Charter,[23] the Budapest Memorandum on Security Assurances,[24] and the Helsinki Accords[25]) in 2014; the Kremlin carried out an impressive conventional and nuclear military modernization in 2010–2016,[26] and occupied Donetsk and Luhansk.[27] Russia deployed large military forces against the Baltic States,[28] achieved victory in Aleppo,[29] and made mischief in the EU and the American 2016 presidential elections,[30] but the establishment refuses to accept any responsibility for these counter-actions or modify its behavior.

It has scolded Russia, imposed toothless economic sanctions,[31] made sundry token military gestures,[32] but consistent with its doctrine of "strategic patience" has chosen to reduce America's military capabilities in order to expand domestic social programs.[33]

Nothing can change the establishment's mind because domestic social programs and the lure of arms reductions take precedence over soft power American global nation hegemony.[34] If as a consequence of these priorities, Russia reconquers the Baltic States and re-annexes all of Ukraine, the establishment will fuss and fume, but do nothing decisive. It will just continue placing its trust in "strategic patience", hoping that the Kremlin will implode tomorrow as it did in 1991.

Those who fret that Donald Trump's election will wreck prospects for amicable Russo-American relations do not appreciate that they are calling the kettle black. The establishment was and remains on a collision course with the Kremlin that is unlikely to have a happy ending for the West.[35] It continues to press color revolutions in Russia's neighborhood and on the Kremlin's home turf.[36] It constantly threatens to intensify sanctions,[37] without mounting credible deterrents to Russian forces facing the Baltic States, Ukraine, Donets and Luhansk. The establishment shows no sign of countering the Kremlin's arms buildup, removing regulatory obstacles to America's economic revitalization or solving the EU crisis.

Trump's statements about Russia indicate that he does not grasp the predicament that the establishment has created. His comments suggest that he has not taken to heart contemporary Russia's resurgent economic and military industrial power,[38] the Kremlin's sophisticated approach to geopolitical domination, and information warfighting capabilities. Trump does not seem to appreciate Putin's tenaciousness, his ability to repress dissent and make opponents vanish,[39] and his willingness to play "Russian roulette." He has offered no comprehensive plan to counter the *siloviki*'s vendetta and settle Cold War II.

Nonetheless, he is in a better position than the establishment to manage the Russo-American relationship. Trump is not married to American soft power global nation hegemony, or the color revolutions and regime change strategies that the establishment has employed in the Kremlin's neighborhood and heartland. He is comfortable with state self-governance and is distrustful of establishment globalist solutions. His preference for delegating responsibility to self-regulating independent entities should facilitate compromise and peaceful coexistence.[40]

Trump will increase American military power giving Putin a pause, and he may succeed in revitalizing the US economic growth with a mix of deregulatory and tax incentive policies. The combined effect of these actions should be stabilizing and create a framework for a more lasting solution. Russian military theoreticians coined the term "correlation of forces" and the Kremlin respects the strength of its foreign rivals. If Trump were an anti-communist ideologue, these positives might be countervailed by a will to eliminate Russia's threat. But he is a businessman driven more by a desire to make a great deal, than to destroy his adversaries, and in this regard is far more sensible than his establishment critics.[41]

Trump cannot settle the Russo-American imbroglio unilaterally because Putin is committed to his great power restoration project and has transformed Russia's military and civilian economies so that they can provide both the guns and butter required for Moscow to hold its own.[42] The Kremlin no longer is the impoverished superpower that Henry Rowan and Charles Wolf, Jr claimed it was in 1990. Putin has successfully created workably competitive markets inside the military industrial complex and parts of the consumer goods sector. Counting on "strategic patience" may have made sense when the Soviet Union was a planned economy, but not today. Russia will not fade quietly into the night.[43] Putin knows this. He is betting on the West's adaptive failure. A great deal therefore will depend on whether his assessment of the West is right; on whether Trump can tilt the correlation of forces back in America's favor.[44]

Endnotes

1. Svetlana Savranskaya and Thomas Blanton, *The Last Superpower Summits: Gorbachev, Reagan, and Bush: Conversations that Ended the Cold War*, Budapest/New York: Central European University Press, 2016. Savranskaya and Blanton show that keeping the Union together, and backing Gorbachev personally, remained at the core of US policy all the way through 1991, for fear of a bloody disintegration that would dwarf the slaughter taking place at that time in Yugoslavia. "Yugoslavia with nuclear weapons," as one official put it. This however does not negate the fact that Reagan and Bush also encouraged Gorbachev in his destructive economic and political policies including German reunification and the liberalization that led to the secession of Estonia, Latvia, Lithuania, Ukraine, and Belarus. On Ukraine see Serhii Plokhy, *The Last Empire: The Final Days of the Soviet Union*, New York: Basic Books, 2014, pp. 158–161. Secretary of Defense Dick Cheney was the strongest proponent of encouraging the rapid disintegration of the USSR because he saw the fracturing of the former enemy as a diminution of threat. See National Security Archive, "The End of the Soviet Union 1991", http://nsarchive.gwu.edu/NSAEBB/NSAEBB576-End-of-Soviet-Union-1991/. Boris Yeltsin played a decisive role in the process of Soviet disunion. See Mikhail Gorbachev, *Zhizn' i Reformy*, Moscow: Novosti, 1995, p. 589. Gennady Burbulis devised Yeltsin's secret memorandum entitled "Strategy for Russia in the Transition Period" to speedily form a Russian state that would be the sole legal heir to the Soviet Union and would embark on a radical economic reform alone, leaving behind the center and the rest of the republics. This was the strategy — to get rid of Gorbachev by dismantling the Union.

2. Boris Yeltsin reduced Russian defense spending by 90 percent in 1992 and throughout the years of his rule. National security advisor Brent Scowcroft confessed he "thought there was positive benefit in the breakup of command and control over strategic nuclear weapons in the Soviet Union to several republics. Anything which would serve to dilute the size of an attack we might have to face was, in my view, a benefit well worth the deterioration of unified control over the weapons." See George Bush and Brent Scowcroft, *A World Transformed*, New York: Alfred A. Knopf, 1998, p. 544. "President Bush saw both the opportunity and the danger. Gorbachev was not going to be around much longer to make the arms-race-in-reverse happen. So Bush insisted on pushing the envelope, and given the reality in the Soviet Union, with so many ideological blinders about Soviet behavior in tatters on the floor of the Situation Room, the NSC agreed with the president's push to offer significant and unilateral disarmament initiatives." National Security Archive, "The End of the Soviet Union 1991", http://nsarchive.gwu.edu/NSAEBB/NSAEBB576-End-of-Soviet-Union-1991/.

3. Serhii Plokhy, *The Last Empire: The Final Days of the Soviet Union*, New York: Basic Books, 2014, p. 26. "Gorbachev probably was the only person at the meeting who still believed in the possibility of integrating the Soviet Union into Europe. In the perceptive words of his spokesman, Andrei Grachev, 'he was inspired by an almost religious faith in the feasibility of finally joining these two separate worlds and a burning desire to bring this about.'"

4. The relationship began in 1991 within the framework of the North Atlantic Cooperation Council (later renamed Euro-Atlantic Partnership Council). In 1994, Russia joined the Partnership for Peace program. On May 27, 1997, at the NATO summit in Paris, NATO and Russia signed the Founding Act on Mutual Relations, Cooperation and Security, a road map for would-be NATO–Russia cooperation.

5. Moldova, Ukraine and Georgia signed Association Agreements with the EU on June 27, 2014, which deepened their trade and political links with the EU, and the European Parliament passed a resolution recognizing the "European perspective" of all three post-Soviet countries.

6. The European Commission controls the Eastern Partnership (EaP). It is an initiative of the EU governing its relationship with the post-Soviet

states of Armenia, Azerbaijan, Belarus, Georgia, Moldova and Ukraine, intended to provide a venue for discussions of trade, economic strategy, travel agreements and other issues between the EU and its Eastern neighbors. The project was initiated by Poland, and a subsequent proposal was prepared in cooperation with Sweden. It was presented by the foreign minister of Poland and Sweden at the EU General Affairs and External Relations Council in Brussels on May 26, 2008. The Eastern Partnership was inaugurated by the EU in Prague on May 7, 2009. The Eastern Partnership consists of the post-Soviet states: Armenia, Azerbaijan, Belarus, Georgia, Moldova, Ukraine and the EU. Russia has voiced concerns over the Eastern Partnership, seeing it as an attempt to expand the EU's "sphere of influence" in the quest for oil. Russia has also expressed concerns that the EU is putting undue pressure on Belarus by suggesting it might be marginalized if it follows Russia in recognizing the independence of the Georgian breakaway regions of Abkhazia and South Ossetia. "Is this promoting democracy or is it blackmail? It's about pulling countries from the positions they want to take as sovereign states," Russian foreign minister Sergei Lavrov has stated. The European Commission portrays its actions as benign globalization; Russia sees the process as malevolent.

7. Putin claims that the West reneged on promises to keep former Soviet republics and satellites out of NATO and the EU. Sarotte reports with regard to East Germany that unwritten promises were made, but quickly shelved. See Sarotte, "A Broken Promise?" Despite this claim, Putin occasionally presses his plan for a Greater Europe co-led by Russia and others spanning the Atlantic to the Pacific.

Marek Menkiszak, Greater Europe: Putin's Vision of European (dis) integration, OSW Number 46, Warsaw, October, 2013. John Mearsheimer asserts that Putin's grievances are well founded. "The United States and its European allies share most of the responsibility for the crisis. The taproot of the trouble is NATO enlargement, the central element of a larger strategy to move Ukraine out of Russia's orbit and integrate it into the West. At the same time, the EU's expansion eastward and the West's backing of the pro-democracy movement in Ukraine — beginning with the Orange Revolution in 2004 — were critical elements, too. Since the mid-1990s, Russian leaders have adamantly opposed NATO enlargement, and in recent years, they have made it clear that they would not stand by while their strategically important neighbor turned into a Western bastion." See John Mearsheimer, "Why the Ukraine Crisis Is the West's Fault: The Liberal Delusions that Provoked Putin", *Foreign Affairs*, Vol. 90, September/ October 2014. Gorbachev concurs. See Nathan Gardels, "Why Gorbachev Feels Betrayed by the Post-Cold War West", *The World Post*, November 7, 2014. http://www.huffingtonpost.com/2014/11/07/ gor-bachev-post-cold-war-west_n_6116654.html. Note that Gorbachev may have a hidden agenda. He could be indicted for treason because of his role in fomenting *katastroika*. See "Russian Parliament Moves to Charge Gorbachev with Treason for Breaking Up U.S.S.R.", April 11, 2014.

8. Bruno Dallago and Steven Rosefielde, *Transformation and Crisis in Central and Eastern Europe: Challenges and Prospects*, London: Routledge, 2016.

9. Steven Rosefielde, *The Kremlin Strikes Back: Russia and the West after Crimea's Annexation*, Cambridge: Cambridge University Press, 2017.

10. Grounds for suspicion are increased by the president's failure to reverse course when confronted with the adverse effects of devolving communist power from the Kremlin to the republics and abolishing command planning. The loss of East Germany on November 9, 1989, and of the Baltic states in September 1991 did not trigger recentralization of Communist Party power, and no effort was made to restore command planning after the economy swooned in 1990. Gorbachev and his supporters of course could and did argue that retreat was unwarranted and advance imperative, but it is difficult to understand how radical reformers maintained their faith amid the evidence to the contrary unless they subconsciously or consciously intended to destroy communism at any price.

11. Alexander Zinoviev, *Katastroika*, London: Claridge Press, 1991.

12. Steven Rosefielde, *Russia in the 21st Century: The Prodigal Superpower*, Cambridge: Cambridge University Press, 2005.

13. Vasily Ivanovich Brezhkov, *Head of the Leningrad KGB Administration: 1954–1996*, Saint Petersburg: Choice, 2004.

14. Steven Rosefielde, *The Kremlin Strikes Back: Russia and the West after Crimea's Annexation*, Cambridge: Cambridge University Press, 2017.

15. Graham Allison and Robert Blackwill, America's Stake in the Soviet Future, *Foreign Affairs*, Vol. 70, No. 3, 1991, pp. 77–79. Graham Allison and Robert Blackwill, "On With the Grand Bargain", *The Washington Post*, August 27, 1991.

16. John Mearsheimer, "Why the Ukraine Crisis Is the West's Fault: The Liberal Delusions that Provoked Putin", *Foreign Affairs*, Vol. 90, September/ October 2014. Gorbachev concurs. See Nathan Gardels, "Why Gorbachev Feels Betrayed by the Post–Cold War West", *The World Post*, November 7, 2014. http://www.huffingtonpost.com/2014/11/07/ gorbachev-post-cold-war-west_n_6116654.html.

17. Joshua R. Itzkowitz Shifrinson, "Deal or No Deal? The End of the Cold War and the U.S. Offer to Limit NATO Expansion", *International Security*, Vol. 40, No. 4, Spring 2016, pp. 7– 44. http://belfercenter.ksg. harvard.edu/files/003-ISEC_a_00236-Shifrinson.pdf.

18. Steven Rosefielde, *Russia in the 21st Century: The Prodigal Superpower*, Cambridge: Cambridge University Press, 2005.

19. The World Bank group encouraged Deng Xiaoping to gradually create a market economy, but encouraged Russia to do the reverse. China prospered; Russia collapsed. Joshua Cooper Ramo, "The Beijing Consensus", *Foreign Policy Centre*, 2004. http://fpc.org.uk/fsblob/244.pdf.

   The Chinese Communist Party rejected shock therapy out of hand, and the West knew Deng Xiaoping could not be persuaded to abandon his gradualist approach to authoritarian market building. Instead of scuttling the command economy in one fell swoop, China chose to turbocharge aggregate economic demand to ease the dislocations cause by orderly marketization. Now that the Chinese approach has been vindicated and shock therapy largely forgotten, Deng Xiaoping's strategy is lauded as the Beijing Consensus. See Stefan Halper, *The Beijing Consensus: How China's Authoritarian Model Will Dominate the Twenty-First Century*, New York: Basic Books, 2010.

20. NATO troops to enter Pristina which was historically part of Russia's sphere of influence in early June 1999. Yeltsin protested, but ultimately capitulated to the *siloviki*'s chagrin.

21. Robert Gates, *Duty: Memoirs of a Secretary at War*, New York, NY: Alfred A. Knopf, 2014.

22. Eugene Kogan, *Russian Military Capabilities*, Tiblisi Georgia: Georgian Foundation for Strategic and International Studies, 2016. "Despite claims to the contrary, Russia is much closer to having the military it needs that has often been suggested. In other words, the Western perception of the not sufficiently prepared Russian military was deeply mistaken. The 2008–2012 military reform prepared the military for the year 2013. The Kremlin began to set up a pool of rapid deployment forces in 2013 in order to be able to intervene in its neighborhood. These well-equipped, well-trained, modern forces consist of Airborne Forces (four divisions, five brigades), Marines (four brigades, eight separate regiments), GRU Intelligence Forces (GRU Spetsnaz) brigades and three or four elite Ground Forces units as well as air and naval support. The MoD planned that, in the coming years, all of these units would be made up of professionals. On this basis, the Airborne Forces already count up to 20 battalions. There is every reason to believe that the 30,000 to 40,000 troops transferred to the south-eastern border of Ukraine in February 2014 were the backbone of these rapid deployment forces that realistically may have 100,000 and more troops ready for rapid deployment. The GRU Spetsnaz forces, in particular, have both expanded — with two new brigades: the 100th and the 25th — and developed. Most of the 15,000 to 17,000 Spetsnaz are essentially very well-trained light infantry and intervention forces. However, a growing awareness of the need for truly 'tier one' special forces able to operate in small teams and complex political environment led to the decision to create the Special Operations Command (or KSO in Russian) in 2010. Becoming operational in 2013, the KSO first saw action in the seizure of Crimea in 2014. Numbering about 500 operators with integral airlift and close air support assets, the KSO represents a genuine enhancement of Russian capabilities and one designed for precisely the kind of military political operations described for the first time in the 2014 doctrine. On the other hand, attempts to increase the proportion of the Armed Forces staffed on a professional, volunteer basis continue to lag behind plans. As of December 2014 the total such kontraktniki in the military numbered 295,000: a solid increase from 2013's 186,000 but still well short of the 499,000 meant to be in the ranks by 2017. As of December 2015 the

total of such kontraktniki in the military numbered 352,000 while their number should reach 384,000 in 2016. It can be assumed that the number of professional soldiers is likely to increase until 2017. Thus, the term lagging behind will become obsolete.

General Yuri Borisov, Deputy Minister of Defence for Procurement (hereafter cited as General Borisov), said in late January 2015 that: 'The segment of modern equipment in the Aerospace Defence Forces (or VKO in Russian), the Navy and the Strategic Missile Forces (or RVSN in Russian) is at the rate of more than 40%.' Currently, only 28% of the Russian Air Force inventory consists of modern equipment while the figure stands at 26% for the Ground Forces and the rest of the Russian military. RIA Novosti reported in early October 2015 by citing General Borisov that: "Modern hardware now makes up 45.8% of the Aerospace Forces (or VKS in Russian)." Finally, in early February 2016 General Sergei Shoigu, Minister of Defence, said that: "Forty seven percent of the country's arms and equipment inventory is now considered 'modern.'" The most modern area is its nuclear deterrent which between the three elements of its nuclear triad are reported to be 55 percent modernized. The Aerospace Forces are at 52 percent with the Navy sitting at 39 percent and the Ground Forces at 35 percent at the close of 2015. The further increase in modern equipment requires substantial funds that, despite the current economic crisis, President Vladimir Putin and his administration are ready to shoulder. Therefore, the pronounced target for the Armed Forces to have 70 percent of modern equipment by 2020 is no longer a far-fetched scenario but a fact that the West at large need to acknowledge, carefully monitor and think through as to what it can do about it. The author's assertion may be dismissed out of hand by the expert community but facts presented above reinforce the author's assertion. Furthermore, the section below, entitled Defence Spending, reinforces the author's view that the reshaping of the Russian military and equipping it with modern weapons is on the right track.

23. Robin Geiß, "Russia's Annexation of Crimea: The Mills of International Law Grind Slowly but They Do Grind", *International Law Studies*, Vol. 91, 2015, pp. 226–249. http://stockton.usnwc.edu/cgi/viewcontent.cgi?article=1377&context=ils.

24. *Budapest Memorandums on Security Assurances, 1994*, December 5, 1994 "1. The Russian Federation, the United Kingdom of Great Britain and Northern Ireland and the United States of America reaffirm their commitment to Ukraine, in accordance with the principles of the Final Act of the Conference on Security and Cooperation in Europe, to respect the independence and sovereignty and the existing borders of Ukraine". http://www.cfr.org/nonproliferation-arms-control-and-disarmament/budapest-memorandums-security-assurances-1994/p32484.

25. The Final Act of the Conference on Security and Cooperation in Europe, August 1, 1975, 14, I.L.M. 1292 (Helsinki Declaration). http://www1.umn.edu/humanrts/osce/basics/finact75.htm. I. Sovereign equality, respect for the rights inherent in sovereignty; II. Refraining from the threat or use of force; III. Inviolability of frontiers; IV. Territorial integrity of States.

26. Julian Cooper, Russia's state armament program to 2020: A quantitative assessment of implementation 2011–2015, FOI, FOI-R-4239-SE, March 2016. "This report provides an overview of the implementation of the Russian state armament programme to 2020 as the end of its first five years approaches. It is an empirical study designed to present data that is not readily accessible to analysts." Julian Cooper reports that Russia exceeded its goal of increasing the modern component of its arsenal to 30 percent in 2015. The new official figure is 47 percent, attributable in part to "accelerated withdrawal of older weaponry for service use. There is clearly much scrapping of old equipment underway at present but some will simply be put in storage. But in addition quite a large volume of repaired and modernised equipment has been procured during the last 2–3 years and all this is considered 'modern', helping to meet the target." Personal correspondence, April 25, 2015.

27. Russia is engaged in a proxy war of attrition in Donbass (Donetsk and Luhansk oblasts) within parameters fixed by the Minsk II process. Full text of the document signed by the leaders of Ukraine, Russia, France, Germany and pro-Russian separatists on February 12, 2015, February 16, 2015. https://www.transcend.org/tms/2015/02/full-text-of-the-minsk-ii-agreement-on-ukraine/.

28. The Kremlin's arms buildup has multiple purposes including the achievement of battlefield escalation dominance with conventional and

nuclear ordnance up to the strategic nuclear threshold (a global recon-
naissance/strike capability to wage intercontinental conventional war
against the US/allies and other adversaries in support of Russian national
interests). See James Howe, "Future Russian Strategic Nuclear and Non-
Nuclear Forces: 2022", paper presented to the American Foreign Policy
Council Conference on "The Russian Military in the Contemporary
Perspective" held May 9–10 in Washington, D.C., 2016.

29. Stephen Blank, "A Clinic on Clausewitz: Lessons of Russia's Syria
Campaign", paper presented to the American Foreign Policy Council
Conference on "The Russian Military in the Contemporary Perspective"
held 9–10 May in Washington, D.C. 2016. "World leaders have hailed
the agreement as a substantive breakthrough to the Syrian impasse. But
the reality is very different; the text of the agreement permits Russia to
continue bombing raids against a broad range of allegedly terrorist targets, effectively giving the Kremlin carte blanche to continue its military
operations directed against all manner of opposition to long-time ally
Bashar Assad. In this way, Russia can continue to shape outcomes in
Syria, and do so with virtual impunity." Sergei Karpukhin, "The Russian
Media and the Fall of Aleppo: State-run outlets are essential to making
the case for Putin's intervention in Syria", *Atlantic*, December 23, 2016.
https://www.theatlantic.com/international/archive/2016/12/russia-
media-putin-aleppo-syria-turkey-isis-karlov/511682/.

30. The Kremlin always has been a propaganda master and ceaselessly
strives to control public perceptions at home and abroad. This has
made it easy for the Democrat Party to blame its electoral defeat on
Russian cyber mischief.

President Obama in the waning days of his administration denounced
Russia for intervening in the November election and imposed eye-
catching sanctions on Moscow's diplomats. Few serious Western
experts on Russian intelligence operations believe Obama's allegation,
dismissing his claims as political theater. White House, Office of the
Press Secretary, "Statement by the President on Actions in Response to
Russian Malicious Cyber Activity and Harassment", December 29,
2016. https://www.whitehouse.gov/the-press-office/2016/12/29/state-
ment-president-actions-response-russian-malicious-cyber-activity.
Jeffrey Carr, "FBI/DHS Joint Analysis Report: A Fatally Flawed Effort",

December 30, 2016. https://medium.com/@jeffreycarr/fbi-dhs-joint-analysis-report-a-fatally-flawed-effort-b6a98fafe2fa#.8l2dzj6rf. "The FBI/DHS Joint Analysis Report (JAR) 'Grizzly Steppe' was released yesterday as part of the White House's response to alleged Russian government interference in the 2016 election process. It adds nothing to the call for evidence that the Russian government was responsible for hacking the DNC, the DCCC, the email accounts of Democratic party officials, or for delivering the content of those hacks to Wikileaks. It merely listed every threat group ever reported on by a commercial cybersecurity company that is suspected of being Russian-made and lumped them under the heading of Russian Intelligence Services (RIS) without providing any supporting evidence that such a connection exists." "As security researchers, what we call 'the Sednit group' is merely a set of software and the related network infrastructure, which we can hardly correlate with any specific organization." "Where's the Evidence?

If the White House had unclassified evidence that tied officials in the Russian government to the DNC attack, they would have presented it by now. The fact that they didn't means either that the evidence doesn't exist or that it is classified.

If it's classified, an independent commission should review it because this entire assignment of blame against the Russian government is looking more and more like a domestic political operation run by the White House that relied heavily on questionable intelligence generated by a for-profit cybersecurity firm with a vested interest in selling 'attribution-as-a-service'." Cf. Dan Goodin, "White House fails to make case that Russian hackers tampered with election", *arsTechnica*, December 30, 2016. http://arstechnica.com/security/2016/12/did-russia-tamper-with-the-2016-election-bitter-debate-likely-to-rage-on/.

31. Susanne Oxenstierna and Per Olsson, *The Economic Sanctions against Russia: Impact and Prospects of Success*, FOI-R-4097-SE, September, 2015. Victor Gorshkov, "Recent Developments in Russia's Financial Sector", in Steven Rosefielde, Masaaki Kuboniwa, Satoshi Mizobata and Kumiko Haba, eds., *The Unwinding of the Globalist Dream: Asian Reverberations* (with Masaaki Kuboniwa, Kumiko Haba and Satoshi Mizobata, eds.), Singapore: World Scientific, 2017.

32. NATO, "Defense Expenditures Data for 2014 and Estimates for 2015", press release, June 22, 2015. www.nato.int/cps/en/natohq/news_120866. htm. Cf. Bryan Bender, "The Secret U.S. Army Study that Targets Moscow", *Politico*, April 14, 2016. http://www.politico.com/magazine/story/2016/04/moscow-pentagon-us-secret-study-213811. Lieutenant General H.R. McMaster told the Senate Armed Services committee last week that lighter armored vehicles like those the Army relied on in Iraq and Afghanistan are vulnerable to Russia's new weapons. And main battle tanks like Russia's T-90 — thought to be an anachronism in recent conflicts— are still decisive. Also "Russia possesses a variety of rocket, missile and cannon artillery systems that outrange and are more lethal than U.S. Army artillery systems and munitions."

33. Strategic patience is the notion that the West should tolerate foreign misbehavior because the West's intrinsic superiority will allow it to always prevail. The term is often attributed to Angela Merkel. Mark Salter, "Merkel Has a Strange View of How the Cold War Was Won", *Business Insider*, February 24, 2015. http://www.businessinsider.com/merkel-has-a-strange-view-of-how-the-cold-war-was-won-and-its-affecting-her-strategy-on-Russian aggression-2015-2. "Merkel reminded the audience that she was a little girl living in East Germany when the Soviets built the Berlin Wall in 1961 and the West had responded appropriately by patiently waiting 28 years for it to come down." Keir Giles, *Russia's 'New' Tools for Confronting the West: Continuity and Innovation in Moscow's Exercise of Power*. London: Chatham House, The Royal Institute of International Affairs, March 2016. Jan Techau, "The Politics of 2 Percent: NATO and the Security Vacuum in Europe", *Carnegie Europe*, September 2, 2015. http://carnegieeurope.eu/2015/08/31/politics-of-2-percent-nato-and-security-vacuumineurope/ifig?mkt_tok=3RkM MJWWfF9wsRogva3BZKXonjHpfsX56OsvXqGg38431UF wdcjKPmjr1YUDTcZ0aPyQAgobGp5I5FEIQ7XYTLB2t60MWA%3 D%3D.

"The members of the North Atlantic Treaty Organization (NATO) pledged in 2014 to increase their defense spending to 2 percent of their gross domestic products by 2024. It is unrealistic to assume that this goal will ever be reached by all 28 allies, and yet the 2 percent metric persists— and it has assumed a significance beyond its face value. It is about addressing Europe's growing security vacuum and defining who will be in charge of European security. The reduction of the U.S. security footprint in Europe and Europeans' dramatic loss of military capability since the 1990s have created a security vacuum in Europe. NATO's 2 percent metric is one instrument to address that. As a way to measure an increase in military capability, the 2 percent metric is barely useful. It does not measure spending in real terms or actual output. The target has had some success in stimulating debate on European security. It has become an important gauge of who is and who is not politically committed to NATO's core task: Europe's security.

"Europeans underestimate the political significance of 2 percent in the U.S. debate over security commitments to Europe. Americans overestimate the political significance of 2 percent among Europeans struggling with austerity and divergent threat perceptions, which make it difficult to increase their defense commitments."

34. Roger Zakheim, "Clinton and Trump Both Offer More of the Same For the Military", *AEI*, September 2, 2016. http://www.aei.org/publication/clinton-and-trump-both-offer-more-of-the-same-for-the-military/?utm_source=paramount&utm_medium=email&utm_content=AEITODAY&utm_campaign=090616. "Those challenges can be broken down into three areas: modernizing and growing our military capability to deter revisionist powers like China and Russia; rebuilding and restoring the readiness of our forces to sustain operations in a low-end terrorism fight as well as high-end warfare; and resourcing a strategy to truly defeat ISIS. In other words, we lack a military capable of deterring adversaries and assuring allies in three key regions of the world. Despite a public record chock full of testimony from military leaders pleading for relief and warning of dire consequences if unaddressed, the administration response to all three challenges has been anemic. It ranges from outright denial, in the case of the readiness crisis, to inadequate, in the case of military modernization."

35. Steven Rosefielde, "Russia and the West after Crimea's Annexation: The Correlation of Military Forces", paper presented at the ASEEES Conference, Washington DC, November 20, 2016.

36. Mark Almond, "Bulgaria & Moldova Switch from Hillary's Euro-Atlantic Column", Ron Paul Institute, November 14, 2016. http://www.

ronpaulinstitute.org/archives/featured-articles/2016/november/14/bul-garia-moldova-switch-from-hillarys-euro-atlantic-column/. "November 13th was as unlucky for stalwart backers of the foreign policy-line embodied by Hillary Clinton just as 8th November was for her domestic supporters. In both Bulgaria and Moldova, the voters rejected candidates for president who had been openly endorsed by Washington and Brussels."

37. "US and Britain Consider New Economic Sanctions on Syria, Russia", *CNBC*, October 16, 2016. http://www.cnbc.com/2016/10/16/us-and-britain-consider-new-economic-sanctions-on-syria-russia.html. "With military options all but eliminated, the United States and Britain on Sunday said they were considering new sanctions to pressure the Syrian and Russian governments to halt an offensive against rebel-held parts of Aleppo, Syria's largest city."

38. Steven Rosefielde, *Russia's Military Industrial Resurgence*: *Evidence and Potential*, Carlisle Barracks: US Army War College, 2016.

39. Doug Stanglin, "Russian Activist Suffers Symptoms of Poisoning for 2nd Time in 2 years", *USA TODAY*, February 3, 2017. http://www.usatoday.com/story/news/2017/02/03/russian-activist-felled-2015-suspected-poisoning-hospitalized-similar-symptoms/97437612/.

40. Cf. Andrew Kuchins, "Elevation and Calibration: A New Russia Policy for America", *Center on Global Interests*, December 2016. http://globalinterests.org/wp-content/uploads/2016/12/CGI_A-New-Russia-Policy-for-America_Andy-Kuchins.pdf.

41. For an amusing establishment spoof of Putin and Trump, see Robert Shrimsley, "Vladimir Putin: The Autocrat's Man of the Year: What Does a Leader Have to Do to Win Some Recognition?" *Financial Times*, December 16, 2016. https://www.ft.com/content/1ef9fb1c-c2b1-11e6-81c2-f57d90f6741a. "In the Kremlin an unhappy Vladimir Putin has summoned his close ally Dmitry Medvedev.

You wanted to see me.

I've been reading the western media.

I wish you would not do that Vladimir Vladimirovich, it's full of fake news. Also it makes you angry.

Angry! I'm astonished. Time, the Financial Times, Chapter 11 Monthly — they've all made Trump Person of the Year. How is this possible? Look at my record: I've invaded Ukraine; stolen Crimea; destabilised western Europe; recreated the Russian sphere of influence; flattened Syria; rigged the US elections, and got my guy in the White House. What does a man have to do to get some bloody recognition?"

42. Steven Rosefielde, *Russia's Military Industrial Resurgence: Evidence and Potential*, Carlisle Barracks: US Army War College, 2016.

43. Charles, Wolf, Jr and Henry Rowen, *The Impoverished Superpower: Perestroika and the Soviet Military Burden*, San Francisco, CA: Institute for Contemporary Studies, 1990.

44. Correlation of forces is a Soviet concept closely related to the Western notion of balance of power. It includes military, economic, political, sociological, ideological and personal factors like leadership. The establishment failed miserably on this score. Perhaps, Trump will do better. N.V. Ogarkov, *Vsegda v golovnosti k zashchite Otechestva*, Moskva, 1982, p. 31; N. V. Ogarkov, *Istoriya Uchit vditel'nosti*, Moskva, 1985, p. 41; Steven Metz and James Kievit, *Strategy and the Revolution in Military Affairs: From Theory to Policy*, Carlisle: US Army War College, June 27, 1995. http://www.strategicstudiesinstitute.army.mil/pubs/summary.cfm?q=236. Stephen Biddle, *Military Power: Explaining Victory and Defeat in Modern Battle*, Princeton, NJ: Princeton University Press, 2006; Donald Rumsfeld, "Transforming the Military", *Foreign Affairs*, Vol. 81, No. 3, May/June 2002, pp. 20–32; Mary FitzGerald, "Marshal Ogarkov and the New Revolution in Soviet Military Affairs", *Defense Analysis*, Vol. 3, No. 1, 1987, pp. 13–19 (Center for Naval Analyses, Alexandria, Virginia, CRM 87-2/January 1987). http://www.tandfonline.com/doi/pdf/10.1080/07430178708405274.

Chapter 11

China

The establishment perceives Xi Jinping's China as an emerging rival for globalist hegemonic power that must be tutored into accepting a subordinate role in the world order,[1] but for the most part the conflict is barely perceptible on the radar screen. The Sino-American relationship is nettlesome, but not openly confrontational, oscillating across a broad spectrum from partnership to Cold Peace (skirmishing without threatening war). Both sides occasionally growl, but have steered clear of the low intensity on-again, off-again Cold War (belligerence without open military conflict) that now characterizes the relationship between Washington and Moscow.

This could change soon regardless of whether the establishment or populists control the White House for the same reason that Russia and America are at loggerheads. On China's side, Beijing refuses to subordinate itself to American hegemony, or abandon its irredentist claims to Taiwan.[2] Xi Jinping believes in China's greatness,[3] contests Washington's globalist values, and Beijing is becoming more assertive, especially regarding Taiwan and the disputed waters of the South China Sea. China's leaders also are sometimes testy because they suspect that the White House is plotting color revolutions against them.[4]

Washington for its part continues America's soft power hegemonic global nation quest, and opposes Taiwan's reunification on Beijing's terms. Both sides are drifting beyond the smiles toward Cold War, especially in the South China Sea.

The establishment is aware of the danger. It acknowledges that China is now the industrial workshop of the world. Washington knows that Beijing is gobbling up natural resource assets across the globe,[5] is rapidly modernizing its military, and is on the cusp of becoming a formidable civilian and military high tech rival, but the establishment however is not prepared to do anything significant about Beijing's challenge because domestic social programs outweigh America's foreign ambitions. The establishment is still hopeful that globalism and "strategic patience" will allow it to realize America's dream of soft power global hegemony, but if temporizing fails, it is prepared to let the chips fall where they may rather than spend the funds needed to create credible military deterrence in China's neighborhood.[6] It is prepared to leave defense ultimately to the nations of the Asia Pacific themselves, accepting restricted American access to the South China Sea from Japan to Australia, and abandoning Taiwan.

Xi Jinping knows this, and he is betting on the West's adaptive failure. Xi is wise to do so as long as the establishment rules America's roost, but now he must consider whether Trump's presidency substantially alters the correlation of forces.

Taiwan's President Tsai Ing-wen initiated a phone conversation with Donald Trump on December 2, 2016 and it illustrates the potential for radical policy change. Trump's gesture was a signature anti-establishment attack on Foggy Bottom foreign policy.[7] It signaled the possibility that Henry Kissinger's "One China formula" underpinning Sino-American relations since 1973 might be scuttled in favor of some ill-defined populist alternative.[8] The gambit caught the world's attention without clarifying whether it served the American middle class or the larger national interest. Was the decision to rattle cages and perhaps dismantle the established order, or a well-conceived strategy to alter the terms of Sino-American endearment for the common man's good? Is Trump an unguided missile? The answers to these questions are yes and maybe.

Trump's repeated desire to renegotiate the terms of bilateral Sino-American trade for the benefit of American workers is populist. By contrast, the establishment's default policy of allowing China to become the region's hegemon (refusal to pay for adequate military deterrence) is anti-populist because it harms ordinary Americans.

Preserving and expanding commercial competition in the Asia Pacific also serves the interest of all Americans, and *ipso facto* the national interest. However, this phone conversation raises the spectre of Sino-American confrontation on a broad array of problematic geo-political issues that boil down to a single question: Is China's re-emergence as Asia's regional hegemon inevitable? The establishment is schizophrenic on the matter. When it is singing the praises of "globalization", American leaders express confidence that China is destined to become a democratic free enterprise nation, a normal non-hegemonic state that harmoniously participates in the new world order obedient to the rule of international law. When the establishment has second thoughts, it laments that regional Chinese hegemony is inevitable and argues that staying the course has the virtue of allowing the world to negotiate the best possible terms of submission.

Trump is unwilling to accept a negative "inevitable" or temporize. This telephone call indicates confidence that America can avert bad outcomes, or successfully renegotiate now instead of postponing to a future where Beijing is more powerful. Only time will tell whether he is right. The establishment is dismayed and accuses Trump of reckless endangerment. It could be correct. The early evidence indicates that Trump and his advisors have given the matter considerable thought. If one believes that China is destined to be a rising authoritarian force, Trump's bold approach may be worth the gamble. Otherwise, the merit of acting now, temporizing, or submitting depends on competing assessments of the correlation of forces in the years ahead.[9]

Taiwan

The Taiwanese dispute has a tangled history. Taiwan became a Japanese prefecture in 1895. It had been under Chinese control since 1683, but was lost after the First Sino-Japanese War (August 1, 1894–April 17, 1895) when the Qing dynasty ceded it to Tokyo in the treaty of Shimonoseki,[10] settling a territorial dispute that had begun in the late 17th century.[11] If Japan had restrained its imperial ambitions during the 1930s, Taiwan today would be a sleepy Japanese backwater prefecture, but it did not. Instead, Japan pursued a policy of imperial expansion leading to the renunciation of its claims to Taiwan and Penghu in the San Francisco Peace Treaty 1952 concluding World War II.[12] Mao's People's Republic of China (PRC) was excluded from the San Francisco Peace Conference and was not a signatory, but this still left open the question of whether Japan had renounced its claims in favor of the PRC or the Republic of China (ROC), headed by Chiang Kai-shek (leader of the Chinese Nationalist Party, Kuomintang).

Although Mao Zedong had defeated Chiang on the mainland in 1949, the ambiguity mattered because the Kuomintang, which asserted that it was the sole legitimate government of China, held *de facto* control over Taiwan under the protection of American post-war occupation forces. Mao was unable to achieve final victory over Chiang under these circumstances, and was compelled to watch the Kuomintang claim sovereignty over Taiwan as China's rightful government during and after American occupation. Matters were complicated further by the Kuomintang's insistence that China and Taiwan were one country, an assertion that became the foundation stone for subsequent efforts to achieve a final settlement,[13] but gradually became obsolete with the passage of time.

Young Taiwanese today no longer harbor any ambition to rule the mainland. They consider themselves an independent nation and do not feel bound by Qing dynasty precedent.[14] Although they acknowledge their Chinese ethnicity, they identify as Taiwanese, not mainland Chinese citizens, a position that has been championed by President Tsai's Democratic Progressive Party (DPP) for several years.

Xi Jinping and Donald Trump both understand this new reality, and the necessity of hard bargaining.[15] Trump has already announced his intention to discard the establishment's "92 consensus" on the "one China" principle,[16] and vastly expand America's navy.[17] On February 9, 2017 Trump reversed himself in a telephone call to Xi and agreed to honor the One-China principle, without abandoning the possibility of promoting Taiwan's independence later. Should he chose to do so, and sufficient new naval forces are deployed to the Asia Pacific, Xi will not be able to stop Taiwan's *de facto* independence without launching a very risky war. The better part of valor from Xi's perspective will be to cut a face-saving deal including postponing formal American recognition of Taiwan's sovereignty, and sundry other concessions.

Trump will enlarge America's navy and there will be intense trilateral bargaining, but the precise terms of agreement are difficult to foresee because there are mixed motives. While Tsai desires Taiwan's independence, she does not want to lose the China trade.[18] Trump wants Xi to compromise on China's subsidized exports, and Xi does not want to be entangled in global economic sanctions. Solutions exist, but they will be difficult to achieve.[19]

South China Sea

The South China Sea currently is another powder keg, where Trump is likely to alter the correlation of forces.[20] The disputes involve a small set of maritime players,[21] but are interlocked with a larger zone extending westward to Laos, Cambodia, Myanmar and India through the Association of Southeast Asian Nations (ASEAN), and north to the two Koreas, Japan and Russia (East China Sea, Yellow Sea and Sea of Japan).

The South China Sea imbroglio from a territorial perspective involves both island and maritime claims among six parties,[22] two of whom do not recognize each other's legitimacy (China, Taiwan). The antagonists are the Nation of Brunei, the PRC, the Republic of China (Taiwan), Malaysia, the Republic of the Philippines, and the Socialist Republic of Vietnam.[23] America does not claim territory in the region, but like Australia and Indonesia participates as an out-of-area stakeholder defending the right of free navigation in international waters, and Washington has collective defense obligations with Thailand and the Philippines.[24]

China's position is simple. It claims the entire South China Sea delineated by the nine-dash red line on Figure 11.1,[25] and rejects rival counterclaims as well as alternative boundaries that can be derived from principles set forth in the United Nations Convention on the Law of the Sea (UNCLOS). It insists that it is the sole owner of the nine-dash zone including underwater mineral rights and has exclusive subsurface and surface naval transit authority. Beijing explicitly denies any intention to resolve the matter by force and recommends bilateral negotiation, an approach that has frozen the conflict for decades.

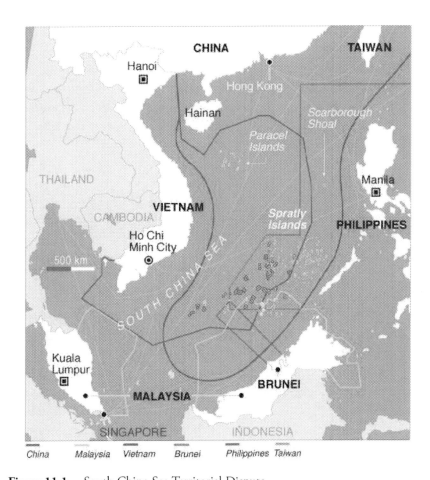

Figure 11.1. South China Sea Territorial Dispute

Source: Voice of America, http://blogs.voanews.com/state-department-news/2012/07/31/challenging-beijing-in-the-south-china-sea/

The territorial counterclaims of the other South China Sea nations are important, but are only part of the larger geostrategic problematic. The principal Southeast Asian claimants do not act independently. Brunei, Malaysia, the Philippines and Vietnam are core members of ASEAN (and the filial Asian Economic Community 2015) and act collectively in the South China Sea dispute together with Indonesia, Singapore, Thailand, Cambodia, Laos and Myanmar (see Figure 11.1).[26] The web is widened further by ASEAN's institutional links with the PRC, Japan, and South Korea (ASEAN + 3),[27] and India, Australia, New Zealand, the United States, and Russia (ASEAN + 8).[28] This daisy chain brings Japan, South Korea, India, Australia, Russia and the United States into the territorial conflict; an expansion complemented by Japan's, South Korea's, North Korea's, Taiwan's and Russia's concern for preserving free navigation in the South China Sea.

The weakening of America's deterrent capabilities in the South China Sea consequently is best construed both as an aspect of a regional property rights dispute and an incipient conflict over the global principle of free navigation. The conflicts, particularly the issue of free navigation, directly affect the security of the entire Asia Pacific region including South Asia, Southeast Asia, Northeast Asia and beyond.

China recently has been trying to change the facts on the ground to compel a resolution on its own terms.[29] It has endeavored to bolster its territorial claims by building artificial islands on reefs in the South China Sea and using them for logistical and military force projection, and its neighbors have responded in kind.[30] Beijing has built at least seven such bases, equipped with access channels, helipads, radar facilities, gun and missile emplacements, piers, military facilities and other objects of strategic importance since 2014.[31] Moreover, China has recently asserted its right to deny warships international access to the nine-dash line zone claiming that the South China Sea is exclusively its property, and not an international waterway.[32] To drive home the point, the People's Liberation Army Air Force scrambled fighter jets in response to a US Navy ship sailing near the disputed Fiery Cross Reef.[33]

China justifies its artificial island building as a necessary measure to deny unauthorized naval operations in its closed South China Sea, taking pains to distinguish commercial from military traffic.[34] The legal skirmishing settles nothing, but is significant suggesting as it does that the battle for the South China Sea is gaining momentum.[35]

Beijing's commitment to pressing the envelop is further confirmed by its response to a decision rendered in July 2016 by the United Nation's Arbitration Tribunal under Annex VII of the UNCLOS in favor of the Philippines' maritime claims against China. Xi Jinping brusquely rejected the UN's jurisdiction, and used China's influence over Cambodia to prevent ASEAN from promulgating a consensus statement urging China to heed the ruling.[36]

The weight of the evidence thus indicates that ASEAN, ASEAN + 3, and ASEAN + 8 are going to find it difficult to offset America's waning deterrent in the Asia Pacific.[37] ASEAN members are trying to rebalance the disequilibrium within the Asia Pacific aggravated by the establishment's plight, but the effort is an uphill struggle because the community is reluctant to oppose Beijing's ambitions openly.

While America's establishment is intent on dithering, China continues to fortify islands in the area it claims and to patrol it with increasingly strong naval forces. *De facto*, China is gradually taking possession of the entire nine-dash line area and infringing the principle of free navigation in international waters.

Trump can be expected to turn the tide. The American navy is going to come back on his watch, and is certain to contest any effort Xi might make to limit freedom of navigation in the South China Sea vigorously. Just as in the case of Taiwan, Xi will not be able to push the envelope very far without launching a risky and senseless war. He will not be pleased, but can afford to be patient hoping for an establishment comeback in 2020, or soon thereafter.

Trump's anti-establishment populist posture will clearly matter in Asia. The change should enhance the autonomy of Asia Pacific nations,[38] and be more broadly positive, even though there will be negative repercussions. Some repolarization will occur, and aspects of China's liberalization may be reversed. Regional and global commerce may be impaired as the price for Taiwan's independence and upholding the principle of free navigation in international waters.

Endnotes

1. America's motivation is often described more benignly as pursuing a grand strategy of maintaining a preponderance of power across Eurasia (in Europe, the Middle East and the Asia-Pacific). Dan Blumenthal, "Testimony before the US-China Economic and Security Review

Commission", *AEI*, March 31, 2016. http://www.aei.org/publication/testimony-before-the-us-china-economic-and-security-review-commission-objectives-and-future-direction-for-rebalance-security-policies/.

2. This is analogous to Russia's irredentist sovereign claims over Novorossiya (most of Ukraine) and the Baltic states.

3. Robert Lawrence Kuhn, "Xi Jinping's Chinese Dream", *New York Times*, June 4, 2013. http://www.nytimes.com/2013/06/05/opinion/global/xi-jinpings-chinese-dream.html?pagewanted=all&_r=0.

"Xi's Chinese Dream is described as achieving the 'Two 100s': the material goal of China becoming a 'moderately well-off society' by about 2020, the 100th anniversary of the Chinese Communist Party, and the modernization goal of China becoming a fully developed nation by about 2049, the 100th anniversary of the People's Republic.

The Chinese Dream has four parts: Strong China (economically, politically, diplomatically, scientifically, militarily); Civilized China (equity and fairness, rich culture, high morals); Harmonious China (amity among social classes); Beautiful China (healthy environment, low pollution)."

4. Nathan Gardels, "Why China Fears a 'Color Revolution' Incited by the West", *Huffington Post*, August 25, 2016. http://www.huffingtonpost.com/nathan-gardels/china-color-revolution-west_b_11597202.html.

"Earlier this month, several Chinese lawyers were convicted of 'subversion' for colluding with 'foreign forces' — read: the United States. The fear is that America's aim is to ultimately foment regime change in Beijing with a popular uprising, like the 'color revolution' in Ukraine and those of the Arab Spring. In what most regard as forced performances, some of the accused even confessed on TV that their legal challenges to the state were opening the doors to the deleterious influence of Western ideas. The Communist Party leadership also sees the promotion of Western-style practices, such as multi-party elections or an independent judiciary, as designed to undermine their rule through a creeping peaceful evolution that will inexorably result in turmoil.

To hammer home that message, China's chief prosecutor's office, the Supreme People's Procuratorate, released a video in tandem with the trials showing the chaos, violence and instability across the world where the West has sought to promote democracy, conveying to Chinese viewers (English subtitles provided by the South China Morning Post) that the stability they enjoy is due to China's one-party system. It is likely such a video was well received. According to a recent Pew Survey, 79 percent of Chinese polled believe their way of life must be protected against 'foreign influence.'

Regime change or fomenting a 'color revolution' in China is not an active U.S. policy, as some top ranks of power in Beijing clearly seem to think. But there is nonetheless an ideological expectation among America's political class that China's governing system is 'on the wrong side of history,' as former U.S. President Bill Clinton once put it, and so destined to fail. And, in the minds of China's leaders, that no doubt amounts to the same thing."

5. Elizabeth C. Economy and Michael Levi, *By All Means Necessary: How China's Resource Quest is Changing the World*, London: *A CFR Book. Oxford University Press*, 2014.

6. This statement includes North Korea, which is not covered in this chapter. Nonetheless, it is worth noting that the establishment's attitude toward China, applies toward its handling of the North Korean nuclear proliferation issue. See Nicholas Eberstadt, "Making the 'North Korea Problem' Smaller", *AEI*, December 30, 2016. http://www.aei.org/publication/making-the-north-korea-problem-smaller/?utm_source=paramount& utm_medium=email&utm_content=AEITODAY&utm_campaign= 010317.

"Two overarching facts frame the recent history of the gradually mounting threat from North Korea:

The first is that Pyongyang has been methodically working for decades to perfect a capability to strike the United States with nuclear weapons. The second is that US 'nonproliferation' policy toward North Korean has been a near-total failure for a full quarter century. There are many reasons for this unhappy state of affairs. One of these, alas, has been the strangely blinkered vision of all recent American administrations, Democrat and Republican alike, for coping with the North Korea problem. It may sound surprising, given the mockability of the Kim family regime in so many other respects: but the plain fact is that America has been outclassed by North Korea on the nuclear chessboard. For better or worse, Pyongyang has demonstrated an innovative, forward-looking and largely strategic approach to 'nuclear breakout' since the end of the Cold

War, while on the other hand Washington's attempted defense of the endangered status quo has been reactive, short-sighted and at times clueless."

7. Douglas Bulloch, "Was Trump-Tsai Phone Call Part of Strategy To Influence 'One China' Policy?" *Forbes*, December 19, 2016. http://www. forbes.com/sites/douglasbulloch/2016/12/19/how-the-trump-tsai-phone-call-changes-u-s-china-relations-and-one-china-policy/#42478112656b.

8. Henry Kissinger, *On China*, New York: Penguin, 2012.

9. Annual Report to Congress, *Military and Security Developments Involving the People's Republic of China 2016*, Office of the Secretary of Defense.
   http://www.defense.gov/Portals/1/Documents/pubs/2016%20 China%20Military%20Power%20Report.pdf.

10. The Treaty of Shimonoseki was a treaty signed between the Empire of Japan and the Qing Empire, ending the peace conference that took place from March 20 to April 17, 1895. This treaty followed and superseded the Sino-Japanese Friendship and Trade Treaty of 1871.

11. Japan had sought to expand its imperial control over Taiwan beginning in 1592, when Toyotomi Hideyoshi undertook a policy of overseas expansion and extending Japanese influence southward. Fu-san Huang, *A Brief History of Taiwan*, Taipei: ROC Government Information Office, 2005. The annexation of Taiwan was an aspect of Japan's "Southern Expansion Doctrine" (*Nanshin-ron*). Because Taiwan was ceded by treaty, the period that followed is referred to by some as the "colonial period", while others who focus on the fact that it was the culmination of a war refer to it as the "occupation period". The cession ceremony took place on board of a Japanese vessel because the Chinese delegate feared reprisal from the residents of Taiwan. James Wheeler Davidson, *The Island of Formosa, Past and Present: History, People, Resources, and Commercial Prospects: Tea, Camphor, Sugar, Gold, Coal, Sulphur, Economical Plants, and Other Productions*, London and New York: Macmillan & Co., 1903.

12. The Soviet Union never signed the treaty and Russia is still technically in an armistice with Japan. The Sino-Japanese war was concluded separately April 28, 1952 by the Treaty of Taipei, signed by Republic of China and Japan.

13. Under Washington's agreement to open full diplomatic relations with Beijing in 1979, the US downgraded its relations with Taiwan. The two, however, maintain close political, economic and military ties on an

"unofficial" basis. Taiwan now has official ties with only 21 countries, most of them small Central American and Caribbean countries as well as Pacific islands.

14. All people have the same moral right, but most independence seekers like the Uyghur and Tibetans are unable to defend themselves.

15. Tsai's DPP supports formal independence from China though the president has been cautious in her dealings with Beijing, vowing to maintain the status quo. That has not been enough for China, which has cut a formal communications channel and discouraged Chinese tourists from visiting the island. Beijing has also tried to limit Taiwan's presence on the global stage, blocking it from attending global health, security and aviation meetings. More recently, China has flexed its military muscles by sending jets and warships, including its only operational aircraft carrier, near the island but outside of Taiwan's airspace and territorial waters. William Kazer, "Taiwan's Leader Says Planned U.S. Stops on Trip Will Be Unofficial, Routine", *Wall Street Journal*, December 31, 2016.

http://www.wsj.com/articles/taiwans-leader-says-planned-u-s-stops-on-trip-will-be-unofficial-routine-1483181381.

16. The 1992 Consensus was the outcome of a November 1992 meeting in British Hong Kong between the mainland China-based Association for Relations across the Taiwan Strait (ARATS) and the Taiwan-based Straits Exchange Foundation (SEF). Three months before the meeting, the Taiwan side (on August 1, 1992) published the following statement in respect of its interpretation of the meaning of "One China":

"Both sides of the Taiwan Strait agree that there is only one China. However, the two sides of the Strait have different opinions as to the meaning of 'one China'. To Peking, 'one China' means the 'People's Republic of China (PRC),' with Taiwan to become a 'Special Administration Region' after unification. Taipei, on the other hand, considers 'one China' to mean the Republic of China (ROC), founded in 1911 and with *de jure* sovereignty over all of China. The ROC, however, currently has jurisdiction only over Taiwan, Penghu, Kinmen, and Matsu. Taiwan is part of China, and the Chinese mainland is part of China as well." China/Taiwan: Evolution of the "One China" Policy — Key Statements from Washington, Beijing, and Taipei by Shirley A. Kan of Congressional Research Service.

17. David B. Larter, "Donald Trump Wants to Start the Biggest Navy Build-up in Decades", *Navy Times*, November 15, 2016 https://www.navytimes.com/articles/donald-trumps-navy-bigger-fleet-more-sailors-350-ships.

"Donald Trump has pledged that he'll lead the biggest U.S. Navy build-up since the Reagan administration, but the details on what's likely to be an expensive and potentially decades-long effort remain to be seen.

Trump vowed to build the 350-ship fleet Republican defense hawks have long sought and reverse decades of fleet contraction which has yielded today's battle force of 272 ships. And while the politics of large increases to the defense budget are dicey in the best of times, Trump sees a naval build-up as part of his agenda to create jobs, according to an October internal Trump campaign memo obtained by Navy Times.

The plan, if enacted, would aim to restore the Navy to a size it hasn't been since 1998, and would mean tens of thousands of new sailor jobs. So far, it remains unclear what mix of ships the incoming administration wants to build more of, from $10 billion Ford-class carriers or $3 billion Virginia-class attack submarines to $500 million littoral combat ships, and how that fleet composition is connected to a strategic vision."

18. Josh Horwitz, "The charts that Show how Trump's 'One China' Statements could Jeopardize Taiwan's Economy", *Quartz*, December 15, 2016. https://qz.com/861507/charted-taiwans-economy-is-more-dependent-on-china-than-ever-before-making-trumps-threats-dangerous/. "Over the past fifteen years Taiwan's economy has become deeply linked with that of its neighbor. China is Taiwan's largest trade partner, absorbing nearly 30% of Taiwan's exports by value. Somewhat ironically, most of this growth took place during the administration of Chen Shui-bian — the island's first president from the Democratic Progressive Party (DPP), which broadly advocates independence from China."

19. The default is a perpetually "frozen conflict".

20. Annual Report to Congress, *Military and Security Developments Involving the People's Republic of China 2016*, Office of the Secretary of Defense, 2016. http://www.defense.gov/Portals/1/Documents/pubs/2016%20China%20Military%20Power%20Report.pdf.

21. The dispute has been affected by Japan's failure to indicate successor states it renounced all claims to the Spratly Islands and other conquered islands and territories in the Treaty of San Francisco and Treaty of Peace

with the Republic of China (Taiwan) signed on September 8, 1951. On August 15, China's Foreign Minister Zhou Enlai in response to unfolding developments declared that "the Chinese government of the day had taken over those islands" and that the PRC's rightful sovereignty "shall remain intact".

22. There are several disputes, each of which involved a different collection of countries:

(1) The nine-dash line area claimed by the Republic of China, later PRC which covers most of the South China Sea and overlaps exclusive economic zone claims of Brunei, Indonesia, Malaysia, the Philippines, Taiwan and Vietnam. Singapore has reiterated that it is not a claimant state in the South China Sea dispute and therefore allows Singapore to play a neutral role in being a constructive conduit for dialogue among the claimant states.

(2) Maritime boundary along the Vietnamese coast between Brunei, Cambodia, China, Malaysia, the Philippines, Taiwan, and Vietnam.

(3) Maritime boundary north of Borneo between Brunei, China, Malaysia, the Philippines, Taiwan and Vietnam.

(4) Islands in the South China Sea, including the Paracels Islands, the Pratas Islands, Scarborough Shoal and the Spratly Islands between Brunei, China, Malaysia, the Philippines, Taiwan and Vietnam.

(5) Maritime boundary in the waters north of the Natuna Islands between Cambodia, China, Indonesia, Malaysia, Taiwan and Vietnam.

(6) Maritime boundary off the coast of Palawan and Luzon between Brunei, China, Malaysia, the Philippines, Taiwan and Vietnam.

(7) Maritime boundary, land territory, and the islands of Sabah, including Ambalat, between Indonesia, Malaysia and the Philippines.

(8) Maritime boundary and islands in the Luzon Strait between China, the Philippines and Taiwan.

(9) Maritime boundary and islands in the Pedra Branca (and Middle Rocks) between Singapore and Malaysia. This was resolved amicably between the countries through the court of arbitration and joint committees.

23. The interests of different nations include acquiring fishing areas around the two archipelagos; the potential exploitation of crude oil and natural

gas under the waters of various parts of the South China Sea, and the strategic control of important shipping lanes.

24. Southeast Asia Treaty Organization (SEATO) was an international organization for collective defense in Southeast Asia created by the Southeast Asia Collective Defense Treaty, or Manila Pact, signed in September 1954 in Manila, Philippines. SEATO was dissolved on June 30, 1977 after many members lost interest and withdrew. The United States still considers the mutual defense aspects of its treaty active for Australia, France, New Zealand, the Philippines, Thailand and the United Kingdom.

25. The nine-dash line was originally an "eleven-dotted-line", first indicated by the then Kuomintang government of the Republic of China in 1947, for its claims to the South China Sea. After the Communist Party of China took over mainland China and formed the PRC in 1949, the line was adopted and revised to nine as endorsed by Zhou Enlai.

26. ASEAN was founded on August 8, 1967 by Indonesia, Malaysia, the Philippines, Singapore and Thailand. It later expanded to include Brunei, Cambodia, Laos, Myanmar (Burma) and Vietnam.

27. Beginning in 1997, ASEAN created "ASEAN Plus Three" adding affiliated organizations to expand the core's reach. The original three affiliates were the PRC, Japan and South Korea. This was followed by the even larger East Asia Summit (EAS), which included ASEAN Plus Three countries as well as India, Australia, New Zealand, the United States, and Russia.

28. ASEAN operates by consensus among the original 5 and core 10 members. The core pays attention to the + 8.

29. "Chinese Warships Enter South China Sea Near Taiwan in Show of Force", *Reuters*, December 16, 2016. https://www.theguardian.com/ world/south-china-sea. "China's air force conducted long-range drills this month above the East and South China Seas that rattled Japan and Taiwan. China said those exercises were also routine.

In December last year, the defence ministry confirmed China was building a second aircraft carrier but its launch date is unclear. The aircraft carrier programme is a state secret."

Hrvoje Hranjski, "Recent Developments Surrounding the South China Sea", *Washington Post*, December 25, 2016. https://www.

washingtonpost.com/world/asia_pacific/recent-developments-surround-ing-the-south-china-sea/2016/12/25/920825fe-cb10-11e6-85cd-e66532e35a44_story.html?utm_term=.899e6dd5725e.

"China has begun daily civilian flights to Sansha city on Woody Island, also known as Yongxing Dao, in the disputed Paracels that are also claimed by Vietnam and Taiwan."

30. However, it should be noted that other nations in the dispute have also built artificial islands. See Derek Watkins, "What China Has Been Building in the South China Sea", *New York Times*, October 27, 2015. http://www.nytimes.com/interactive/2015/07/30/world/asia/what-china-has-been-building-in-the-south-china-sea.html.

31. "China's Man-Made Islands in the South China Sea", *South Front*, https://southfront.org/chinas-artificial-islands-south-china-sea-review/. David Larter, "U.S. Wary of Chinese Moves Near Disputed South China Sea Reef", *Navy Times*, September 7, 2016. https://www.navytimes.com/articles/us-wary-of-chinese-moves-near-disputed-south-china-sea-reef. Jane Perlez, "New Chinese Vessels Seen Near Disputed Reef in South China Sea", *New York Times*, September 5, 2016. Building up the reefs in the South China Sea, China pursues multiple objectives, including ensuring the safety of expanding shipping lanes, extending maritime protection to its regional waters, and developing capabilities to conduct non-conventional security operations outside the region. The PLA Navy has sufficient self-defense capabilities, but deficiency in cross-region operations and force projection is evident, [though] Beijing is trying to change that.

32. Julian G. Ku, M. Taylor Fravel and Malcolm Cook, "Freedom of Navigation Operations in the South China Sea Aren't Enough: The U.S. Will Need to Do More if It's to Stop Chinese Overreach", *Foreign Policy*, May 16, 2016. http://foreignpolicy.com/2016/05/16/freedom-of-navigation-operations-in-the-south-china-sea-arent-enough-unclos-fonop-philip-pines-tribunal/.

33. *Ibid.*

34. *Ibid.*

35. "China Says Japan Trying to 'Confuse' South China Sea Situation", *Reuters*, September 19, 2016. "China on Monday accused Japan of try-ing to 'confuse' the situation in the South China Sea, after its neighbor

said it would step up activity in the contested waters, through joint training patrols with the United States." http://www.businessinsider.com/r-china-says-japan-trying-to-confuse-south-china-sea-situation-2016-9.

36. Alex Willemyns, "Cambodia Blocks ASEAN Statement on South China Sea", *Cambodia Daily*, July 25, 2016. https://www.cambodiadaily.com/news/cambodia-blocks-asean-statement-on-south-china-sea-115834/.

"Cambodia has blocked any reference to a U.N.-backed court's ruling against Beijing's claims to the South China Sea in an ASEAN statement and is pushing to remove a previously routine phrase expressing concern about the sea's 'militarization,' according to reports." China owns much of Cambodia's business assets.

37. The statement of course excludes China which is a member of ASEAN +3. India is only peripherally concerned with the Asia Pacific.

38. Olli Suorsa, "Hedging against Over-dependence on US Security: Thailand and [the] Philippines", *RSIS* Commentary 317/2016, December 29, 2016. "Thailand and the Philippines are seen distancing from the US and leaning toward China. This should not be understood as switching allegiances but as refusing to choose sides and diversifying their economic, diplomatic and military relations with multiple regional powers."

Chapter 12

Islam

America's first significant involvement with the Islamic world dates to the First Barbary War (1801–1805) long before the emergence of today's establishment.[1] During the ensuing 140 odd years, relations were minimal and might have remained so if World War II had not wrecked the West's colonial system in the Muslim Middle East, Africa, India, Malaysia and Indonesia, and communism had been contained within Soviet borders after 1945. Neither happened. Muslim nations across the globe acquired national independence in the early post-war era, and communism spread to Eastern and Central Europe, the Baltic States, Balkans, the Middle East (Arab socialism), Iran, North Korea, China, Indochina, Malaysia and Indonesia.

The combination of these forces created a political vacuum and prodded America into action. Suddenly, and with little preparation the United States was presented with an opportunity to penetrate previously closed societies and simultaneously contain the spread of communism. This entailed the use of soft and hard power.[2] America as the world's richest post-war nation provided foreign assistance to the Muslim world directly and via international organizations like the World Bank Group (created 1944) and the United Nations (established 1945). Hard power was exercised by US forces,[3] and through participation in Central Treaty Organization (CENTO),[4] North Atlantic Treaty Organization (NATO, Turkish dimension), and Southeast Asia Treaty Organization (SEATO).[5]

The American Central Intelligence Agency was also employed. It organized a *coup d'etat* (Operation Ajax) that overthrew Iran's Prime Minister Mohammed Mossadeq to strengthen the monarchical rule of Mohammad Reza Pahlavi.[6]

The fall of Saigon on April 30, 1975, marking the end of America's intervention in the Vietnamese civil war profoundly altered the establishment's post-war approach to global engagement. It generated what Ronald Reagan called the "Vietnam syndrome",[7] an aversion to the use of American military force as an instrument of diplomacy,[8] and an upgrading of "soft power", which morphed into an inclusive strategy of economic,[9] social (cultural),[10] and political "globalization" in the mid-1970s.[11] The transformation marked the establishment's switch from the traditional American Dream to its current globalist variant that fused the goal of American global hegemony with the formation of a culturally blended, affirmative action, restorative justice one world order.

This transformation is the key to understanding the gulf separating the establishment's and Donald Trump's perception of the global Islamic challenge. The American establishment gradually adopted the position that the 1.6 billion strong Islamic community was a colonialist victim, a blot that needed to be rectified through open immigration to America, affirmative action and restorative justice.[12]

The new mandate led to a spate of American-supported color revolutions and regime changes in the post-colonial Islamic sphere, but results did not match expectations.[13] The establishment wanted a world populated by "good Muslims"; that is, secularized cosmopolitans with Islamic pedigrees who would open their markets, democratize and add a dash of spice to the global blend. This was wishful thinking. The real Islamic universe that Trump perceives is heterogeneous and ridden with political intrigue. It contains some secularized cosmopolitans comfortable with the globalist outlook, but the majority of the world's Muslims self-identify with authoritarianism, socially conservative Islam, Islamic fundamentalism and militant radicalism. They are not swayed by the establishment's charm offensive, leaving America's relations with the Islamic world in disarray.

Establishment policies which mixed color revolutions, regime change and the "War on Terror",[14] failed in Syria,[15] Libya,[16] Egypt,[17] Yemen,[18] Saudi Arabia,[19] Turkey,[20] Iraq,[21] Iran[22] and Afghanistan,[23] preventing America from becoming the soft power hegemon of the Muslim world. Russia's re-entry into the Islamic fray concomitant with its rapid arms build-up (2010–2016),[24] and the imperatives of the "War on Terror" were contributing factors to the establishment's woes. Nonetheless, the evidence suggests that Samuel Huntington's assessment of Islam's tenacity was more accurate than the establishment's quixotic belief in the potency of globalist cultural change.[25] Neither color revolutions nor economic enticements have transformed Muslims into pliable secular cosmopolitans.

The establishment does not deny this, but still has faith that its strategy is the only viable path forward. If Hillary Clinton had won the 2016 presidential election, she would have stayed the globalist regime change course, and the establishment is hoping that experience will soon tutor Donald Trump that globalist engagement with the Islamic world is irreversible.

The establishment is right in its belief that there will be some continuity. Trump will find it difficult to extricate the United States from the "War on Terror",[26] and will likely use force across the Islamic world to deter terrorism and Russian expansion, but little else will be the same. Trump rejects the establishment's globalist mission of transforming Muslims into secularized cosmopolitans. He holds soft power in low regard,[27] and will deal with Muslim issues case by case,[28] instead adopting a one-size-fits all strategy.

The domestic implications of ditching globalism are obvious. Trump will curb Muslim immigration,[29] keeping it well below what it might have been,[30] and will terminate affirmative action benefits to America's Muslim community. He will not mince words, labeling Islamic terrorism "radical Islam", freeing himself from the restraint of having to deal leniently with terrorism to placate Muslim sensibilities.

Trump also will discard the globalist social justice agenda abroad, with potentially profound ramifications. The establishment is sympathetic with radical Islam whenever militancy is used as a cudgel against kings like Salman of Saudi Arabia, and authoritarians like Syria's Bashar al-Assad. It is willing to "sleep with its terrorist enemies" if this advances modernization, democratization, globalization and ultimately secularization of the Islamic world.

Trump looks at the matter just the other way round. He perceives Islamic terrorism, especially Islamic fundamentalist terrorism as America's principal foe, and is chary of re-engineering Islamic civilization. The reversal of priorities in all likelihood will prod him to pursue more cordial relations with Syria, Libya, Egypt, Yemen, Saudi Arabia, Turkey, Iraq, Iran, Afghanistan, Jordan, the Emirates, Kuwait, Pakistan and Afghanistan. He will confront Iran's *mullahs* over Shiite terrorism, its meddling in Levant, and may well undo the Obama–Kerry Iran nuclear deal (Joint Comprehensive Plan of Action (JCPOA)).[31] The Iranian Shiite tilt in Obama's Middle East policy that seemed to emerge in 2015 is likely to be reversed.[32]

The establishment views all Trump's impending Islamic policy changes with dismay not as it says because they will inflame conflicts, but because Trump intends to jettison the globalist version of the American Dream and hew a less doctrinaire populist course. The issue is not war or peace. It is populism versus globalism. The establishment is committed to the victory of its version of the American Dream; Trump to pragmatic pluralism and the suppression of Islamic terrorism. The establishment was not, but Trump is willing to employ sufficient hard power to achieve his objectives.

Israel

The looming tidal change in America's Islamic policy will prompt a thorough re-examination of Israel's future role as an enclave in an overwhelmingly Muslim Middle East. For the first quarter century after the founding of the Jewish state in 1947, Israel's survival depended on repeling attacks from Egypt, Syria and Jordan. Israel defeated the trio in the Six-Day War (June 5–10, 1967),[33] and Egypt–Syrian duo during the Yom Kippur War (October 6–23, 1973).[34] However, these victories did not pacify the region. They caused a significant refugee problem,[35] setting the stage for an entirely different trilateral struggle among Palestinian advocates for an independent Palestinian state carved out of Israel and conquered territories, Israel and various stakeholders including the United States and the United Nations. In the first "land for peace" phase of the post-Yom Kippur war struggle which culminated in the Camp David Accords,[36] Israel secured recognition and peace by returning Sinai to Egypt, but Syria, Jordan and the Palestinians could not come to terms. This led to a second phase dedicated to brokering a "Two State solution" that exchanged formal recognition of Israel's sovereignty with the creation of a Palestinian state.[37] All parties, including stakeholders, agreed to the Two State, a framework for settlement of the "Israeli–Palestinian Conflict", but agreement could not be reached because various spokesmen for the Palestinians refused to accept anything less than a full loaf. They demanded that Israel should cede the entire West Bank and Gaza to their authority. They demand control over parts of Jerusalem,[38] and the right of Palestinians who had fled the area in 1947 and their descendants to return to Israel with full restoration of property.[39]

The deadlock disappointed hopes on all sides, but also resulted in a fundamental change in the ground rules. The Palestinians were permitted to govern Gaza (financed mostly by the United States),[40] while Israeli settlers slowly moved into the West Bank and East Jerusalem dimming prospects for an amicable settlement.[41] The security problems changed too. At the time of the Camp David Accords, it seemed that Syria and other parts of the Middle East would successfully transition into peaceful democratic states, but the region instead descended into chaos. There now is no basis other than establishment's wishful thinking for supposing that a final settlement of the Israeli–Palestinian along the lines stipulated in the United Nations Security Council Resolution 2334 constitutes a viable framework for resolving the Israeli–Palestinian conflict as Barack Obama and John Kerry claim.[42] Demography and internecine Islamic warfare have changed the correlation of regional forces precluding settlement on the obsolete terms jointly favored by the establishment and Palestinian authorities.[43]

Donald Trump sees the reality better than his critics.[44] He has announced three steps that reveal his intentions. He has designated David Friedman, a staunch opponent of the Two State solution to be America's ambassador to Israel.[45] He has announced that the United States' embassy in Tel Aviv will be moved to Jerusalem,[46] and that he will defund the United Nations Relief and Works Agency for Palestine Refugees.[47] The first action speaks for itself. The second supports Israel's 1980 declaration asserting that "Jerusalem, complete and united, is the capital of Israel", and contravenes United Nations Security Council Resolution 2334 contrary to Obama and Kerry wishes.[48] The third initiative withdraws American economic assistance needed by Palestinian authorities to press their case for a Palestinian-friendly settlement. The gesture signals Trump's intention to discard the Camp David Accords and substitute a resolution process based on the new reality on the ground, allowing Israel to retain prize territories conquered in the 1973 Yom Kippur War, while leaving the Palestinians with a self-governing Gaza (but not sovereign Palestinian state), and sparsely inhabited parts of the West Bank.[49]

The establishment is in a tizzy, warning that Trump's three-fold plan threatens to subvert the peace process. The alert is justified. This is precisely what Trump intends to do and more.[50] Trump is going to discard a peace process that has not brought peace and has no prospect of ever succeeding in an attempt to test a more pragmatic alternative. It remains to be seen whether he will fare any better than his predecessors, but it is already clear that Trump will matter for Israel and the larger issue of how best to engage Islamic civilization going forward.[51]

Endnotes

1. David Smethurst, *Tripoli: The United States' First War on Terror*, New York: Presidio Press, 2006; Michael Oren, *Power, Faith, and Fantasy: The United States in the Middle East, 1776 to 2006*, New York: W.W. Norton & Co., 2007.

   Frank Lambert, *The Barbary Wars: American Independence in the Atlantic World*, New York: Hill and Wang, 2005.

2. Joseph Nye, *Bound to Lead: The Changing Nature of American Power*, New York: Basic Books, 1990. Joseph Nye, *Soft Power: The Means to Success in World Politics*, New York: Public Affairs, 2004.

3. The toppling of a pro-Western government in Iraq's 14 July Revolution in 1958, along with the internal instability, caused Lebanon's President Chamoun to call for American assistance. US President Eisenhower responded by authorizing Operation Blue Bat on July 15, 1958. This was the first application of the Eisenhower Doctrine under which the US announced that it would intervene to protect regimes it considered threatened by international communism. The goal of the operation was to bolster the pro-Western Lebanese government of President Camille Chamoun against internal opposition and threats from Syria and Egypt. The plan was to occupy and secure the Beirut International Airport, a few miles south of the city, then to secure the port of Beirut and approaches to the city. The operation involved approximately 14,000 men, including 8,509 United States Army personnel, a contingent from the 1st Airborne Battle Group, 187th Infantry from the 24th Infantry Division (based in West Germany) and 5,670 officers and men of the United States Marine Corps (the 2nd Provisional Marine Force, of Battalion Landing Teams 1/8 and 2/2).

4. CENTO originally known as the Baghdad Pact was formed in 1955 by Iran, Iraq, Pakistan, Turkey and the United Kingdom.

5. SEATO was an international organization for collective defense in Southeast Asia created by the Southeast Asia Collective Defense Treaty, or Manila Pact, signed in September 1954 in Manila, the Philippines. Primarily created to block further communist gains in Southeast Asia, SEATO is generally considered a failure because internal conflict and dispute hindered general use of the SEATO military; however, SEATO-funded cultural and educational programs left long-standing effects in Southeast Asia. SEATO was dissolved on June 30, 1977 after many members lost interest and withdrew. The United States still considers the mutual defense aspects of its treaty active for Australia, France, New Zealand, the Philippines, Thailand and the United Kingdom.

6. Hugh Wilford, *America's Great Game: The CIA's Secret Arabists and the Making of the Modern Middle East*, Paris: Basic Books, 2013.

7. Norman Podhoretz, "Making the World Safe for Communism", *Commentary*, Vol. 61, No. 4, April 1976. Ronald Reagan, "PEACE: Restoring the Margin of Safety", Speech to Veterans of Foreign Wars Convention, Chicago, Illinois, August 18, 1980. https://reaganlibrary. archives.gov/archives/reference/8.18.80.html.

   "For too long, we have lived with the 'Vietnam Syndrome'. Much of that syndrome has been created by the North Vietnamese aggressors who now threaten the peaceful people of Thailand. Over and over they told us for nearly 10 years that we were the aggressors bent on imperialistic conquests. They had a plan. It was to win in the field of propaganda here in America what they could not win on the field of battle in Vietnam. As the years dragged on, we were told that peace would come if we would simply stop interfering and go home. It is time we recognized that ours was, in truth, a noble cause. A small country newly free from colonial rule sought our help in establishing self-rule and the means of self-defense against a totalitarian neighbor bent on conquest. We dishonor the memory of 50,000 young Americans who died in that cause when we give way to feelings of guilt as if we were doing something shameful, and we have been shabby in our treatment of those who returned. They fought as well and as bravely as any Americans have ever fought in any war. They deserve our gratitude, our respect, and our continuing concern. There is a lesson for all of us in Vietnam. If we are forced to fight, we must have the means and the determination to prevail or we will not have what it takes to secure the peace. And while we are at it, let us tell those who fought in that war that we will never again ask young men to fight and possibly die in a war our government is afraid to let them win".

8. Clausewitz, Carl von, *Principles of War*, Translated by Hans Gatske, Mechanicsburg: The Military Service Publishing Company, 1942. Originally "Die wichtigsten Grundsätze des Kriegführens zur Ergänzung meines Unterrichts bei Sr. Königlichen Hoheit dem Kronprinzen" (written 1812).

9. Economic globalization is the increasing economic integration and interdependence of national, regional and local economies across the world through an intensification of cross-border movement of goods, services, technologies and capital. Paul James and Barry Gills, *Globalization and*

Economy, Vol. 1: Global Markets and Capitalism, London: Sage Publications, 2007.

10. Martin Albrow and Elizabeth King, eds., *Globalization, Knowledge and Society,* London: Sage, 1990. Paul James, *Globalism, Nationalism, Tribalism,* London: Sage Publications, 2006.

11. Political globalization centers are the desirability of reducing the importance of nation states. Supranational institutions such as the European Union, the WTO, the G8 or the International Criminal Court replace or extend national functions to facilitate international agreement. See Jan-Aart Scholte, Jan-Aart, *Globalization: A Critical Introduction,* London: Palgrave, 2005. Nicola Acocella, *Economic Policy in the Age of Globalization,* London: Cambridge University Press, 2005. Joseph Stiglitz, *Globalization and Its Discontents,* New York: W.W. Norton, 2002. Joseph Stiglitz, *Making Globalization Work,* New York: W.W.Norton, 2006.

12. Michael Lipka, "Muslims and Islam: Key Findings in the U.S. and around the World", *Pew Research Center,* July 22, 2016. http://www.pewresearch.org/fact-tank/2016/07/22/muslims-and-islam-key-findings-in-the-u-s-and-around-the-world/. The 1.6 billion figure (23 percent of the global population) is for 2010. The establishment has considerable sympathy for compensating Palestinians for their grievances.

13. The failure of the establishment's globalist stratagem was anticipated by Samuel Huntington. During 1993, Huntington provoked great debate among international relations theorists by arguing that after the fall of the Soviet Union, Islam would become the biggest obstacle to Western domination of the world. The West's next big war therefore, he said, would inevitably be with Islam. His prophecy controverted Francis Fukuyama's claim that history had ended. It also conflicted with the establishment's outlook, but the two views can be reconciled by supposing that the Islamic threat Huntington perceived could be countered by gradually taming transforming the faithful into secularized cosmopolitans. Samuel Huntington, *The Clash of Civilizations and the Remaking of World Order,* New York: Simon & Schuster, 1996. Samuel Huntington, "The West: Unique, Not Universal", *Foreign Affairs,* Vol. 75, No. 6, November/December 1996, pp. 28–46. Francis Fukuyama, *The End of History and the Last Man,* New York: Free Press, 1992.

14. The War on Terror is a metaphor for the international military campaign that started after the September 11 attacks on the United States. It was originally delimited to countries associated with Islamic terrorism organizations including al-Qaeda and like-minded organizations.

15. The Syrian Civil War grew out of the unrest of the 2011 Arab Spring and escalated to armed conflict after President Bashar al-Assad's government violently repressed protests calling for his removal. The Syrian government has since then refused efforts to negotiate with what it describes as armed terrorist groups. The war is being fought by several factions: the Syrian Government and its various supporters, a loose alliance of Sunni Arab rebel groups (including the Free Syrian Army), the majority-Kurdish Syrian Democratic Forces, Salafi jihadist groups (including al-Nusra Front) who often co-operate with the Sunni rebels, and the Islamic State of Iraq and the Levant (ISIL). The factions receive substantial support from foreign actors, leading many to label the conflict a proxy war waged by both regional and global powers.

    Hassan Hassan, "Why the United States Must Change Its Failed Policy in Syria", *CNN*, August 16, 2016. http://www.cnn.com/2016/08/16/opinions/syria-aleppo-united-states/. "Over the course of the Syrian conflict, the US has failed to match words with action, such as when President Barack Obama declared that Bashar Al Assad was no longer a legitimate ruler and when he reversed his decision to punish the regime for attacking civilians with chemical weapons. Policy inconsistencies, intermittent support for the rebels, confused messaging, and the absence of strong international leadership have contributed to this protracted conflict and allowed space for regional and international actors to rip the country apart."

16. On March 19, 2011, a multi-state coalition began a military intervention in Libya's civil war, ostensibly to implement United Nations Security Council Resolution 1973. The goal was "an immediate ceasefire in Libya, including an end to the current attacks against civilians, which it said might constitute crimes against humanity" ... "imposing a ban on all flights in the country's airspace — a no-fly zone — and tightened sanctions on the Qadhafi regime and its supporters." Military operations began, with American and British naval forces firing over 110 Tomahawk cruise missiles, the French Air Force, British Royal Air Force, and Royal

Canadian Air Force undertaking sorties across Libya and a naval blockade by Coalition forces. The intervention ended in October, but the country descended into chaos. See Dominic Tierney, "The Legacy of Obama's 'Worst Mistake'", *The Atlantic*, April 15, 2016. http://www. theatlantic.com/international/archive/2016/04/obamas-worst-mistake-libya/478461/.

"In 2014, Obama said: '[W]e [and] our European partners underestimated the need to come in full force if you're going to do this. Then it's the day after Qaddafi is gone, when everybody is feeling good and everybody is holding up posters saying, 'Thank you, America.' At that moment, there has to be a much more aggressive effort to rebuild societies that didn't have any civic traditions." In recent interviews with The Atlantic's Jeffrey Goldberg on the 'Obama Doctrine,' the president bluntly said the mission in Libya 'didn't work.' Behind closed doors, according to Goldberg, he calls the situation there a 'shit show.'" "What went wrong? Obama has placed the responsibility on the entrenched tribalism of Libyan society, as well as the failure of America's NATO allies to step up to the plate."

17. The Egyptian revolution of 2011, (Lotus color revolution) began on January 25, 2011 and took place across all of Egypt. It consisted of demonstrations, marches, occupations of plazas, riots, non-violent civil resistance, acts of civil disobedience and strikes. Millions of protesters from a range of socio-economic and religious backgrounds demanded the overthrow of Egyptian President Hosni Mubarak. The revolution included Islamic, liberal, anti-capitalist, nationalist and feminist elements. Violent clashes between security forces and protesters resulted in at least 846 people killed and over 6,000 injured. The protesters' primary demands were the end of the Mubarak regime and emergency law, freedom, justice, a responsive non-military government and a voice in managing Egypt's resources.

Mubarak dissolved his government and did not intend to seek re-election. On May 24, 2011, Mubarak was ordered to stand trial on charges of premeditated murder of peaceful protesters and, if convicted, could face the death penalty. He was found guilty of complicity in the murder of protesters and sentenced to life imprisonment, but the sentence was overturned on appeal and a retrial ordered. Mubarak was eventually cleared of all charges on November 29, 2014. After the revolution against Mubarak and a period of rule by the Supreme Council of the Armed Forces, the Muslim Brotherhood took power in Egypt through a series of popular elections, with Egyptians electing Islamist Mohamed Morsi to the presidency in June 2012. On July 3, 2013, Morsi was deposed by a *coup d'état* led by the minister of defense, General Abdel Fattah El-Sisi, who became Egypt's *de facto* strongman and was eventually elected president himself in a 2014 election.

18. The Yemeni Civil War is an ongoing conflict that began in 2015 between two factions claiming to constitute the Yemeni government, along with their supporters and allies. Houthi forces controlling the capital Sana'a and allied with forces loyal to the former president Ali Abdullah Saleh have clashed with forces loyal to the government of Abdrabbuh Mansur Hadi, based in Aden. Al-Qaeda in the Arabian Peninsula (AQAP) and the Islamic State of Iraq and the Levant have also carried out attacks, with AQAP controlling swaths of territory in the hinterlands, and along stretches of the coast. On 21 March, after taking over Sana'a and the Yemeni government, the Houthi-led Supreme Revolutionary Committee declared a general mobilization to overthrow Hadi and further their control by driving into southern provinces. The Houthi offensive, allied with military forces loyal to Saleh, began on the next day with fighting in Lahj governorate. By March 25, Lahij fell to the Houthis and they reached the outskirts of Aden, the seat of power for Hadi's government; Hadi fled the country the same day. Concurrently, a coalition led by Saudi Arabia launched military operations by using airstrikes to restore the former Yemeni government and the United States provided intelligence and logistical support for the campaign. According to the UN, from March 2015 to August 2016, over 10,000 people have been killed in Yemen, including 3,799 civilians.

19. In October 2013, Saudi intelligence chief Prince Bandar bin Sultan suggested a distancing of Saudi Arabia–United States relations as a result of differences between the two countries over the Syrian civil war and diplomatic overtures between Iran and the Obama administration.

20. On July 15 2016, a *coup d'état* was attempted in Turkey against state institutions, including, but not limited to the government and President Recep Tayyip Erdoğan. The attempt was carried out by a

faction within the Turkish Armed Forces that organized themselves as the Peace at Home Council. They attempted to seize control of several key places in Ankara, Istanbul and elsewhere, but failed to do so after forces loyal to the state defeated them. The Council cited an alleged erosion of secularism, the elimination of democratic rule, a disregard for human rights, and Turkey's loss of credibility in the international arena as reasons for the coup. The government accused the coup leaders of being linked to the Gülen movement, which is designated as a terrorist organization by the Republic of Turkey and led by Fethullah Gülen, a Turkish businessman and cleric who lives in Pennsylvania, United States. Erdoğan accuses Gülen of being behind the coup — a claim that Gülen denies — and accused the United States of harboring him. Events surrounding the coup attempt and the purges in its aftermath reflect a complex power struggle between Islamist and ultranationalist elites in Turkey.

21. Dominic Tierney, "The Legacy of Obama's 'Worst Mistake'", *The Atlantic*, April 15, 2016. http://www.theatlantic.com/international/archive/2016/04/obamas-worst-mistake-libya/478461/. "Two years later, in 2003, Washington again failed to prepare for the day after, or post-conflict stabilization. The Bush administration was eager to overthrow Saddam Hussein, and equally determined to avoid getting bogged down in a prolonged nation-building mission in Iraq. The result was a 'small-footprint' invasion plan aimed at leaving as quickly as possible. There was little or no preparation for the possible collapse of Iraqi institutions, widespread looting, or an organized insurgency. The first U.S. official in charge of Iraqi reconstruction, Jay Garner, summarized the thinking: '[S]tand up a government in Iraq and get out as fast as we can.' Symbolizing the lack of concern for rebuilding the country, Bush's pick for Garner's successor was L. Paul Bremer — a man Bush had never met, who wasn't an expert on Iraq or post-conflict reconstruction, and didn't speak Arabic. Bremer decided to purge members of Saddam's Baath Party from public-sector work and disband the Iraqi army, thereby creating a mass of unemployed, resentful, and armed men, furthering the spiral into instability.

Obama was elected on a 'no more Iraqs' platform, but he repeated the same mistake of winning the war and losing the peace."

In a major split in the ranks of Al Qaeda's organization, the Iraqi franchise, known as Al Qaeda in Iraq covertly invaded Syria and the Levant and began participating in the ongoing Syrian Civil War, gaining enough support and strength to re-invade Iraq's western provinces under the name of the Islamic State of Iraq and the Levant (ISIS/ISIL), taking over much of the country in a *blitzkrieg*-like action and combining the Iraq insurgency and Syrian Civil War into a single conflict. Due to their extreme brutality and a complete change in their overall ideology, Al Qaeda's core organization in Central Asia eventually denounced ISIS and directed their affiliates to cut off all ties with this organization. The Obama administration began to reengage in Iraq with a series of air-strikes aimed at ISIS beginning on August 10, 2014. On September 9, 2014 President Obama said that he had the authority he needed to take action to destroy the militant group known as the Islamic State of Iraq and the Levant, citing the 2001 Authorization for Use of Military Force Against Terrorists, and thus did not require additional approval from Congress. The following day on September 10, 2014 President Barack Obama made a televised speech about ISIL, which he stated, "Our objective is clear: We will degrade, and ultimately destroy, ISIL through a comprehensive and sustained counter-terrorism strategy." Obama has authorized the deployment of additional US Forces into Iraq, as well as authorizing direct military operations against ISIL within Syria. On the night of September 21/22 the United States, Saudi Arabia, Bahrain, the UAE, Jordan and Qatar started air attacks against ISIS in Syria.

22. America and the Islamic Republic of Iran have been at sword points since the Iranian Revolution in 1979. The Obama administration nudged the two sides towards reconciliation by initiating and signing a deal on nuclear weapons development that has been the source of considerable acrimony. Donald Trump has pledged to renegotiate what he considers a very bad the deal. For another assessment see Henry Kissinger and George P. Shultz, "The Iran Deal and Its Consequences Mixing Shrewd Diplomacy with Defiance of U.N. Resolutions, Iran Has Turned the Negotiation on Its Head", *Wall Street Journal*, April 7, 2015. http://www.wsj.com/articles/the-iran-deal-and-its-consequences-1428447582. "Yet negotiations that began 12 years ago as an interna-tional effort to prevent an Iranian capability to develop a nuclear arsenal

are ending with an agreement that concedes this very capability, albeit short of its full capacity in the first 10 years." "Until clarity on an American strategic political concept is reached, the projected nuclear agreement will reinforce, not resolve, the world's challenges in the region. Rather than enabling American disengagement from the Middle East, the nuclear framework is more likely to necessitate deepening involvement there — on complex new terms. History will not do our work for us; it helps only those who seek to help themselves."

23. Dominic Tierney, "The Legacy of Obama's 'Worst Mistake'", *The Atlantic*, April 15, 2016. http://www.theatlantic.com/international/archive/2016/04/obamas-worst-mistake-libya/478461/. In 2001, the United States toppled the Taliban in Afghanistan but gave little thought about how to stabilize the country. In a memo to Secretary of Defense Donald Rumsfeld early in that campaign, Under Secretary of Defense for Policy Douglas Feith argued that Washington "should not allow concerns about stability to paralyze U.S. efforts to oust the Taliban leadership. ... Nation-building is not our key strategic goal." "With the Taliban on the run, decision-makers in Washington behaved as if the mission was over. A year later, in 2002, there were just 10,000 US troops and 5,000 international soldiers trying to provide security to a population of about 20 million. With the new government in Afghanistan unable to provide basic services outside of the capital, the almost inevitable result was a Taliban recovery, which set the stage for today's stalemated conflict."

24. Steven Rosefielde, *The Kremlin Strikes Back: Russia and the West after Crimea's Annexation*, Cambridge: Cambridge University Press, 2017.

25. Samuel Huntington, *The Clash of Civilizations and the Remaking of World Order*, New York: Simon & Schuster, 1996.

26. The establishment is opposed to Islamic terrorism in part because Al Qaeda and other want to forestall American global hegemony.

27. Joe Crowe, "Trump Aims for 'Peace Through Strength,' Not 'Soft Power'", *Washington Post*, December 29, 2016. http://www.newsmax.com/Politics/trump-aims-peace-strength/2016/12/29/id/766078/.

28. Joe Crowe, "Trump Aims for 'Peace Through Strength,' Not 'Soft Power'", *Washington Post*, December 29, 2016. http://www.newsmax.com/Politics/trump-aims-peace-strength/2016/12/29/id/766078/. "Trump said that Obama refusing to use the term 'radical Islam' plays

into their hands, while the president has said that inflammatory language would turn more young people against the U.S., the Post reported."

29. Tal Kopan, "Donald Trump: Syrian Refugees a 'Trojan Horse'", *CNN*, November 16, 2016. http://www.newsmax.com/Politics/trump-aims-peace-strength/2016/12/29/id/766078/. http://www.cnn.com/2015/11/16/politics/donald-trump-syrian-refugees/. "Donald Trump says he's now more against allowing Syrian refugees into the U.S. than ever, warning it could be a way for terrorists to sneak into the country. We have no idea who these people are, we are the worst when it comes to paperwork," Trump said Monday on CNBC. "This could be one of the great Trojan horses." "The mogul also slammed German Chancellor Angela Merkel, one of the most powerful leaders in Europe, for allowing refugees into Germany. She has been under pressure to reverse an open-door policy. 'As far as Merkel's concerned, she ought to be ashamed of herself, what she's done,' Trump said, saying there are 'riots in the street' in Germany over refugees."

30. Carol Morello, "U.S. Surpasses Syrian Refugee Goal Set by Obama, Expects More Next Year", *Washington Post*, September 27, 2016. https://www.washingtonpost.com/world/national-security/us-surpasses-syrian-refugee-goal-set-by-obama-expects-more-next-year/2016/09/27/59cedeb8-84e7-11e6-ac72-a29979381495_story.html?utm_term=.38f88b512b46.

"The United States has admitted 12,500 refugees from war-ravaged Syria over the past year, surpassing President Obama's target, and expects to admit even more next year, a State Department official said Tuesday.

The Syrians are among 85,000 refugees from all over the world who have been resettled in the fiscal year that ends late this week, said Ann Richard, the assistant secretary of state for population, refugees and migration. That is up from 70,000 in the previous year. The White House aims to admit 110,000 refugees over the next 12 months.

Though goals are typically set for regions rather than specific countries, Obama last September asked the State Department to admit 10,000 Syrians in response to the humanitarian crisis consuming the country after five years of conflict. 'This administration has been clear it wants more Syrians,' Richard told reporters. 'My guidance is we want to bring even more than we brought this year, without having a target.' At the United Nations last week, Obama hosted a summit in which the leaders of 49 countries pledged more humanitarian aid, education opportunities and legal jobs for Syrian refugees in their midst."

31. The JCPOA is an international agreement on the nuclear program of Iran reached in Vienna on July 14, 2015 between Iran, the P5+1 (the five permanent members of the United Nations Security Council — China, France, Russia, the United Kingdom, the United States — plus Germany), and the European Union.

32. Andrew Tilghman, "Shiite Militias, Once a Foe, May Now Get U.S. Support", *Military Times*, May 20, 2015. http://www.militarytimes. com/story/military/pentagon/2015/05/20/shiite-militias-us-support-iraq-ramadi-islamic-state/27651319/. "Just a couple of months ago, the top U.S. commander in the Middle East said Iraq's Shiite militias have American blood on their hands and he hoped today's U.S. strategy to defeat the Islamic State extremists will not involve an alliance with those groups. 'The U.S. has effectively changed its position, coming to the realization that Shiite militias are a necessary evil in the fight against ISIS,' Mardini told Military Times in an email Wednesday."

For the opposite viewpoint see Harold Rhode, "The U.S. Role in the Sunni-Shi'ite Conflict With Allies Like These...", Gatestone Institute, May 2013. https://www.gatestoneinstitute.org/3708/the-us-role-in-the-sunni-shiite-conflict.

33. The Six-Day War was fought between June 5 and 10, 1967 by Israel and the neighboring states of Egypt (known at the time as the United Arab Republic), Jordan and Syria. Relations between Israel and its neighbors had never fully normalized following the 1948 Arab–Israeli War. In the period leading up to June 1967, tensions became danger-ously heightened. In reaction to the mobilization of Egyptian forces along the Israeli border in the Sinai Peninsula, Israel launched a series of pre-emptive airstrikes against Egyptian airfields. The Egyptians were caught by surprise, and nearly the entire Egyptian air force was destroyed with few Israeli losses, giving the Israelis air superiority. Simultaneously, the Israelis launched a ground offensive into the Gaza Strip and the Sinai, which again caught the Egyptians by surprise. After some initial resistance, Egyptian leader Gamal Abdel Nasser ordered the evacuation of the Sinai. Israeli forces rushed westward in pursuit of the Egyptians, inflicted heavy losses, and conquered the

Sinai. Nasser induced Syria and Jordan to begin attacks on Israel by using the initially confused situation to claim that Egypt had defeated the Israeli air strike. Israeli counterattacks resulted in the seizure of East Jerusalem as well as the West Bank from the Jordanians, while Israel's retaliation against Syria resulted in its occupation of the Golan Heights.

34. The Yom Kippur War, Ramadan War, was a war fought by a coalition of Arab states led by Egypt and Syria against Israel from October 6 to 25, 1973. The fighting mostly took place in the Sinai and the Golan Heights, territories that had been occupied by Israel since the Six-Day War of 1967. Egyptian President Anwar Sadat also wanted to reopen the Suez Canal. Neither specifically planned to destroy Israel, although the Israeli leaders could not be sure of that.

   The war began when the Arab coalition launched a joint surprise attack on Israeli positions in the Israeli-occupied territories on Yom Kippur, the holiest day in Judaism, which also occurred that year during the Muslim holy month of Ramadan. Egyptian and Syrian forces crossed ceasefire lines to enter the Sinai Peninsula and the Golan Heights respectively. Both the United States and the Soviet Union initiated massive resupply efforts to their respective allies during the war, and this led to a near-confrontation between the two nuclear superpowers.

35. The displacement of civilian populations resulting from the war would have long-term consequences, as 300,000 Palestinians fled the West Bank and about 100,000 Syrians left the Golan to become refugees. Across the Arab world, Jewish minority communities were expelled, with refugees going to Israel or Europe.

36. The Camp David Accords were signed by Egyptian President Anwar El Sadat and Israeli Prime Minister Menachem Begin on September 17 1978, following 12 days of secret negotiations at Camp David. The two framework agreements were signed at the White House, and were witnessed by the United States President Jimmy Carter. The second of these frameworks (A Framework for the Conclusion of a Peace Treaty between Egypt and Israel) led directly to the 1979 Egypt–Israel Peace Treaty. The first framework (A Framework for Peace in the Middle East), which dealt with the Palestinian territories, was written without participation of the Palestinians and was condemned by the United Nations.

37. The two-state solution refers to a solution of the Israeli–Palestinian conflict which calls for "two states for two groups of people." The two-state solution envisages an independent State of Palestine alongside the State of Israel, west of the Jordan River. The boundary between the two states is still subject to dispute and negotiation, with Palestinian and Arab leadership insisting on the "1967 borders", which is not accepted by Israel. The territory of the former Mandate Palestine which shall not form part of the Palestinian State, shall be part of Israeli territory. The framework of the solution is set out in UN resolutions on the "Peaceful settlement of the question of Palestine", going back to 1974. The resolution calls for "two States, Israel and Palestine ... side by side within secure and recognized borders" together with "a just resolution of the refugee question in conformity with UN resolution 194". There have been many diplomatic efforts to realize a two-state solution, starting from the 1991 Madrid Conference. There followed the 1993 Oslo Accords and the failed 2000 Camp David Summit followed by the Taba negotiations in early 2001. In 2002, the Arab League proposed the Arab Peace Initiative. The latest initiative, which also failed, was the 2013–2014 peace talks.

38. There is significant disagreement in the international community on the legal and diplomatic status of Jerusalem. Legal scholars disagree on how to resolve the dispute under international law. Many United Nations (UN) member states formally adhere to the United Nations proposal that Jerusalem should have an international status. The chief dispute revolves around the legal status of East Jerusalem, while broader agreement exists regarding future Israeli presence in West Jerusalem. *De jure*, the majority of UN member states and most international organizations do not recognize Israel's ownership of East Jerusalem which occurred after the 1967 Six-Day War.

   As a result, foreign embassies are generally located in Tel Aviv and its suburbs. Jerusalem is one of the key issues in the Israeli–Palestinian peace process. Both Israelis and the Palestinians want it as their capital.

   The European Union has stated that Jerusalem's status is that of *corpus separatum*.

39. The Palestinian right of return is the political position or principle that Palestinian refugees, both first-generation refugees (30,000 to 50,000

people as of 2012) and their descendants (5 million people as of 2012), have a right to return, and a right to the property they themselves or their forebears left behind or were forced to leave in what is now Israel and the Palestinian territories (both formerly part of the British Mandate of Palestine), as part of the 1948 Palestinian exodus, a result of the 1948 Palestine war, and due to the 1967 Six-Day War. Proponents of the right of return hold that it is a "sacred" right, as well as an inalienable and basic human right, whose applicability both generally and specifically to the Palestinians is protected under international law. This view holds that those who opt not to return or for whom return is not feasible, should receive compensation in lieu. Opponents of the right of return hold that there is no basis for it in international law, and that it is an unrealistic demand.

40. The Gaza Strip, or simply Gaza, is a small self-governing Palestinian territory on the eastern coast of the Mediterranean Sea that borders Egypt on the southwest for 11 km (6.8 mi) and Israel on the east and north along a 51 km (32 mi) border. Gaza, together with the West Bank, comprise the Palestinian territories claimed by the Palestinians as the State of Palestine. The territories of Gaza and the West Bank are separated from each other by Israeli territory. Both fall under the jurisdiction of the Palestinian Authority, but Gaza has since June 2007 been governed by Hamas, a Palestinian Islamic organization which came to power in free elections in 2006. It has been placed under an Israeli and US-led international economic and political boycott from that time onwards. Most of the Gaza Strip administration funding comes from outside as an aid, with large portion delivered by UN organizations directly to education and food supply. Most of the Gaza GDP of $700 million comes as foreign humanitarian and direct economic support. Of those funds, the major part is supported by the US and the European Union. The United Nations Relief and Works Agency for Palestine Refugees (UNRWA) was founded in 1949 and was meant to be temporary. UNRWA's directors hijacked the group to use it as a political hammer against the Jewish state. With time, UNRWA began to view international support as an entitlement. Today, its annual budget is $1.4 billion. Michael Rubin, "Dump UNRWA, Vote on 2008 Peace Agreement?", *AEI*, January 2, 2017. http://www.aei.org/publication/dump-unrwa-vote-on-2008-peace-

agreement/?utm_source=paramount&utm_medium=email&utm_content=AEITODAY&utm_campaign=010317.

41. In January 2015, the Israeli Interior Ministry gave figures of 389,250 Israeli citizens living in the West Bank and a further 375,000 Israeli citizens living in East Jerusalem. Ahuva Balofsky, "Jewish Population in Judea & Samaria Growing Significantly", *Breaking Israel News*, January 5, 2015. https://www.breakingisraelnews.com/26966/jewish-population-in-judea-and-samaria-growing-significantly/#Cfviilb2dxzut183.99.

42. United Nations Security Council Resolution 2334 was adopted on December 23, 2016. It concerns the Israeli settlements in "Palestinian territories occupied since 1967, including East Jerusalem." The resolution passed in a 14–0 vote by members of the UN Security Council (UNSC); the United States, which has veto power, abstained.

The resolution states that Israel's settlement activity constitutes a "flagrant violation" of international law and has "no legal validity". It demands that Israel should stop such activity and fulfill its obligations as an occupying power under the Fourth Geneva Convention. It was the first UNSC resolution to pass regarding Israel and the Palestine territories since 2009, and the first to address the issue of Israeli settlements with such specificity since Resolution 465 in 1980. While the resolution did not include any sanction or coercive measure and was adopted under non-binding Chapter VI of the United Nations Charter, Israeli newspaper Haaretz stated it "may have serious ramifications for Israel in general and specifically for the settlement enterprise" in the medium-to-long term.

43. Michael Rubin, "What Kerry Got Wrong in His Israel Speech", *AEI*, December 28, 2016. http://www.aei.org/publication/what-kerry-got-wrong-in-his-israel-speech/?utm_source=paramount&utm_medium=email&utm_content=AEITODAY&utm_campaign=122916. "Here is what Obama and Kerry get wrong:

Intransigence: Who is holding up peace? After long and careful negotiations between Israel and the Palestinian Authority brokered by the United States and the broader international community, Israeli leaders offered their Palestinian counterparts peace deals in 2000 and 2008. Both the late Palestinian Chairman Yasser Arafat and his successor Mahmoud Abbas rejected the offers and walked away, without offering a counter proposal. When Israeli Prime Minister Benjamin Netanyahu froze settlement construction upon Obama's request, Abbas again refused for nine months to even talk to the Israelis.

Diplomacy: The Palestinian Authority was created as a result of the Oslo Accords. By walking away from that agreement, both in terms rejecting terrorism and acting unilaterally, the Palestinian Authority have done away with the foundational document which legalizes their existence. By acquiescing to unilateral Palestinian actions and revising the basis of Palestinian–Israeli peace, Kerry has shown that U.S. diplomacy and commitments can never be trusted.

Law: The West Bank and Jerusalem are technically disputed territories, rather than occupied Palestinian land. That is why the Oslo Accords called for bilateral negotiations. Kerry is also confused about settlements. If it is illegal to build on disputed land, then all building, be it by Israelis or Palestinians, should be treated similarly. To suggest Jews cannot live in disputed land, as Kerry does, is akin to supporting religious apartheid. Kerry's notion of mutuality when it comes to "natural growth" is bizarre. Israel is a sovereign state. The Palestinians are not.

Demography: Underlying Kerry's argument is that peace is necessary to keep Israel Jewish and democratic. To support this argument, Kerry appears to be relying on a false understanding of Palestinian demography. The numbers he appear to rely on are false: The Palestinian Central Bureau of Statistics double-counts Arabs in Jerusalem, continues to count emigrants, and regularly adjusts its counts across censuses to confirm to the Palestinian Authority's arguments. Kerry also appears not to recognize that Israel does not occupy the Gaza Strip. And while Kerry is talking Gaza and its plight, remember how much better off it is than so many other places: Turkey, Bosnia, and Brazil, for example.

Context: Neither Obama nor Kerry are students of history. With last week's U.N. Security Council Resolution 2234, Obama and Kerry for the first time have denied Israel's rights to the Western Wall, Judaism's holiest site. Kerry appears unaware that Jordan — which occupied the Old City of Jerusalem but whose possession was not internationally recognized — had blown up synagogues and religiously cleansed the city. What Obama and Kerry do [has] legitimize[d] this.

Motivation for terrorism: Is terrorism caused by the Israel–Palestinian conflict? If so, why did the U.S. intelligence community identify Islamist ideology as motivating terrorism a year before the partition of Palestine and two years before Israel's independence?

U.S. credibility: Everyone can see what a final agreement looks like — both Presidents Clinton and George W. Bush helped negotiate it. Why can't we impose that and just offer guarantees? Here's the problem: It's hard to talk about the ability of any state in the region to trust American security guarantees or red lines given Obama and Kerry's reversal on the Syria chemical weapons red line.

It is deeply ironic that Kerry seeks to make peace between Israel and Arabs when ties have never been better between Israel, Egypt, Jordan, Morocco, Tunisia and the Gulf Cooperation Council despite the U.S. rather than because of it. What Obama and Kerry have achieved is manna for rejectionists and a huge setback for those who seek to build upon diplomatic precedent. Kerry's ban on settlements, if confirmed by the United Nations, will be the death blow to diplomacy and a guarantee that unilateral actions determine the future of the region. Kerry will have blood on his hands."

44. Omri Ceren, "Kerry on Israel: An Alternate Universe", *The Daily Beast*, December 29, 2016.

http://www.thedailybeast.com/articles/2016/12/29/kerry-on-israel-an-alternate-universe.html. The real Resolution 2334 describes all of East Jerusalem and the West Bank as occupied Palestinian territory. Nonetheless, Kerry said that a previous resolution built to avoid exactly that conclusion, Resolution 242, was still "enshrined in international law … and remains the basis for an agreement today. The real Resolution 2334 calls for a Palestinian state but not a Jewish state. Nonetheless Kerry said that a previous resolution, which calls for both, Resolution 181, was still 'fundamental… [and] incorporated into the foundational documents of both the Israelis and Palestinians.' A little while after Kerry finished speaking Wednesday, Mustafa Barghouti, a member of the Palestine Liberation Organization executive committee, reportedly rejected the idea of recognizing Israel as a Jewish state." Cf. Glenn Kessler, "Fact-checking John Kerry's Speech on the Israeli-Palestinian Conflict", *Washington Post*, January 3, 2017. https://www.washingtonpost.com/

news/fact-checker/wp/2017/01/03/fact-checking-john-kerrys-speech-on-the-israeli-palestinian-conflict/?utm_term=.7631a5052128.

45. Josh Lederman, "David Friedman, Donald Trump's Pick for Ambassador to Israel, Has All Sides on Edge", *Washington Times*, December 26, 2016. http://www.washingtontimes.com/news/2016/dec/26/trumps-pick-for-ambassador-to-israel-has-all-sides/. "If President-elect Donald Trump wanted to show he planned to obliterate President Barack Obama's approach to Israel, he may have found his man to deliver that message in David Friedman, his pick for U.S. ambassador. The bankruptcy lawyer and son of an Orthodox rabbi is everything Obama is not: a fervent supporter of Israeli settlements, opponent of Palestinian statehood and unrelenting defender of Israel's government. So far to the right is Friedman that even many Israel supporters worry he could push Israel's hawkish Prime Minister Benjamin Netanyahu to be more extreme, scuttling prospects for peace with Palestinians in the process."

46. Felicia Schwartz, "Trump: Moving U.S. Embassy in Israel to Jerusalem 'Very Big Priority'", *Wall Street Journal*, December 12, 2016. http://www.wsj.com/articles/trump-considers-moving-u-s-embassy-in-israel-to-jerusalem-a-very-bigpriority-adviser-says-1481579944. "President-elect Donald Trump considers moving the U.S. embassy in Israel to Jerusalem from Tel Aviv a 'very big priority,' senior adviser Kellyanne Conway said in a radio interview Monday, describing a step that would represent a major reversal of longstanding U.S. policy. Both Israel and the Palestinians have claims to the contested city, and the U.S. has held that Jerusalem's final status should be the subject of broader international negotiations aimed at resolving the long-simmering dispute."

47. Funding for the Palestinian authorities fell by half in 2016, suggesting that the Islamic community is deserting the Palestinian cause. See "Drop in Foreign Funding to Force Cuts in Palestinians' Budget", *Reuters*, January 3, 2017. "'We had expected to get $1.2 billion in [external] support and offers but we have only received $640 million so far,' Prime Minister Rami al-Hamdallah told the Al-Quds newspaper".

Saudi Arabia has in the past been a reliable supporter of the Palestinians, as have the United Arab Emirates and Turkey, but it has cut back its contributions sharply in recent months. http://www.voanews.com/a/drop-foreign-funding-force-cuts-palestinians-budget/3661598.

html. Sarah Lee, "Donald Trump Issues Veiled Twitter Warning to the United Nations", *The Blaze*, December 24, 2016. http://www.theblaze. com/news/2016/12/24/donald-trump-issues-veiled-twitter-warning-to-the-united-nations/. "On Friday, President-elect Donald Trump used his favorite source of communication to let the United Nations — and the world — know that he intends to make changes that will affect the U.N. after he's inaugurated in January 2017. The only thinly-veiled threat comes as a response to the unprecedented move made by the Obama administration this week in declining to vote on a resolution before the international body that mandated Israel cease settlement building in Palestinian-occupied areas. The U.S. has traditionally protected Israel when similar resolutions have been presented before the UN. This marks the first time the U.S. has allowed a resolution of this kind to be passed. The vote has led to international outcry from Israeli Prime Minister Benjamin Netanyahu, Trump, top Trump surrogate Newt Gingrich and South Carolina Senator Lindsey Graham, who suggested on Saturday defunding the U.N. The United States maintains its embassy in Tel Aviv, and a Consulate General in Jerusalem as part of the 'Consular Corps of the Corpus Separatum.' Under the Constitution of the United States the President has exclusive authority to recognize foreign sovereignty over territory. The Congress has adopted a number of concurrent resolutions which support recognition of a united Jerusalem as the capital of Israel and urging Jerusalem as the site of the US embassy. The resolutions expressed the 'sense' of the House or Senate but had no binding effect. The Jerusalem Embassy Act of 1995 stated that 'Jerusalem should be recognized as the capital of the State of Israel; and the United States Embassy in Israel should be established in Jerusalem no later than May 31, 1999.' The Justice Department Office of Legal Counsel concluded that the provisions of the bill invade exclusive presidential authorities in the field of foreign affairs and are unconstitutional. The fact that a US embassy is located in a particular city, like Tel Aviv, does not legally mean that the US recognizes that city as a capital. Experts in the field of foreign relations law have said that, faced with congressional force majeure, the State Department could simply construct another embassy in Jerusalem and continue to argue that the U.S. does not recognize Jerusalem as the capital. The U.S. Consulate relocated to the neighborhood of Talpiot to provide visa and other consular services to residents of Jerusalem and the Palestinian Territories."

48. Chris Enloe, "Ted Cruz: History will Record President Obama, John Kerry as 'relentless enemies' of Israel", *The Blaze*, December 31, 2016. http://www.theblaze.com/news/2016/12/31/ted-cruz-history-will-record-president-obama-john-kerry-as-relentless-enemies-of-israel/. "History will record and the world will fully understand Obama and Kerry as relentless enemies of Israel." "According to Cruz, Obama and Kerry intentionally designed their foreign policy to 'weaken and marginalize' Israel, while 'emboldening' Israel's enemies".

Cruz said "he believes that Kerry's Wednesday speech, where he called Israel's government the 'most right-wing extreme' in Israeli history, will 'enflame rising anti-Semitism' in Europe and across the world." "Kerry's speech drew a stunning moral equivalence between our great ally Israel and the Palestinian Authority, currently formed in a 'unity' government with the vicious terrorists of Hamas. Secretary Kerry declared the Hamas regime in Gaza 'radical,' in the same way he declared the duly-elected government of Israel 'extreme.' He declared vicious terrorism sponsored by Hamas equal to Israeli settlements in West Bank. And he equated Israel's celebration of its birth with the Palestinian description of this event as the 'disaster.' His speech attempted to lay out an historic and seismic shift towards the delegitimization of our ally, Israel, and the further empowerment of the Palestinian Authority." "Kerry's central conclusion, that 'Israel can either be Jewish or democratic, it cannot be both' is an inanity that passes as profound only in Ivory Tower faculty lounges. There are roughly 50 majority-Muslim countries in the world. There is one — only one — Jewish state. And yet, for Kerry and Obama, that is too much. The Israeli Knesset has 17 elected Arab members. It has Muslim members and Christian members. In contrast, one searches in vain for Muslim countries that have elected Jewish representatives."

49. Griff Witte, "Israeli Settlements Grew on Obama's Watch. They May be Poised for a Boom on Trump's", *Washington Post*, January 2, 2017. https://www.washingtonpost.com/world/middle_east/israeli-settlements-grew-on-obamas-watch-they-may-be-poised-for-a-boom-on-trumps/2017/01/02/24feeae6-cd23-11e6-85cd-e66532e35a44_story.

html?utm_term=.ccd30e713fbe. "Instead, Bennett (Israel's Education Minister) argues for unilateral Israeli annexation of 'Area C' — the 60 percent of West Bank land where Israeli settlements are concentrated. The vast majority of the West Bank's 2.5 million Palestinians live in Areas A and B, where Bennett says they should be able to have autonomy but not a state".

"We have to say, 'This is what we want, and this is what we are going to do,' he said. 'You can't go on saying how the world is wrong, this is ours, and then at the end you forget to kick the ball into the net.'"

50. Michael Rubin, "Eight Possible Trump Responses to the UN Israel Vote", *AEI*, December 24, 2016. http://www.aei.org/publication/eight-possible-trump-responses-to-the-un-israel-vote/?utm_source=paramount& utm_medium=email&utm_content=AEITODAY&utm_campaign= 122816. "President-elect Trump's team has said that he will retaliate against the United Nations, and perhaps the Palestinian Authority, in response to the Security Council vote. He should. The vote was meant to undermine peace, rather than build it. Here's what he can do:

(1) Cut all funding for The United Nations Relief and Works Agency for Palestine Refugees in the Near East, which was supposed to close shop 60 years ago, as well as all U.N. agencies that have unilaterally recognized Palestine.

(2) Move forward with plans to place the U.S. Embassy in Jerusalem and recognize Jerusalem, including the Old City, as Israel's capital.

(3) Close the Palestinian Authority's shadow embassy in Washington, D.C. After all, the Palestinian Authority has violated agreements dating back more than two decades.

(4) The U.S. could recognize that the Oslo Accords are now null and void and that Israel can take unilateral actions in the West Bank and Gaza given that the Palestinians have walked away from the agreement that established the Palestinian Authority in those territories.

(5) The U.S. could end all programs administered through its consulate in East Jerusalem.

(6) The U.S. Congress could take a no-nonsense approach toward the Palestinian Authority's support for terrorism by implementing the Palestine Liberation Organization Commitments Compliance Act

and cut off all funding to the Palestinian Authority until it ceases all support for terrorism, especially the payment of pensions to imprisoned terrorists.

(7) The new State Department could designate the Palestine Liberation Organization as a terrorist group.

(8) The US could suspend funding for the U.N. until it institutes internal reforms, such as a ban on business- or first-class travel for its employees."

51. Oren Liebermann, Amir Tal and Abeer Salman, "Israel Announces First New Settlement Construction since Trump's Inauguration", *CNN*, January 24, 2017. http://www.cnn.com/2017/01/24/middleeast/israel-approves-west-bank-construction/.

"Just days after US President Donald Trump was sworn into office, Israel approved the construction of approximately 2,500 new housing units in West Bank settlements Tuesday, according to a statement from Defense Minister Avigdor Liberman and Prime Minister Benjamin Netanyahu. 'We are building — and we will continue to build,' said Netanyahu in a tweet. The planned new homes mark one of the largest settlement expansions since 2013, according to the settlement watchdog Peace Now. It comes just days after Trump's inauguration and two days after he spoke with Netanyahu, a conversation which Trump described as 'warm' and during which he invited Netanyahu to the White House early next month. Most of the housing units are in the main settlement blocs, Liberman said, but approximately 100 units are in Beit El, a settlement outside of Ramallah, which received a $10,000 donation in 2003 from the Trump Foundation — Trump's charitable organization — according to the foundation's publicly available tax return."

Chapter 13

Europe

Russia, China and Islam all reject America's globalist hegemonic ambitions. The establishment engages them to achieve its global nation notion of the American Dream. The transatlantic relationship between the US and Europe is fundamentally different. The establishment — until Trump's election — partnered with Europe's elites for a common hegemonic purpose. Each side within the transatlantic relationship had its own sub-agenda, and everyone bickered about obligations and spoils, but America and Europe were allies, and will remain so under Trump, despite a great deal of grumbling. They will not become enemies, or even frenemies, even though they are going to strongly disagree about how best to manage Russia, China, Islam, Israel, North Atlantic Treaty Organization (NATO),[1] the Transatlantic Trade and Investment Partnership,[2] the Paris Climate Agreement,[3] populism[4] and possibilities for further EU desertions.[5]

The American establishment is no longer in command of the United States, creating a transatlantic schism that replicates the split between the hegemonic global nation and populism at home. Just as the Democrats and many Republicans will tenaciously resist all Trump's populist policies, European Union (EU) insiders and sympathizers in the United Kingdom (UK) will staunchly defend their programs.[6] They will uphold their existing policies toward Russia, China, Islam, Israel, NATO,[7] the Transatlantic Trade and Investment Partnership, the Paris

Climate Agreement, populism, and opposition to EU secession. They will fight a rearguard resistance.

Trump will have less leverage over Europe than at home, with his clout varying issue by issue. The EU cannot stay Trump's populist hand in China, Israel, NATO, the Transatlantic Trade and Investment Partnership, and the Paris Climate Agreement. EU leaders will object, but Trump can press forward on his own on these matters. Europe probably will be relieved if America curbs or eliminates economic sanctions against Russia,[8] and both sides should be able to cooperatively forge a mutually acceptable joint containment program for the Baltic States and Ukraine (de facto conceding Crimea's annexation). The main joust therefore will be over talking Trump into holding his punches over globalism because his vocal assaults against Europe's immigration and refugee policies on one hand, and his distaste for transnational institutions on the other abet European populism and encourage EU desertion.[9] European elites are vulnerable on these scores and will need to tread gingerly, even though there is no reason to believe that Trump intends to crusade against them.

Europe is suffering through a time of troubles mostly of its own making. It is mired in secular economic stagnation and its internal contradictions are increasingly polarizing national and transnational affairs.[10] Globalist EU leaders will be sorely tempted to blame Trump for their woes,[11] and foment anti-Americanism,[12] but the fault is primarily theirs.[13]

Endnotes

1. Tyler Durden, "How Trump Will Impact the European Union", *Zero Hedge*, November 15, 2016. http://www.zerohedge.com/news/2016-11-15/how-trump-will-impact-european-union.

   "US complaints about European NATO member states relying too heavily on US defence support aren't new, but never before have they featured so prominently. Trump has warned that: 'The countries we are defending must pay for the cost of this defense. And if not, the US must be prepared to let these countries defend themselves.' He even made US defense of the Baltics dependent on this, saying that if Russia attacked them, he would decide whether to come to their aid only after reviewing whether these countries 'have fulfilled their obligations to us.' One of his senior allies, Newt Gingrich, who's being touted as the new American Secretary of State, has called NATO enlargement to the Baltics an 'emotional' decision, adding 'I'm not sure I would risk a nuclear war over some place which is [in] the suburbs of St. Petersburg'.

If countries are already reluctant to pay for financial transfers or accept that the EU can tell them how many refugees they need to take, they naturally don't enjoy the idea of being forced to send their young people abroad if their own government is outvoted by foreign leaders. Sure, a lot of lip service has been paid over the years to this particular EU pipe dream, and we have 'Eurocorps' and all kinds of other forms of voluntary cooperation, but none of this goes beyond what NATO already does. NATO itself consistently stays clear from the supranationalism pushed for by the EU Commission. A number of EU member states, including the Netherlands, have already rejected the plans, so if Trump is serious (which is unclear, given that his running mate Mike Pence is more of a hawk towards Russia), EU member states will strengthen their own defence capacity first."

2. Tyler Durden, "How Trump Will Impact the European Union", *Zero Hedge*, November 15, 2016. http://www.zerohedge.com/news/2016-11-15/how-trump-will-impact-european-union. "EU–US trade deal TTIP, which currently is under negotiation, is already struggling with many hurdles in Europe. Now it faces a possible US veto, given Donald Trump's skepticism towards trade deals. Current EU Trade Commissioner Cecilia Malmstroem has said that 'we frankly don't know' if Trump wants to continue negotiations, while former EU Trade Commissioner Karel De Gucht thinks 'TTIP is now dead'. Juncker has urged Trump to provide some clarity on the issue, adding that with regards to 'the trade deal with the United States, I do not view that as something that would happen in the next two years'".

3. Tyler Durden, "How Trump Will Impact the European Union", *Zero Hedge*, November 15, 2016. http://www.zerohedge.com/news/2016-11-15/how-trump-will-impact-european-union.

"It's no big secret that Trump thinks 'global warming was created by and for the Chinese in order to make US manufacturing non-competitive.' There are some question marks about whether he has the legal power to withdraw from the Paris Agreement on climate change, but he'll probably try to do so, with a number of lawsuits from Democratic-run states likely. If that takes too long, he's able to withdraw unilaterally from the 1992 UN Framework Convention on Climate Change itself within one year. Either way, he may just ignore international climate commitments. This would increase the opposition in Europe against respecting those, as it would put Europe's industry at a disadvantage, despite the fact that EU Climate and Energy Commissioner Miguel Arias Cañete has reacted to Trump's victory by promising that 'the world can count on the EU to continue to lead on climate.' Trump has also pledged to cancel billions in payments to UN climate change programs, again likely to increase doubts in Europe about whether it should pay the rest of that bill. With Open Europe, we've made clear how any advantages from EU climate changes rules are closely dependent on what the rest of the world does, which would be another reason for EU climate policies to come under fire."

4. Tyler Durden, "How Trump Will Impact the European Union", *Zero Hedge*, November 15, 2016. http://www.zerohedge.com/news/2016-11-15/how-trump-will-impact-european-union.

"Trump's victory is a great boost for the so-called 'populist' forces who're haunting Europe's mainstream politicians and were among the first to congratulate Trump. On Sunday December 4, Austria may well elect a far right President, while Italy could vote no against an electoral reform which may lead to the resignation of Italian PM Renzi, possibly followed by new elections propelling Italy's populist 'Five-star movement' to power. In March 2017, the Netherlands is electing a new Parliament. While far the right populist PVV formation of Geert Wilders' was for a long time polling as the biggest party, he has been recently losing ground a bit. But the situation is unstable, as Wilders is currently being tried for inciting hatred and as a result of the Dutch government's refusal to respect a referendum vote against the EU–Ukraine Treaty. Then there's also Marine Le Pen in France, who doesn't stand a great chance to be elected but may well make it to the final round. Europe's mainstream politicians should maybe look in the mirror and acknowledge that, at least when it comes to the prevailing anger against the EU, they are far from innocent. Instead of considering euro exits and government defaults as a solution, eurozone politicians decided to organize transfers between countries that weren't popular in countries paying for it nor in countries that had to respect the condition to allow intervention in domestic spending. During the refugee crisis, mainstream politicians dragged their feet, resulting in chaos. It took until Spring 2016 for EU governments to take strong action, which has resulted in refugee drownings ending between Greece and Turkey, but until then the EU's focus was to harmonise asylum rules and try to impose refugee quotas that are pointless, given that we're speaking of countries sharing a passport free zone. The chaos and the EU's eagerness not to waste a good crisis served as a boost for populism in the countries of the Schengenzone, which almost collapsed. It also may have helped to make the British even more hostile to the EU than they already were, even though the UK isn't even in Schengen. In the same way, Trump's anti-establishment victory may now have much more of an effect outside of the US than mainstream politicians assume." John Henley, "Marine Le Pen Promises Liberation from the EU with France-first Policies", *Guardian*, February 5, 2017. https://www.theguardian.com/world/2017/feb/05/marine-le-pen-promises-liberation-from-the-eu-with-france-first-policies. Le Pen "pledges to take France out of the eurozone and — unless the EU agrees to revert to a loose coalition of nations with neither a single currency nor a border-free area — to hold a referendum on France's EU membership."

5. Tyler Durden, "How Trump Will Impact the European Union", *Zero Hedge*, November 15, 2016. http://www.zerohedge.com/news/2016-11-15/how-trump-will-impact-european-union

   "Trump and his allies have raised doubts about US protection of the Baltics raises the UK's value as a military power in Europe, and that's something Britain can use in Brexit negotiations. On the other hand, of course, the US election result may fuel the concern of EU leaders about the prospect of having their own difficult domestic elections, and therefore prompt a further stubbornness with regards to Brexit. Either way, a positive UK–EU relationship in a post-Brexit world will be needed, and Trump may upset that."

6. Clemens Wergin, "For Europe, Trump's Election Is a Terrifying Disaster", *New York Times*, November 10, 2016. http://www.nytimes.com/2016/

11/11/opinion/for-europe-trumps-election-is-a-terrifying-disaster. html?_r=0.

7. Soeren Kern, "Donald Trump and the Return of European Anti-Americanism", *Gatestone Institute*, November 21, 2016. https://www. gatestoneinstitute.org/9372/trump-europe-anti-americanism. "For the past seven decades, the United States has spent hundreds of millions of dollars annually to guarantee German security, although Germany steadfastly refuses to honor a NATO pledge to spend a minimum of 2% of GDP on defense spending. Germany spent only 1.16% of GDP on its own defense in 2015 and 1.15% in 2016. German officials are now offended that Trump is asking them to pay their fair share for their own defense."

8. EU globalists fault Trump for being too cozy with Putin, but most of them favor relaxing sanctions because they harm EU exporters.

9. Daniel Gros, "Can the EU Survive Populism?", *Project Syndicate*, January 4, 2017. https://www.project-syndicate.org/commentary/european-union-populist-target-by-daniel-gros-2017-01?utm_source=Project+Syndicate +Newsletter&utm_campaign=2697d604ef-roubini_america_first_ 8_1_2017&utm_medium=email&utm_term=0_73bad5b7d8-2697d 604ef-93559677. "Another year, another threat to the European Union's survival. The good news is that the greatest disruption of 2016, Britain's vote to exit the EU, appears manageable. The bad news is that both France and Italy face the prospect of a populist political takeover this year. Either outcome could well spell the end of the EU."

10. Clemens Wergin, "For Europe, Trump's Election Is a Terrifying Disaster", *New York Times*, November 10, 2016. http://www.nytimes.com/2016/11/ 11/opinion/for-europe-trumps-election-is-a-terrifying-disaster.html?_r=0.

"Chancellor Angela Merkel of Germany knows how grave the situation is. As she congratulated Mr. Trump on his victory on Wednesday, she also lectured him on the elements of liberal democracy that form the basis of the American-European relations. 'Germany and America are bound by their values: democracy, freedom, the respect for the law and the dignity of human beings, independent of their origin, skin color, religion, gender, sexual orientation or political position,' Ms. Merkel said. 'On the basis of these values I offer the future president of the United States, Donald Trump, close cooperation. Ms. Merkel realizes that right-wing populists are on the rise across Europe, threatening the existing liberal order. And at the very moment the West goes through a severe identity crisis, Mr. Trump, an expression of that crisis, has removed the possibility that the United States can act as a democratic example or a possible savior.'"

11. Richard A. L. Williams, "Donald Trump: European President Jean Claude Juncker Says US-EU relationship at Risk after Election", *Independent*, November 11, 2016. http://www.independent.co.uk/news/ world/europe/donald-trump-european-president-claude-juncker-says-us-eu-relationship-at-risk-after-election-a7412601.html#commentsDiv.

12. Soeren Kern, "Donald Trump and the Return of European Anti-Americanism", *Gatestone Institute*, November 21, 2016. https://www. gatestoneinstitute.org/9372/trump-europe-anti-americanism. "European anti-Americanism is certain to escalate in the years ahead, not because of Trump or his policies, but because 'globalists' appear desperate to save the failing European Union, an untransparent, unaccountable, anti-democratic, sovereignty-grabbing alternative to the nation state."

13. Steven Rosefielde, "Grexit and Brexit: Rational Choice, Compatibility, and Coercive Adaptation", *Acta Oeconomica*, 66(1), September 2016, pp. 77–91.

Part III

Tomorrow

Chapter 14

Turning Point

The establishment and Donald Trump offer America and the world a clear choice between yesterday and a brave new age. The alternatives are black and white across the boards both in domestic and foreign affairs. The traditional and global national versions of the American Dream are mutually exclusive. American populism and establishment globalism preclude one another. Establishment/populist agendas cannot be reconciled. Privilege for some is incompatible with equal opportunity for all.

The decoded policy preferences and priorities of both camps are plain enough despite obligatory double talk and visionary rhetoric.[1] The establishment is the voice of its "adorables" (minorities, activist women, bisexuals, the under-privileged, poor, immigration advocates, politically correct educators, environmental activists, Wall Street, globalist nation supporters and soft power imperialists). It is committed to building a globalist hegemonic order ruled from Washington unaccountable to the people at home and abroad, disclaimers to the contrary notwithstanding, with zero tolerance for domestic and foreign "deplorables". The establishment supports privileges for the adorables; repression and over-taxation for deplorables, and tailors its policies accordingly.

Trump is the voice of American populism. Ordinary people are his adorables; overzealous special interest groups his *bete noir*, and Trump's policies likewise are compatibly designed to protect and empower the common man, while restraining privilege seekers. He wants America to defend itself against terrorism and foreign aggression vigorously. He desires to lead, but is not a cold warrior. He is prepared to co-exist with Russia, China and the Islamic world if they refuse to follow.

The endgames and policy consequences of the establishment's and Trump's paradigms are polar opposites. The establishment wants open global migration; populists demand strict immigration quotas. The establishment wants tariff free international trade; populists want labor protection. The establishment insists on the primacy of international law (and transnationalism); populists demand complete democratic national sovereignty. The establishment touts inclusive economic growth that leaves no one behind, even if this means glacial progress; populist only require fair competition. The establishment wants doctrinal education imposed by federal authorities; populists desire pluralist local alternatives. The establishment supports federal environmental activism; populists insist on maximizing expected net benefit (risk weighted calculation of net national benefits and costs). The establishment wants a fully egalitarian society with selective affirmative action for the "deserving" disadvantaged and restorative justice; populists draw the line at equal opportunity. The establishment wants to rid the world of spheres of influence by subordinating Russia, China and Islamic civilization to its hegemonic "rule of law"; populists prefer peaceful co-existence to Cold War and hegemonic globalization. The establishment aggressively employs covert action and low intensity military force ("intervention") in pursuance of its hegemonic agenda; populists do not have a parallel mission. The establishment is unwilling to use the threat of large-scale military force against powerful adversaries like Russia and China; populists are prepared to contain more vigorously.

Both camps when push comes to shove prioritize domestic electoral preferences over foreign concerns. The establishment's electoral constituency favors subordinating national security considerations to social welfare programs, especially affirmative action and restorative justice. If the establishment is compelled to choose between defending the right of free navigation in the South China Sea or cutting social programs; national security will be shortchanged. America's populists place greater trust in defense against enemy nations and foreign terrorists. If compelled to choose between guns and butter when security is on the line, they prefer the Spartan option.

Neither camp is irrational, or foolish. Their behavior is consistent, given their disparate ambitions. Neither camp is better nor worse than the other from a positive (scientific) perspective, given their priorities. The comparative merit of the establishment's yesterday and the Trump's tomorrow turns solely on normative judgments about individual and national well-being.

It is unwise to expect normative unanimity about the merit of yesterday's and tomorrow's social agendas, even though some wrong-headedly contend that this can be accomplished with neo-Kantian hocus pocus.[2] There are no universally accepted norms (ethics) or reliable measures of well-being that take inclusive account of material, psychological, social, ethical and spiritual factors.[3] Nonetheless, there is room for constructive normative debate about the comparative merits of yesterday's establishment epoch and perhaps tomorrow's brave new age, as well as prospects for mutual evolutionary accommodation on principle and policy. A full-fledged assessment is premature, but the rudiments are considered in the next chapter.[4]

Endnotes

1. Nouriel Roubini, "'America First' and Global Conflict Next", *Project Syndicate*, January 2, 2017. https://www.project-syndicate.org/commentary/trump-isolationism-undermines-peace-worldwide-by-nouriel-roubini-2017-01?utm_source=Project+Syndicate+Newsletter&utm_campaign=2697d604ef-roubini_america_first_8_1_2017&utm_medium=email&utm_term=0_73bad5b7d8-2697d604ef-93559677. "Donald Trump's election as President of the United States does not just represent a mounting populist backlash against globalization. It may also portend the end of Pax Americana — the international order of free exchange and shared security that the US and its allies built after World War II. That US-led global order has enabled 70 years of prosperity. It rests on market-oriented regimes of trade liberalization,

increased capital mobility, and appropriate social-welfare policies; backed by American security guarantees in Europe, the Middle East, and Asia, through NATO and various other alliances."

2. John Rawls, *A Theory of Justice*, Cambridge MA: Harvard University Press, 1971; Michael Sandel, *Justice: What's the Right Thing to Do?* New York: Farrar, Straus and Giroux, 2009.

3. Measures of well-being should include per capita income and work-related stress, appreciativeness, physical and mental health, external economies and diseconomies, social comforts and socially induced anxieties, liberty, civil rights, moral imperatives and dilemmas, altruism, martyrdom, and faith based fears and benefits. Some people are libertines and others are puritans. Some people are egalitarians; others believe that individuals deserve whatever they competitively earn. Some people are intolerant in pursuit of their beliefs; others are open-minded.

4. A box score of winners and losers can be compiled. The realities of winning and losing can be deconstructed with Karl Popper's critical reason, and a set of mutual satisfactory compromises identified to assist leaders advance the cause of global well-being. Karl Popper, "The Rationality Principle", in David Miller, ed., *Popper Selections*, Princeton: Princeton University Press, 1985. Abram Bergson, "Social Choice and Welfare Economics under Representative Government", *Journal of Public Economics*, Vol. 6, No. 3, October, 1976, pp. 171–190.

Chapter 15

Prospects

The feasibility, broad contours and potential merits of Trump's populist tomorrow are clear. Although American populism contests some establishment values, it is not deplorable and offers a legitimate democratic path forward, but some details require further consideration. Who are the likely winners and losers? Will America and the world be more tranquil, prosperous, and tolerant? Can America's populist agenda be modified to accommodate positive aspects of the establishment vision? The answers to these questions are mildly reassuring. Trump's curtailment of social transfers is unlikely to be catastrophic. His policies should increase net global well-being judged from a neutral perspective. Populism should be able to accommodate the legitimate needs of the disadvantaged and reduce national and global polarization.

Winners and Losers

American populism is the winner and the establishment the loser of the 2016 US presidential election. Its agenda has triumphed and the establishment's vision has lost. This means that the traditional American Dream is in, and the establishment's global nation counter-vision is out. Pluralist democracy, open society, self-reliance, competition, equal opportunity and the founding principles of the American constitution are on the domestic front; peaceful co-existence, containment, support for democratic allies and the War on Terror are the winners in international affairs. Dogmatism has been rebuffed at home, and hegemonic globalism abroad has been set back.

There have also been socio-economic victors and victims. The productive middle class has won an important battle in an ongoing war. It will receive substantial tax relief and increased economic, civic and social liberty. Intrusive, burdensome, and morally offensive government regulation, manipulation, repression, social coercion and control will be lightened. The productive middle class will have greater democratic clout. It will enjoy greater freedom of thought, speech and action, increased job security and relief from the pressures of immigration, globalism, and the furies of political correctness.

Speculators and the rich more broadly are victors too. They are apt to fare even better under Trump than they did under Obama.[1] Trump is likely to continue federal deficit spending,[2] loose-money policy, and lax financial regulations that favor large speculative profits on Wall Street,[3] in the real estate and other tangible asset markets. He has promised to cut income tax rates substantially,[4] and may abolish inheritance taxes.[5] American populism historically has opposed extreme wealth, but Trump himself appears to be the rich man's bosom buddy.

The victims of American populism will be activists associated with establishment immigration, environmental, education and social welfare programs, politically correct non-governmental organizations (NGOs) and public institutions, bureaucrats, and beneficiaries of affirmative action, entitlements and restorative justice transfers. Potential victims include both existing and prospective members (new immigrants and those hoping to benefit from further relaxation of eligibility requirements). Establishment public service providers and their outsourcees will lose income, status and influence. Privileged minorities of sundry types, individuals wrongly classified as disabled, and those accustomed to long-term unemployment and social welfare benefits will be hardest hit. There are widespread fears that Medicaid,[6] Medicare and Social Security recipients will be savaged, but the handwringing is unwarranted. Current recipients of these transfers will be grandfathered, and cuts be glacial. Despite cuts, the poor, disabled, incompetent and unemployed will remain protected regardless of race, religion or creed.

Finally, it should be noted that Americans and foreigners alike are apt to enjoy the fruits of populist economic policies. Establishment over regulation has mired much of the world in secular economic stagnation. Deregulation offers hope for happier days.

Net Assessment

There is no denying that tomorrow will not be victim free. The establishment can be counted on to never let us forget this. Nonetheless, on balance Trump's populist age holds considerable promise. It should alleviate the plight of America's productive middle class and other establishment victims across the globe, without exacting an onerous toll on the entitled or jeopardizing world peace. It will restore an open society, equal opportunity and self-reliance, and provide hope for those losing faith in democracy.

Moreover, a society that encourages responsible social discourse is in a good position to mend fences. There is nothing reprehensible in the establishment's social justice advocacy. Populists through reasoned discourse, can be sensitized to grievances and persuaded to take more extensive remedial action than seems warranted to them at the moment. Likewise, establishment activists who no longer have the upper hand can be coached to rethink the wisdom of pressing the globalist cause against resilient adversaries like Russia, China and the Islamic world.

American populism is not a panacea; nothing is. Nonetheless, in an imperfect universe, it provides a sound framework for solving legitimate problems and advancing global well-being.

Endnotes

1. Thomas Piketty, *Capital in the Twenty-First Century*, Cambridge, MA: Belknap Press, 2014.
2. David Davenport, "One Thing to Expect From President Trump: More Debt and Deficits", *Forbes*, November 30, 2016. http://www.forbes.com/

sites/daviddavenport/2016/11/30/one-thing-to-expect-from-president-trump-more-debt-and-deficits/#7348565342b8. "But one thing seems fairly certain: a Donald Trump presidency is likely to have little regard for decreasing the national debt (the cumulative amount owed by the federal government) or the annual budget deficit. Some of us are shocked that the national debt has nearly doubled (from roughly $10 trillion to nearly $20 trillion) on President Obama's watch, but that number will likely grow under President Trump, perhaps even on a similar scale. Why do I say this? First, consider what Trump himself had to say on the subject during the campaign: 'I'm the king of debt; I understand debt probably better than anybody. I know how to deal with debt very well. I love debt.'"

3. Brent A. Sutton, "8 Questions about the Future of Banking Regulation under Trump", *Washington Post*, November 23, 2016. https://www.washingtonpost.com/news/monkey-cage/wp/2016/11/23/8-questions-about-the-future-of-banking-regulation-under-trump/?utm_term=.93d9f898395e. "The key changes Republicans want are in the Financial CHOICE Act, drafted by Rep. Jeb Hensarling (R-Tex.), chair of the House Financial Services Committee. In September, the committee passed that bill largely along party lines. The act would gut Dodd-Frank in a variety of ways, including reducing the number of banks covered by its supervision; ending the special resolution mechanism, gutting the powers of the Consumer Financial Protection Bureau; forcing all regulatory agencies to be funded specifically by congressional appropriations; requiring detailed cost-benefit analysis of proposed regulations; and repealing the Volcker Rule, which prohibits proprietary trading and places severe limits on investments in hedge funds and private equity funds."

4. John Ydstie, "Who Benefits from Donald Trump's Tax Plan?", *National Public Radio*, November 13, 2016. http://www.npr.org/2016/11/13/501739277/who-benefits-from-donald-trumps-tax-plan.

5. Ashlea Ebeling, "Will Trump Victory Yield Estate Tax Repeal?", *Forbes*, November 9, 2016. http://www.forbes.com/sites/ashleaebeling/2016/11/09/will-trump-victory-yield-estate-tax-repeal/#5af96d892bf2. "Trump's tax plan calls for repealing the estate tax, and imposing a capital gains tax on assets left to heirs above a $10 million threshold." "If estate tax repeal

happens, it would be a tremendous gimme to the rich (including eventually Trump and his family). In tax year 2015, just 4,918 estates paid $17 billion in estate taxes (less than 1% of federal revenue). More than a third was raised from the richest of the rich — the 266 estates valued at $50 million or more brought in $7.4 billion to the Treasury." "Maybe Congress will just bite the bullet and say 'Get rid of the estate tax because it affects so few,' says Charles 'Skip' Fox, an estate lawyer with McGuire Woods in Charlottesville, Va." "Under current law, for 2017, the estate and gift tax exemption is $5.49 million per individual, up from $5.45 million in 2016. That means an individual can leave $5.49 million to heirs and pay no federal estate or gift tax. Surviving spouses can carry over each other's unused exemptions, allowing a couple to shield just shy of $11 million ($10.98 million) from federal estate and gift taxes. For taxable estates, the rate is 40%. Assets get a "stepped up basis" that allows capital gains to escape taxation if passed to heirs. If you bought stock for $100,000 and it's worth $1 million when you die, the $900,000 appreciation escapes capital gains taxation — but could be subject to the estate tax depending on the value of your estate."

6. Benedic N. Ippolito, Jeffrey Clemens, "Medicaid Reform: The Elephant in the Room", *AEI*, January 4, 2017.

Conclusion

Donald Trump stunned the world on morrow of the November 7, 2016 American presidential election by upsetting the establishment juggernaut. The meaning and implications of Trump's victory were blurred at first by finger pointing and lamentations. However, it soon became clear to many observers that Trump had triumphed by tapping a wellspring of populist discontent invisible on establishment radar screens, but conspicuous in rural America where "Thank you Jesus" signs dotted the post-election landscape. Trump and "populism" swiftly became political synonyms. The identity is imperfect because neither Trump, nor American populism is unambiguous. Nonetheless, our inquiry into the meaning and significance of Trump's tomorrow has revealed that American populism is an authentic ground swell and a useful concept for understanding why Trump's victory may be a major historical turning point. Trump has planted a stake in the heart both of the establishment's globalist hegemonic ambitions, and self-serving domestic political correctness.

The establishment bemoans populism as the end of days. It is sounding the call for its troops to seize victory from the jaws of defeat. This is understandable from the standpoint of identity politics, but still seems unwise. Recent Polish experience with populism suggests that the globalist cause would be better served by acknowledging past excesses and making the global nation agenda more electorally palatable.[1] Unless globalists learn how to compromise, Trump's populist America could dominate the scene for a very long time.

Endnote

1. Sławomir Sierakowski, "The Five Lessons of Populist Rule", *Project Syndicate*, January 2, 2017. https://www.project-syndicate.org/commentary/lesson-of-populist-rule-in-poland-by-slawomir-sierakowski-2017-01?utm_source=Project+Syndicate+Newsletter&utm_campaign=2697d604ef-roubini_america_first_8_1_2017&utm_medium=email&utm_term=0_73bad5b7d8-2697d604ef-93559677. "Jarosław Kaczyński, Poland's *de facto* leader, has become, next to Donald Trump, an avatar of the populist threat to the Western democratic model. As we await Trump's inauguration as US president on January 20, it is worth pondering the first year of populist rule in Poland. The results have run contrary to expectations. The conventional view of what awaits the US (and possibly France and the Netherlands) in 2017 is an erratic ruler who enacts contradictory policies that primarily benefit the rich. The poor will lose, because populists have no hope of restoring manufacturing jobs, despite their promises. And massive inflows of migrants and refugees will continue, because populists have no plan to address the problem's root causes. In the end, populist governments, incapable of effective rule, will crumble and their leaders will either face impeachment or fail to win re-election.

Kaczyński faced similar expectations. Liberal Poles thought that he would work for the benefit of the rich, create chaos, and quickly trip himself up — which is exactly what happened in 2005–2007, when Kaczyński's Law and Justice Party (PiS) last governed Poland. But the liberals were wrong. PiS has transformed itself from an ideological nullity into a party that has managed to introduce shocking changes with record speed and efficiency. Other countries currently anticipating populist rule should take note of its key hallmarks."

Bibliography

Acocella, Nicola, *Economic Policy in the Age of Globalization*, London: Cambridge University Press, 2005.

Action, James, "Can Trump Enforce His Red Line on North Korea?", *The Atlantic*, January 5, 2017.

Ahlburg, Dennis, "Simon and the Population Growth Debate", *Population and Development Review*, Vol. 24, No. 2, 2002, pp. 317–327.

Albrow, Martin and King, Elizabeth (eds.), *Globalization, Knowledge and Society*, London: Sage, 1990.

Allison, Graham and Blackwill Robert, "America's Stake in the Soviet Future", *Foreign Affairs*, Vol. 70, No. 3, 1991, pp. 77–79.

Altman, Roger, "The Great Crash 2008", *Foreign Affairs*, January/February 2009.

Alvarez, Robert, "An Energy Department Tale: Captain Perry and the Great White Whale", *Bulletin of Atomic Scientists*, December 1, 2016.

Axelrod, Robert, *The Evolution of Cooperation*, New York: Basic Books, 1984.

Barfield, Claude, "The Case for a Rump TPP", *AEI*, November 30, 2016.

Barth, James R., Li Tong, Phumiwasana, Triphon and Yago, Glenn, *A Short History of the Subprime Mortgage Market Meltdown*, Santa Monica: Milken Institute, 2008.

Bergson, Abram, "Social Choice and Welfare Economics under Representative Government", *Journal of Public Economics*, Vol. 6, No. 3 (October), 1976, pp. 171–190.

Berezhkov, Vasilii Ivanovich, *Rukovoditeli Lenigradskovo upravleniia KGB: 1954–1991 (Leaders of the Leningrad KGB: 1954–1991)*, Saint Petersburg: Vybor, 2004.

Biddle, Stephen, *Military Power: Explaining Victory and Defeat in Modern Battle*, Princeton, NJ: Princeton University Press, 2006.

Blumenthal, Dan, "Testimony before the US–China Economic and Security Review Commission", *AEI*, March 31, 2016.

Blumenstyk, Goldie, "What's In and What's Out for Colleges as Trump Takes Office", *Chronicle of Higher Education*, December 21, 2016.

Borjas George, *We Wanted Workers: Unraveling the Immigration Narrative*, New York: W.W. Norton, 2016.

Boyd, Richard, "John Stuart Mill on Economic Liberty and Human Flourishing", *AEI*, November 23, 2016.

Bucci, Alberto, "Population Growth in a Model of Economic Growth with Human Capital Accumulation and Horizontal R&D", *Journal of Macroeconomics,* Vol. 30, 2008, pp. 1124–1147.

Bush, George and Scowcroft, Brent, *A World Transformed*, New York: Alfred A. Knopf, 1998.

Chomsisengphet, Souphala and Pennington-Cross, Anthony, "The Evolution of the Subprime Mortgage Market", *Federal Reserve Bank of St. Louis Review*, Vol. 88, No. 1 (January/February), 2006, pp. 31–56.

Clark, John, "Toward a Concept of Workable Competition", *The American Economic Review*, Vol. 30, No. 2, Part 1 (June), 1940, pp. 241–256.

Clausewitz, Carl von, *Principles of War*, Translated by Hans Gatske, Harrisburg: The Military Service Publishing Company, 1942.

Coase, Ronald, "The Problem of Social Cost", *Journal of Law and Economics,* Vol. 3, 1960, pp. 1–44.

Coulter, Ann, *In Trump We Trust: E Pluribus Awesome!,* New York City: Sentinel, 2016.

Coulter, Coulter Ann, *Adio. America: The Left's Plan to Turn Our Country into a Third World Hellhole*, Washington, DC: Regnery Publishing, 2015.

Cowell, Edward, *Stories of the Buddha's Former Births*, Cambridge: Cambridge University Press, Vol. 3, No. 322, 1897, pp. 49–52.

Dallago, Bruno and Rosefielde, Steven, *Transformation and Crisis in Central and Eastern Europe: Challenges and Prospects*, London: Routledge, 2016.

Dallago, Bruno and McGowan, John, J. (eds.), *Crises in Europe in the Transatlantic Context: Economic and Political Appraisals*, London: Routledge, 2016, pp. 119–136.

Daniels, Robert, *The Conscience of the Revolution: Communist Opposition in Soviet Russia*, Cambridge, Mass: Harvard University Press, 1960.

Davidson, James, *The Island of Formosa, Past and Present: History, People, Resources, and Commercial Prospects: Tea, Camphor, Sugar, Gold, Coal, Sulphur, Economical Plants, and Other Productions*, London and New York: Macmillan & Co., 1903.

Delmon, Jeffrey, *Public Private Partnership Programs: Creating a Framework for Private Sector Investment in Infrastructure*, Amsterdam: Kluwer, 2014.

Dollar, David and Kraay, Aart, "Spreading the Wealth", *Foreign Affairs*, Vol. 81, No. 1 (January/February), 2002, pp. 120–133.

Eberstadt, Nicholas, "Making the 'North Korea Problem' Smaller", *AEI*, December 30, 2016.

Economy, Elizabeth and Levi, Michael, *By All Means Necessary: How China's Resource Quest is Changing the World*, London: A CFR Book, Oxford University Press, 2014.

Faragher, John (ed.), *Rereading Frederick Jackson Turner: The Significance of the Frontier in American History*, New York: H. Holt and Company, 1984.

Fitzgerald, F. Scott, *The Great Gatsby*, New York: Charles Scribner's Sons, 1925.

FitzGerald, Mary, "Marshal Ogarkov and the New Revolution in Soviet Military Affairs", *Defense Analysis*, Vol. 3, No. 1, 1987, pp. 13–19.

Frank, Lambert, *The Barbary Wars: American Independence in the Atlantic World*, New York: Hill and Wang, 2005.

Galbraith, John Kenneth, *The New Industrial State*, Princeton, NJ: Princeton University Press, 1967.

Gates, Robert, *Duty: Memoirs of a Secretary at War*, New York, NY: Alfred A. Knopf, 2014.

Geib, Robin, "Russia's Annexation of Crimea: The Mills of International Law Grind Slowly but They Do Grind", *International Law Studies*, Vol. 91, 2015, pp. 226–249.

Goldberg, Jonah, "History's Lessons on Trump's Wealthy Cabinet", *AEI*, December 16, 2016.

Gorbachev, Mikhail, *Zhizn'i Reformy (Life and Reforms)*, Moscow: Novosti, 1995.

Gorki, Maxim, *The Lower Depths*, Wellesley, MA: Branden Publishing Company, 1906.

Gorshkov, Victor, "Recent Developments in Russia's Financial Sector", in Steven Rosefielde, Masaaki Kuboniwa, Satoshi Mizobata and Kumiko Haba (eds.), *The Unwinding of the Globalist Dream: Asian Reverberations*, Singapore: World Scientific, 2017.

Grundmann, Reiner, "Climate Change and Knowledge Politics", *Environmental Politics*, Vol. 16, No. 3, 2007, pp. 414–432.

Gwartney, James, "Supply-Side Economics", in David R. Henderson (ed.), *Concise Encyclopedia of Economics* (2nd edn.), Indianapolis: Library of Economics and Liberty, 2008.

Haas, Richard, *A World in Disarray: American Foreign Policy and the Crisis of the Old Order*, New York: Penguin Press, 2017.

Haberler, Gottfried von, *Prosperity and Depression: A Theoretical Analysis of Cyclical Movements* [1937], New Brunswick, NJ: Transaction Publishers, 2011.

Haberler, Gottfried von, *The Theory of International Trade*, Geneva: League of Nations, 1936.

Hassett, Kevin, "Recovery through Tax Reform", *AEI*, December 9, 2016.

Holzman, Franklyn, *Foreign Trade under Central Planning*, Cambridge: Harvard University Press, 1974.

Huntington, Samuel, *The Clash of Civilizations and the Remaking of World Order*, New York: Simon & Schuster, 1996.

Huntington, Samuel, "The West: Unique, Not Universal", *Foreign Affairs*, Vol. 75, No. 6 (Nov/Dec), 1996, pp. 28–46.

Howe, James, "Future Russian Strategic Nuclear and Non-Nuclear Forces: 2022", paper presented to the American Foreign Policy Council Conference on "The Russian Military in the Contemporary Perspective" held May 9–10 in Washington DC, 2016.

Ippolito, Benedic and Clemens, Jeffrey, "Medicaid Reform: The Elephant in the Room", *AEI*, January 4, 2017.

Itzkowitz Shifrinson, Joshua, "Deal or No Deal? The End of the Cold War and the U.S. Offer to Limit NATO Expansion", *International Security*, Vol. 40, No. 4 (Spring), 2016, pp. 7–44.

James, Paul, *Globalism, Nationalism, Tribalism*, London: Sage Publications, 2006.

James, Paul and Gills, Barry, *Globalization and Economy, Vol. 1: Global Markets and Capitalism*, London: Sage Publications, 2007.

Karpukhin, Sergei, "The Russian Media and the Fall of Aleppo: State-run Outlets are Essential to Making the Case for Putin's Intervention in Syria", *Atlantic*, December 23, 2016.

Kelley, A., McGarry, K., Fahle, S., Marshall, S., Du, Q. and Skinner, S., "Out-of-Pocket Spending in the Last Five Years of Life", *Journal of General Internal Medicine*, Vol. 28, No. 2, 2012, pp. 304–309.

Keynes, John Maynard, *The General Theory of Employment, Interest and Money*, London: Macmillan Cambridge University Press, for Royal Economic Society, 1936.

Kindleberger, Charles, *The World in Depression: 1929–1939*, Berkeley, CA: University of California Press, 1973.

Kissinger, Henry, *On China*, New York: Penguin, 2012.

Kogan, Eugene, *Russian Military Capabilities*, Tiblisi Georgia: Georgian Foundation for Strategic and International Studies, 2016.

Kremer, Michael, "Population Growth and Technological Change: One Million B.C. to 1990", *The Quarterly Journal of Economics*, Vol. 108, No. 3, 1993, pp. 681–716.

Ku, Julian, Fravel, M. Taylor and Cook, Malcolm, "Freedom of Navigation Operations in the South China Sea Aren't Enough: The U.S. Will Need to Do More if It's to Stop Chinese Overreach", *Foreign Policy*, May 16, 2016.

Liu, Yiyi, *Public Private Partnerships and Joint Ventures: Smart Asian Governance*, in Steven Rosefielde, Masaaki Kuboniwa, Satoshi Mizobata and Kumiko Haba (eds.), *Western Economic Stagnation, Social Strife and Decline: Asian Reverberations*, Singapore: World Scientific, 2017.

Mahbubani, Kishore and Quah, Danny, "The Geopolitics of Populism", *Project Syndicate*, December 9, 2016.

Mathur, Aparna, "Making Manufacturing Great Again Will Require a Two-Pronged Approach", *AEI*, December 21, 2016.

Mearsheimer, John, "Why the Ukraine Crisis is the West's Fault: The Liberal Delusions that Provoked Putin", *Foreign Affairs*, Vol. 90 (September/October), 2014.

Metz, Steven and Kievit, James, *Strategy and the Revolution in Military Affairs: From Theory to Policy*, Carlisle Barracks: US Army War College, 1995.

Mills, Quinn and Rosefielde, Steven, *The Trump Phenomenon and Future of US Foreign Policy*, Singapore: World Scientific, 2016.

Müller, Jan-Werner, *What is Populism?* Philadelphia: University of Pennsylvania Press, 2016.

Navarro, Peter, *Crouching Tiger: What China's Militarism Means for the World*, Amherst, NY: Prometheus, 2015.

Navarro, Peter and Autry, Greg, *Death by China*, Upper Saddle River, NJ: Pearson Education, 2011.

Nye, Joseph, *Bound to Lead: The Changing Nature of American Power*, New York: Basic Books, 1990.

Nye, Joseph, *Soft Power: The Means to Success in World Politics*, New York: Public Affairs, 2004.

OECD, *All on Board: Making Inclusive Growth Happen*, Geneva: OECD, May 29, 2015.

Office of the Secretary of Defense, *Military and Security Developments Involving the People's Republic of China 2016*, Annual Report to Congress, 2016.

Ogarkov, Nikolai, *Vsegda v gotovnosti k zashchite Otechestva (Eternally at the Vanguard of the Nation's Defense)*, Moskva: Voyenizdat, 1982.

Ogarkov, Nikolai, *Istoriya Uchit bditel'nosti (Historical Lessons of Vigilence)*, Moskva, 1985.

Oren, Michael, *Power, Faith, and Fantasy: The United States in the Middle East, 1776 to 2006*, New York: W.W. Norton & Co., 2007.

Oxenstierna, Susanne, and Olsson, Per, *The Economic Sanctions against Russia: Impact and Prospects of Success*, FOI-R-4097-SE, September, 2015.

Piattoni, Simona, "Institutional Innovations and EU Legitimacy after the Crisis" in Bruno Dallago and John McGowan, J. (eds.), *Crises in Europe in the Transatlantic Context: Economic and Political Appraisals*, London: Routledge, 2016, pp. 119–136.

Piketty Thomas, *Capital in the Twenty-First Century*, Cambridge, MA: Belknap Press, 2014.

Plokhy, Serhii, *The Last Empire: The Final Days of the Soviet Union*, New York: Basic Books, 2014.

Podhoretz, Norman, "Making the World Safe for Communism", *Commentary*, Vol. 61, No. 4, April 1976.

Popper, Karl and Bergson, Henri, *Les Deux Sources de la morale et de la Religion*, Paris: Félix Alcan, 1937.

Popper, Karl, *The Open Society and Its Enemies*, London: Routledge, 1945.

Popper, Karl, "The Rationality Principle", in David Miller (ed.), *Popper Selections*, Princeton: Princeton University Press, 1985.

Rapoport, Anatol, *Fights, Games and Debates*, Ann Arbor: University of Michigan Press, 1960.

Rawls, John, *A Theory of Justice*, Cambridge, MA: Harvard University Press, 1971.

Razin, Assaf and Rosefielde, Steven, "Israel and Global Developments 1990–2015: Riding with the Global Flows", in Avi Ben-Bassat, Reuven Grunau, Asaf Zussman (eds.), *Israel Economy in the 21st Century*, Cambridge: MIT Press, 2017.

Robinson, Joan, "Beggar-My-Neighbour Remedies for Unemployment", in *Essays in the Theory of Employment* (2nd edn.), Oxford, UK: Basil Blackwell, 1947, pp. 156–170.

Rodrik, Dani, "Don't Cry Over Dead Trade Agreements", *Project Syndicate* (December 8, 2016).

Rogoff, Kenneth, "The Trump Boom", *Project Syndicate*, December 7, 2016.

Rosefielde, Steven, "China's Perplexing Foreign Trade Policy: Causes, Consequences and a Tit for Tat Solution", *American Foreign Policy Interests*, Vol. 33, No. 1 (January/February), 2011, pp. 10–16.

Rosefielde, Steven, *"Export-led Development and Dollar Reserve Hoarding"*, in Steven Rosefielde, Masaaki Kuboniwa and Satoshi Mizobata (eds.), *Two Asias: The Emerging Postcrisis Divide,* Singapore: World Scientific, 2012, pp. 251–266.

Rosefielde, Steven, "Grexit, Brexit: Rational Choice, Compatibility, and Coercive Adaptation", *Acta Oeconomica*, September, 2016.

Rosefielde, Steven, *Russia in the 21st Century: The Prodigal Superpower*, Cambridge: Cambridge University Press, 2005.

Rosefielde, Steven, *Russian Economy from Lenin to Putin*, New York: John Wiley, 2007.

Rosefielde, Steven, *The Kremlin Strikes Back: Russia and the West after Crimea's Annexation*, Cambridge: Cambridge University Press, 2017.

Rosefielde, Steven and Mills, Quinn, *Democracy and Its Elected Enemies*, Cambridge: Cambridge University Press, 2014.

Rosefielde Steven and Mills, Quinn, *Global Economic Turmoil and the Public Good*, Singapore: World Scientific, 2015.

Rosefielde, Steven, *Russia's Military Industrial Resurgence: Evidence and Potential*, Carlisle Barracks: US Army War College, 2016.

Rosefielde, Steven and Pfouts, Ralph W., *Inclusive Economic Theory*, Singapore: World Scientific, 2014.

Rosefielde, Steven and Zhou, Huan, "*Global Imbalances*", in Steven Rosefielde, Masaaki Kuboniwa and Satoshi Mizobata (eds.), *Prevention and Crisis Management: Lessons for Asia from the 2008 Crisis*, Singapore: World Scientific, 2012.

Rubin, Michael, "Dump UNRWA, Vote on 2008 Peace Agreement?", *AEI*, January 2, 2017.

Rubin, Michael, "Eight Possible Trump Responses to the UN Israel Vote", *AEI*, December 24, 2016.

Rubin, Michael, "What Kerry Got Wrong in His Israel Speech", *AEI*, December 28, 2016.

Rumsfeld, Donald, "Transforming the Military", *Foreign Affairs*, Vol. 81, No. 3 (May/June), 2002, pp. 20–32.

Samuelson, Paul, *Foundations of Economic Analysis*, Cambridge: Harvard University Press, 1947.

Savranskaya, Svetlana and Blanton, Thomas, *The Last Superpower Summits: Gorbachev, Reagan, and Bush: Conversations that Ended the Cold War*, Budapest/New York: Central European University Press, 2016.

Sandel, Michael, *Justice: What's the Right Thing to Do?*, New York: Farrar, Straus and Giroux, 2009.

Say, Jean-Baptiste, *A Treatise on Political Economy* (*Traité d'économie Politique*), Philadelphia: Lippincott, Grambo & Co., 1803.

Scholte, Jan-Aart, *Globalization: A Critical Introduction*, London: Palgrave, 2005.

Scissors, Derek, "China Edges Toward a Big Mistake", *AEI*, November 22, 2016.

Shiller, Robert and Akerlof, George, *Animal Spirits: How Human Psychology Drives the Economy and Why It Matters for Global Capitalism*, Princeton, NJ: Princeton University Press, 2009.

Shiller, Robert, *Irrational Exuberance*, Princeton, NJ: Princeton University Press, 2005.

Simon, Herbert, "A Mechanism for Social Selection and Successful Altruism", *Science*, Vol. 250, No. 4988, 1990, pp. 1665–1668.

Simon, Herbert, "Bounded Rationality and Organizational Learning", *Organization Science*, Vol. 2, No. 1, 1991, pp. 125–134.

Simon, Herbert, *Models of Man: Social and Rational — Mathematical Essays on Rational Human Behavior in a Social Setting*, New York: John Wiley, 1957.

Sinn, Hans-Werner, *The Euro Trap: On Bursting Bubbles, Budgets, and Belief*, London: Oxford University Press, 2014.

Smethurst, David, *Tripoli: The United States' First War on Terror*, New York: Presidio Press, 2006.

Smith, Adam, *An Inquiry into the Nature and Causes of the Wealth of Nations*, Book IV, Chapter III (Part II), London: William Strahan, 1776.

Spense, Michael, "Donald Trump and the New Economic Order", *Project Syndicate*, November 29, 2016.

Stiglitz, Joseph, *Globalization and Its Discontents*, New York: W.W. Norton, 2002.

Stiglitz, Joseph, *Making Globalization Work*, New York: W.W. Norton, 2006.

Stiglitz, Joseph, "What America's Economy Needs from Trump", *Project Syndicate*, November 13, 2016.

Strain, Michael, *The US Labor Market: Questions and Challenges for Public Policy*, Washington DC: AEI, 2016.

Tierney, Dominic, "The Legacy of Obama's 'Worst Mistake'", *The Atlantic*, April 15, 2016.

Trump, Donald, *Art of the Deal*, New York: Random House, 1987.

Trump, Donald, *Great Again*, New York: Simon and Schuster, 2015.

Trump, Donald, *Think Big and Kick Ass in Business and Life*, New York: First Collins, 2007.

Varoufakis, Yanis, "Trump, the Dragon, and the Minotaur", *Project Syndicate*, November 28, 2016.

Weidenbaum, Murray, "The Employment Act of 1946: A Half Century of Presidential Policy Making", *Presidential Studies Quarterly*, Vol. 26, No. 3 (Summer), 1996, pp. 880–885.

Wilford, Hugh, *America's Great Game: The CIA's Secret Arabists and the Making of the Modern Middle East*, Paris: Basic Books, 2013.

Wolf, Jr, Charles and Rowen, Henry, *The Impoverished Superpower: Perestroika and the Soviet Military Burden*, San Francisco, CA: Institute for Contemporary Studies, 1990.

Wolverson, Roya, "Outsourcing Jobs and Taxes", Council on Foreign Relations, February 11, 2011.

Zakheim, Roger, "Clinton and Trump Both Offer More of the Same for the Military", *AEI*, September 2, 2016.

Zinoviev, Alexander, *Katastroika*, London: Claridge Press, 1991.

Zong Jie and Batalova, Jeanne, *Frequently Requested Statistics on Immigrants and Immigration in the United States*, Washington, DC: Migration Policy Institute, May 26, 2016.

Zycher, Benjamin, "Trump Nominee Scott Pruitt will Clean Up the EPA", *AEI*, December 14, 2016.

Index

About the Author

Steven Rosefielde received an AM degree in Soviet Regional Studies (1967) and PhD in Economics from Harvard University (1972). His special areas were Soviet economy and comparative systems theory including Asian economic systems, labor managed firms and international trade. He was trained by Abram Bergson, working as well with Wassily Leontief, Alexander Gerschenkron, Simon Kuznets, Gottfried von  Haberler and Evsei Domar. He is Professor of Economics at the University of North Carolina at Chapel Hill, and has served simultaneously as Adjunct Professor at various universities including the US Naval Postgraduate School, Monterey. He has taught widely across the globe in Russia, Japan, China, and Thailand, and has been a visiting research scholar at the Stockholm School of Economics, Bank of Finland, Trento University, Central Economics and Mathematics Institute (Moscow). During the Soviet era, he was an advisor to the Office of the American Secretary of Defense and FOI (Swedish Defense Institute), also serving as Coordinator of the US–USSR Joint Cooperative Research Program on Science and Technology (between the National Science Foundation and the Soviet Academy of Sciences), Topic 1, subtopic 3, "enterprise modeling," 1977–1981. In 1997, he was inducted into the Russian Academy of Natural Sciences [Rossiiskaia

Akademiia Estestvennykh Nauk (RAEN)]. After the Soviet Union collapsed, he refocused his attention on Asia and the European Union while remaining actively engaged with Russia and Eastern Europe. Throughout his career, he has striven to integrate the lessons learned in high level government service with advanced economic theory.

Professor Rosefielde is a prolific author and his latest publications include four books co-authored with Professor Daniel Quinn Mills from the Harvard Business School: *The Trump Phenomenon and the Future of US Foreign Policy* (World Scientific); *Democracy and Its Elected Enemies: American Political Capture and Economic Decline* (Cambridge University Press); *Masters of Illusion: American Leadership in the Media Age* (Cambridge University Press); *Global Economic Turmoil and Public Good* (World Scientific). He is also single author for the books: *Comparative Economic Systems: Culture, Wealth, and Power in the 21st Century (Wiley-Blackwell); The Kremlin Strikes Back: Russia and the West After Crimea's Annexation (Cambridge University Press); The Russian Economy: From Lenin to Putin (Wiley-Blackwell), Red Holocaust (Routledge); Asian Economic Systems (World Scientific).*

Printed in the United States
By Bookmasters